CROSSING THE **CLASS** AND **COLOR LINES**

CROSSING THE

CLASS AND COLOR LINES

From Public Housing to White Suburbia

Leonard S. Rubinowitz and James E. Rosenbaum

With Shirley Dvorin, Marilynn Kulieke, Alicia McCareins, and Susan Popkin
And with a Foreword by Alex Kotlowitz

THE UNIVERSITY OF CHICAGO PRESS / CHICAGO AND LONDON

Leonard S. Rubinowitz is professor of law at Northwestern University School of Law.
James E. Rosenbaum is professor of sociology, education, and social policy at the Institute for Policy Research at Northwestern University.

The University of Chicago Press, Chicago 60637
The University of Chicago Press, Ltd., London
© 2000 by The University of Chicago
All rights reserved. Published 2000
Printed in the United States of America
09 08 07 06 05 04 03 02 01 00   5 4 3 2 1

ISBN (cloth) : 0-226-73089-1

Library of Congress Cataloging-in-Publication Data

Rubinowitz, Leonard S.
    Crossing the class and color lines : from public housing to white suburbia / Leonard S. Rubinowitz and James E. Rosenbaum with Shirley Dvorin . . . [et al.].
        p.   cm.
    Includes index.
    ISBN 0-226-73089-1
    1. Residential mobility—Illinois—Chicago Metropolitan Area.   2. Public housing—Illinois—Chicago Suburban Area.   3. Afro-Americans—Housing—Illinois—Chicago Suburban Area.   I. Rosenbaum, James E., 1943–   II. Title.

HD7288.92.U62 C487   2000
363.5'996073077311—dc21

                                                99-053847

This book could not have been written without the willingness of the participants in the Gautreaux program—families who moved to the suburbs and those who stayed in Chicago—to share their experiences openly and frankly. In many ways, this book is their story, and their willingness to tell it to strangers made it possible. We dedicate this book to the parents and children of the Gautreaux program, who showed the possibilities for crossing the class and race lines in American society.

CONTENTS

FOREWORD

ALEX KOTLOWITZ

I remember so clearly my first visit to Chicago's public housing. It was a spring afternoon in 1985, and I was visiting a ten-year-old boy, Lafeyette, who was the subject of a local magazine's photo essay for which I was writing the text. When I walked into his seven-story high-rise at the Henry Horner Homes, the smells overwhelmed me: spilt wine, urine, fetid puddles. The darkness enveloped me; I navigated the halls by running my hands along the dirtied cinderblock walls. One elevator didn't work. The breezeway cut through the building like an open tunnel, as if the architects had forgot to design doors for the lobby. And the stories I heard astonished me. In the couple of hours I had with Lafeyette, he told me of a young girl who just a couple of weeks earlier had been shot in the leg while skipping rope outside the building, and of a teenaged boy who, after being shot in a gang altercation, stumbled into the breezeway and died on the stairwell. Lafeyette sensed my horror—my disbelief. He took me by the arm, walked me to the stairwell, and pointed out the brownish blood stains on the steps. He wanted me to believe.

I can't imagine that any reasonable person familiar with Chicago public housing wouldn't suggest that all things being equal we shouldn't tear down most of it and begin from scratch. Rebuild community, if you will. But things haven't been equal, and until very recently razing even the worst of the high-rises wasn't an option. The dreams harbored by those like Lafeyette were straightforward: to leave public housing, to move to a neighborhood in which gunfire was not a daily occurrence, to live in a community in which the schools demanded of the students that they read and write at grade levels, schools that had enough money to offer art and music classes.

The Gautreaux program, which came along in 1976 as the result of a lawsuit that argued in essence that the construction of public housing— the bulk of it built in the 1950s and 1960s—in already existing slums only served to further residential segregation, had this elemental, if not noble notion in mind: it allowed families to depart public housing for city neighborhoods and suburbs that were financially better off. The program was so popular that in 1984, on the one day families could en- roll, so many showed up they had to cancel registration because the po- lice feared they couldn't control the crowd. When registration was made possible by phone, upwards of 10,000 people called in that one day. The lines would get so tied up that I knew people who assigned children and relatives to call from different phones with the hope that one of them would get through. The Gautreaux program embraced a rather simple concept: rather than build new public housing, find housing for families in other communities, communities which both by race and class stood as polar images to those of the inner-city. Gautreaux became a labora- tory, a social experiment, one that hoped to better the lives of the poor while also spurring on residential integration. And while in the end this program, which lasted twenty-two years, involved only 7,000 families, policy makers and activists looked to it as an exemplar. Could we im- prove the lot of some poverty-stricken families by helping them move to middle-class communities? Could we help nurture tolerance by opening up wealthier communities to poor, black families?

It's these questions which Len Rubinowitz and Jim Rosenbaum so adroitly wrestle with in these pages, and in doing so touch on some of the more perplexing issues of our time. Their interviews with families who have made the transition from ghetto to suburb make it clear that this is not a program that takes families from hell to heaven, but rather, given the troublesome issues of race and class, it's a program whose par- ticipant experiences have been, well, not uncomplicated. The women— most of the families are single-parent households—talk despairingly of the relentless crime and violence in their public housing neighborhoods, and clearly the safety of their suburban communities is the most talked- about and the most dramatic change for them. One mother reveled in the simple pleasure of lounging on her suburban patio without the fear of bearing witness to a crime. But as you listen to the voices in these pages, as the mothers talk about their new communities, their new schools, their new neighbors, you detect their ambivalence. While they praise the quality of the suburban schools, they wonder if too many of their children are being placed in special education classes. While they take comfort in the low crime rates, they talk of racial harassment, some of it quite frightening. While they mention the friendliness of some neighbors—one recounts a neighbor delivering a casserole on the day she moved in—they also talk of feeling isolated and alone. It is these paradoxes which make Gautreaux an unusual window onto America's fault lines.

Rubinowitz and Rosenbaum, in the end, speak favorably of the Gautreaux program, and rightfully point out that for anyone committed to the ideals of fairness and tolerance it is a start, a program we can look to as an example, as a model. And, indeed, other cities have looked to Gautreaux and the experience of its participants as they embark on their own efforts to provide opportunity for those who have been left behind. Implicit in all this is that we still live in a world which can best be described as separate and unequal. While it's been some forty years since the dismantling of the legal apartheid of the Jim Crow era, we find our nation still divided, still segregated. As Rubinowitz and Rosenbaum so underscore in this book, many blacks simply don't have the same access to the resources—whether it be good schools or jobs or police protection—as their white suburban neighbors. The Gautreaux program is an effort at leveling the playing field—and for that reason alone we should be thankful that Rubinowitz and Rosenbaum have recorded its history, replete with the voices of its participants who have in the spirit of a distinctly American ethos moved from inner-city to suburb pursuing, as the authors write, a better life. But, as we find in these pages, given our nation's troubling racial history, such a search is neither neat nor linear.

The Gautreaux program, in all its layers, reminds us how far we've come and how far we still have to go.

ACKNOWLEDGMENTS

This book exemplifies the phrase *collaborative effort*. It is the product of the work of many people at various times over an extended period.

The following Northwestern University students and graduates provided invaluable research assistance, including, in some cases, carrying out interviews which serve as the basis for the second part of the book: Alison Brett, Aimee Buehl, Faith Bugel, Diane Butler, Lisa Bynum, Britt Cibulka, Jennifer Cohn, Colleen Connolly, Ben Cooper, Maxine Crump, Jeff Cummings, Michael Evans, Nancy Fishman, Adam Glazer, Victoria Gwiasda, Danika Haueisen, Julie Kaufman, Sheila McCraven, Karen McCurdy, Patricia Meaden, Deidre Michael, Rhonda Miller, Corie Morman, Jeff Osterkamp, Jeff Potts, Patricia Rim, Jennifer Rusin, Deborah Sager, Tara Simmons, Amy Skaggs, Nora Sosnoff, Rob Stonebraker, Jon Streeter, Natasha Tarpley, Karen Taylor, Reenie Terjak, Francine Twine, Carol Uyeno, Natalie Williams, Sarah Willie, and Tom Wilson. Special thanks go to Betsy Lassar, who joined the project in its later stages and made great contributions to its completion.

Cheryl Coppell and Galen Carey played essential roles in designing and carrying out the initial empirical research. Bill Stiers provided computing assistance at that stage. Dan Lewis provided invaluable guidance and counsel on the design of the project.

Many thanks go to Pat Franklin for her great patience, persistence, and good humor in typing many versions of the manuscript. Sang Kim, Maggie Malley, Kathy Polit, Elizabeth Rutenberg, Rob Steiner, Madelyn Townsley, Carmen Velez, and Suzanne Williams also helped with the typing. Paul King provided valuable logistical assistance.

Thanks also to Audrey Chambers of Northwestern University's Institute for Policy Research, who assisted with the research and its dissemination in many ways, and to Judy Rosenbaum for her excellent job on the index.

The authors are grateful for the generous financial support for the underlying research to the Ford Foundation, the Mott Foundation, the Spencer Foundation, and Northwestern University.

The authors are very grateful for the assistance and support of Alex Polikoff, lead counsel for the public housing residents in a lawsuit spanning the last third of the twentieth century, who conceived the research and assisted in securing initial funding for it. The Leadership Council for Metropolitan Open Communities, under the leadership of Kale Williams and his successor, Aurie Pennick, cooperated fully with this research from the outset, and provided assistance and support in many ways throughout the project. Among the Leadership Council staff who were especially helpful were Mary Davis, Harry Gottlieb, Carole Hendrix, John Melcher, and Hank Zuba.

A number of colleagues made helpful suggestions regarding various versions of the manuscript, especially Cynthia Bowman and Florence Roisman, each of whom made exceptionally detailed and invaluable comments on the entire manuscript. Others who reviewed portions of the manuscript include Kathy Abrams, Paul Fischer, Harry Gottlieb, Alex Kotlowitz, Alex Polikoff, Richard Sander, and Ada Skyles. Other colleagues gave helpful suggestions at various stages of the research: Thomas Cook, David Cordray, Andrew Gordon, Christopher Jencks, Paul Lavrakas, James Pitts, and Wesley Skogan.

The authors are grateful to John Tryneski, our editor at the University of Chicago Press, for his wise counsel and infinite patience in helping bring this project to fruition, as well as to the anonymous reviewers, whose suggestions helped to improve the book significantly, to Claudia Rex, Senior Production Editor, and to Nicholas Murray for his very helpful copyediting.

Many thanks, as always, to Linda and Edie Rubinowitz and Ginny and Janet Rosenbaum for their support and counsel throughout the extended gestation period of this book.

Chapter 9 contains some material from Julie E. Kaufman and James E. Rosenbaum, "The Education and Employment of Low-Income Black Youth in White Suburbs," *Educational Evaluation and Policy Analysis* 14, no. 3 (1992). Permission to use this material is gratefully acknowledged.

ONE

Introduction: A Modern Odyssey

When Harriet Tubman, the famous "conductor" of the Underground Railroad, escaped from slavery to the North in 1849, she encountered a different reality than she had envisioned: "I had crossed de line of which I had so long been dreaming. I was free; but dere was no one to welcome me to de land of freedom. I was a stranger in a strange land."[1]

A century and a quarter later, low-income African-American women and their families began to move from Chicago's inner city to mostly white, middle-class suburbs as part of the largest and most innovative housing desegregation program in the country's history. Like Harriet Tubman, they left one world for another that they hoped would be far better; but, as Black women in a white society they also often thought of themselves as "strangers in a strange land."[2]

Families began the trek to Chicago's suburbia in 1976 because a decade earlier Dorothy Gautreaux, a Black community activist and public housing resident on the city's south side, lent her name to a class action lawsuit filed in federal court on behalf of more than forty thousand African-American families who were residents of, or applicants for, Chicago public housing. The suit charged that the Chicago Housing Authority (CHA), with the financial support and approval of the federal Department of Housing and Urban Development (HUD), had engaged in systematic and illegal segregation. The Gautreaux story was to become an extraordinary legal and social odyssey, spanning several decades. In 1969, Judge Richard Austin concluded that CHA had located its buildings and assigned tenants on a racially segregated basis.[3] Later that year, he ordered the CHA to build and buy housing on a desegregated basis, so that Black families could move into predominantly white

Chicago neighborhoods.[4] This effort came to be known as the "scattered site" program because the locations were to be "scattered" throughout the city rather than in a few Black neighborhoods.

After dealing with CHA's responsibility, the courts took up the question of HUD's responsibility for the segregation of public housing in Chicago, finding that agency liable as well. That part of the litigation culminated in a landmark 1976 United States Supreme Court decision permitting the trial court to require HUD to develop and implement a program that would enable low-income Black families to relocate beyond the city limits and throughout the six-county Chicago metropolitan area.[5] This marked the first time that the Supreme Court had ever authorized a school or housing desegregation remedy to extend beyond the community where the violation of law had taken place.

The metropolitan-wide effort, which soon eclipsed the scattered site program in scale and prominence, became known as the Gautreaux Assisted Housing Program, or simply the Gautreaux program. While the stated purpose of the Gautreaux program was racial integration, the consequence was class mixing as well. The program became the country's largest and longest-running residential, racial, and economic integration effort. In the program's more than twenty-year lifetime, about seven thousand low-income Black families moved from the inner city, the majority to the suburbs and the rest to other parts of Chicago. The Gautreaux program also fostered dozens of progeny around the country, as courts, HUD, and other public and private agencies used it as a model for their own local initiatives. These efforts to assist low-income families to move out of the inner city came to be called mobility-based housing programs.

This book, based upon an in-depth study of participants in the Gautreaux program, examines the interdependent factors that affect the ability to implement and sustain mobility-based programs, as exemplified by the remedial efforts in the Gautreaux case. The main remedy in Gautreaux sought to enable low-income Black families to move from Chicago's inner city to middle-income, predominantly white communities—primarily in the suburbs. More generally, however, mobility-based initiatives involve the movement of low-income households of any racial or ethnic group into predominantly working-class, middle-class, or upper-class areas, often composed primarily of other racial or ethnic groups. In light of the history and demographics of many American metropolitan areas—including pervasive patterns of racial segregation in many urban areas—the Gautreaux initiatives represent the paradigm of the mobility-based program: low-income Black families moving into predominantly white middle-class areas.

This book looks at mobility programs largely from the perspective of the opportunities they afford to low-income people of color entering middle-class, predominantly white communities. From that vantage point, sustaining these efforts depends on the continued presence of these families over time—through their staying in the communities in which they relocate or through additional families making similar moves. That continuity depends both on a continuation of the conditions that permitted the initial round of moves and on the quality of movers' experiences.

The factors affecting the implementation of mobility-based programs are both contextual, or external (such as legal and demographic), and programmatic, or internal (such as demand, supply, and resources) to these initiatives. While there is not always a clear line between these two types of factors, contextual factors serve as the stage on which mobility programs operate. They pre-date mobility programs; they have ongoing effects on them, and may be affected by the programs in turn. Administrators take contextual factors into account in designing and implementing programs, but such factors are largely outside of the program structure itself. By contrast, programmatic factors are specific to individual programs: they directly influence program design, day-to-day implementation, and ultimate outcomes.

CONTEXTUAL FACTORS

Contextual factors vary across time and place; they provide the backdrop for and interact with individual programs. These "givens" within which local programs operate include area demographic and developmental patterns, the applicable law, and the local political and governmental structures.

Demographic and Developmental Patterns

Mobility programs take place in the context of an area's historically shaped and evolving demographic and developmental patterns. The demographics include the population size; its composition by race, ethnicity, family status, and class; and the distribution of these groups within and across neighborhoods and municipalities. These spatial arrangements are reflected in developmental patterns, such as the pace and direction of growth; the location and amount of vacant land; the quantity, types, quality, and cost of the housing supply, both publicly assisted housing and the private market; and related public facilities and private institutions.

Moreover, the forces shaping those processes and patterns include governmental policies and practices as well as private market structures and institutional and individual attitudes and actions. As demographic patterns have formed with various degrees of concentration by race, class, and ethnicity, living conditions have varied dramatically across the places where different groups reside—a disparity referred to by one commentator as "spatial inequality."[6]

Mobility-based programs take into account these demographic and developmental patterns and the underlying dynamics that drive a region's spatial distribution. The greater the physical separation of people by race and class, the more deeply embedded and resistant to change may be the structures and attitudes that have created and maintained these patterns. On the other hand, rapid suburban growth may result in the presence of fewer long-standing racial and ethnic enclaves where people try to defend historic "claims" on their communities and thus allow more opportunities for a variety of households to move into the area.

The Chicago region represented a vast territory—and a population to match—within which to operate a housing program. While racial and economic segregation were deeply embedded in both the city and the suburbs, the region's dramatic post-war growth included some movement of African-Americans to the suburbs as well as the construction of a great deal of rental housing beyond the city limits. The Gautreaux initiative began at a time of some lowering of the historic barriers to Blacks' mobility. Moreover, because of the expanding suburban apartment market, a large supply of rental housing was potentially available to the program.

The Law

The legal context within which mobility programs operate consists of federal, state, and local law related to housing discrimination based on race, gender, family status, and class. By 1968, federal constitutional and statutory law prohibited racial discrimination in both publicly assisted and private housing.[7] Even with this apparent uniformity, local variations may occur. For example, federal litigation resulting in race-based remedial obligations can significantly change a local legal landscape.

While most intentional and some inadvertent housing discrimination based on race, sex, or family status is illegal, federal, state, and local law do not generally bar class-based discrimination in either the development or occupancy of housing. Local governments are largely free to regulate land use and building requirements in ways that add to the cost of housing and exclude potential residents based on their income. Moreover, private housing providers are generally free to discriminate against purchasers or renters based on their income. However, a few states and localities prohibit housing discrimination based on source of income. In such places, landlords may not refuse to rent to prospective tenants because they receive government benefits or housing subsidies. Similarly, some state courts have struck down local zoning ordinances and practices that exclude the construction of housing for low- and moderate-income people.[8]

The Gautreaux case dramatically altered Chicago's legal terrain in some ways and left other aspects untouched. The finding that HUD had violated the plaintiffs' rights led to the creation of an unprecedented local program. At the same time, the Chicago region's public and private institutions generally retained their ability to engage in class-based decision-making. For the most part, local governments could continue to zone out affordable housing, and landlords could reject potential tenants based on their income.

Political and Governmental Structures

The number, size, and legal authority of local governmental units, such as municipalities and specialized entities like public housing agencies, can also affect mobility programs. Coordination or cooperation among these bodies may facilitate implementation. On the other hand, fragmentation and lack of coordination may decrease programs' visibility and the possibilities for adverse community response to them.

The six-county Chicago metropolitan area is extremely fragmented, with over two hundred municipalities and multitudes of overlaying specialized governmental units. Coordinating these bodies for implementation purposes would have been impractical, but that did not pose a problem for the Gautreaux program, which relied heavily on the private market. Moreover, this balkanization reduced the possibility of concerted public resistance to the program.

At the same time, the region had more than a dozen public housing agencies. Those agencies traditionally played a significant role in administering the federally funded Section 8 rent subsidy program, and they continued to do so in the Gautreaux initiative. Coordinating their activities posed substantial challenges for Gautreaux program administrators.

PROGRAMMATIC FACTORS

Programmatic factors affecting mobility-based initiatives involve demand, supply, administration, community response, and resources. These factors operate both in the initial entry of low-income families into predominantly middle-class areas and in sustaining their presence there.

Demand

Mobility programs generally depend on voluntary participation. Thus, there must be families willing and able to move into areas with very different class, racial, or ethnic composition, as well as out of the city and into the suburbs if the program requires that.[9] The level of interest may depend on a family's expectations about the benefits to be obtained and the costs to be incurred. Program administrators may affect demand by providing counseling and other assistance.

After some initial uncertainty about whether eligible families would be interested in the Gautreaux program, the demand for the program increased dramatically and remained high throughout the more than two decades of its existence. The program provided much-needed housing subsidies that were not otherwise available because of cutbacks in federal housing programs and very long waiting lists for other programs. Moreover, many families expected that the benefits of relocating to the program's prescribed destinations—improved quality of housing, greater opportunities for education, employment, and safety—would outweigh the costs to be incurred, such as racial discrimination, social isolation, and distance from family, friends, and church. In addition, program administrators undertook counseling initiatives that assisted families in making moves and coping with their new environments. Many families had the confidence and the ability to make these moves, so demand was never a limiting factor in implementing the program.

Supply

Mobility programs also depend on the availability of housing that is of appropriate size, quality, and cost in areas designated as destinations because of their racial or class composition. Programs that rely on new or rehabilitated housing depend on interested developers and receptive local regulatory environments. Other programs depend on the composition and cost of the existing housing stock and on the willingness of housing providers to participate in the program. Landlords' initial and ongoing willingness to rent to program participants may depend on their tolerance for diversity (race, class, family composition, single-parent family, children); their expectations about reactions of present and future middle-class white tenants towards diverse groups; the administrative procedures designed to reduce the perceived costs and risks of participating; the anticipated cost of complying with program requirements; vacancy rates in designated destination areas; and their own experience or accounts of other landlords' experiences with the program.

Gaining sufficient access to appropriate housing proved to be one of the Gautreaux program's major challenges. The race-based locational limitations and HUD's rent ceilings excluded large portions of the region's rental housing. There was little housing available for large families. Moreover, as a primarily demand-side initiative, the Gautreaux program depended heavily on landlords' voluntary participation. Landlords in predominantly white middle-class areas showed substantial reluctance to participate. While there were few overt instances of racial discrimination, all of the factors suggested above seemed to have played a part in many landlords' unwillingness to accept Gautreaux families.

Program administrators and participating families tried various strategies to overcome this resistance. Their efforts resulted in securing a steady, modest supply of housing for the program, especially in times and places with loose rental markets; but there were no breakthroughs such as those that occurred on the demand side.

Administration

Mobility programs depend on administrators' having the authority, commitment, and competence to carry them out. First, the geographical scope of a program's operation affects the opportunities for implementation. Second, administrators may have authority to limit participants' locational options, including placing neighborhoods or communities off limits to relocatees in order to advance racial or economic integration objectives. Agencies may also have the authority to disperse participants within or among communities—limiting the numbers that may move to particular places.

Moreover, agencies may be able to develop a system for selecting program participants, including financial and lifestyle criteria. Such screening may increase the supply of housing available to the program by reducing landlords' risks and cost, but it may also make the program less accessible or less attractive to low-income homeseekers.

In addition to their authority, administrators' commitment is central to programs' chances. Since their participation may be compelled or voluntary, administrators may have widely varying degrees of enthusiasm and energy for the enterprise. Of course, a program's progress also depends on administrators' competence, including their ability to coordinate numerous agencies' activities.

The Leadership Council for Metropolitan Open Communities, a nonprofit fair housing organization founded a decade earlier in the aftermath of open housing marches led by Dr. Martin Luther King, administered the Gautreaux program throughout its life. The agreement establishing the program gave substantial authority to the Leadership Council, starting with the key issue of metropolitanization. Metropolitanization expanded the available housing supply substantially and increased opportunities for community acceptance.

The Leadership Council had a mandate to facilitate integrationist moves. In pursuit of that objective, it could place areas off limits and disperse participants across the region. The Leadership Council also had the authority to screen prospective participants to include those who would be most acceptable to the private market. The demand for the program was so large that the screening process did not result in too few participants.

While the Leadership Council's commitment to the program was never in doubt, neither it nor any other agency had any experience in running such a mobility program. The agency had to create the program before it could operate it. However, as it gained experience with this new initiative, the Leadership Council proved its administrative capability in carrying out this first program of its kind.

Community Response

Implementation of mobility-based programs depends heavily on community reactions—including those of public bodies and officials, such as mayors, city councils, school officials, and police departments, as well as private institutions, organizations, and individuals. Underlying these reactions and responses are community attitudes toward low-income families, particularly people of color. Anticipated or actual response may affect families' willingness to make integrationist moves and thus demand for the program.

Community response may in turn be shaped by contextual factors such as demographic and developmental patterns, the law, and political and governmental structures. Local reactions may also depend on a program's design and implementation, including its scale, pace, duration, and the extent to which it clusters or disperses families within and among communities.[10] Moreover, the information that administrators provide to communities may affect public reaction. To minimize resistance, administrators may engage in public education, or they may provide little information, on the assumption that participants should be no more visible than other families entering these communities.

The characteristics of participating families—their race, class, gender (such as single-parent, female-headed families), and family size and composition (the number, age, and gender of the children)—may affect the responses of communities as well as landlords. Responses to supply-side and demand-side programs may be different. If construction of low-income housing is contemplated, for example, public officials and residents may have opportunities to participate in the local approval processes that they do not have with less visible programs relying on the existing housing market.

While many participating families encountered racism in the suburbs, the overall Gautreaux program elicited very limited community opposition, especially in comparison to the intense resistance to the scattered site program in the city. The Gautreaux program's use of the existing private housing market, its modest pace and scale, its screening of families and dispersal of them across the region, and its commitment to families' confidentiality all contributed to its low visibility, which in turn led to only sporadic and limited opposition to the program itself.

Resources

Mobility programs require funding for both housing subsidies and administrative costs. The rate and duration of spending set the outer limits on the pace and scale of these efforts. The depth of the subsidies affects the amount of housing available to programs. Deep, continuing subsidies are necessary to enable low-income people to enter and remain in predominantly working-class and, especially, middle-class neighborhoods and communities.

Administrative funding levels affect agencies' ability to foster housing development or landlord participation, to increase demand for the program by providing counseling or post-move support and assistance in employment, child care, and transportation, and to maximize community acceptance. Funding sources may be public, including federal agencies such as HUD, as well as state and local coffers, or they may be private—including foundations and individual contributors.

The agreement establishing the Gautreaux program provided for

HUD funding of both the rent subsidies and administrative costs. The amount of subsidy funds constituted the ultimate limiting factor on the program's pace and scale, but access to sufficient housing sometimes acted as a short-term limiting factor. HUD's funding of the Leadership Council enabled the agency to assist families and solicit landlord participation in ways that had not previously been undertaken. At the same time, limitations on the resources available constrained the Leadership Council's operations, especially in the support and assistance it could provide to families after their moves.

Thus, contextual and programmatic factors combined to enable the Gautreaux program to *achieve* a measure of racial and economic integration. A key element in *sustaining* this integration is the quality of the experience of families who participated in the program. This may depend on families' coping capacities as well as on community responses to them—including their safety, schooling, and social experiences.

A substantial portion of Gautreaux families who moved to the suburbs gained benefits that outweighed the costs to them, leading them to stay there for an extended period of time. Thus, the Gautreaux program supports the premise that there is a "geography of opportunity"—that the places in which people live affect their opportunities and life outcomes. Contrary to the claims of "culture of poverty" theorists, many participating low-income Blacks showed the motivation and capacity to take advantage of the opportunities available in the predominantly white, middle-class, suburban communities to which they moved. For many families, the benefits of being there outweighed the racism and other costs they encountered in making these moves. Their accounts of the experience specify the extent to which and the ways in which this is so.

The degree of safety experienced by Gautreaux program participants who moved to the suburbs differed dramatically from what they had experienced in the inner city. Crime and violence presented a constant, pervasive threat in the city, both during the day and at night, with no place—even the confines of their own homes—offering security. Many of the women feared that they or their children would be attacked, robbed, or harmed as innocent bystanders in gang violence. Indeed, a number of the women were victims of crime in their former neighborhoods. Many continually worried that their children—particularly their sons—would be vulnerable to gang recruitment.

In contrast to the city, the suburbs provided freedom from the fear of crime and violence and relief from gang activity. While a significant number of suburban movers experienced incidents of racial harassment and threats, some of which were quite frightening, these incidents were not as common or as dangerous as the threats they had confronted in the city.

A mixed picture emerges from examining the social integration of Gautreaux families into their suburban communities. Most of the suburban movers were accepted by their white neighbors. Women experienced a variety of positive interactions with adults and children, friendships with both whites and Blacks, and a feeling of community connectedness with neighbors helping each other and looking out for each other's children and property.

Yet a significant number of families encountered racial prejudice and harassment. Animus took a variety of forms, ranging from racial epithets to discriminatory treatment when shopping to stone throwing and fighting. Particularly painful were the barriers erected by some white parents which excluded Gautreaux children from playing in their homes or participating with their children in activities. Over time, the number of negative incidents declined, suggesting increased social acceptance within their communities. How the movers coped and helped their children cope with the racism they experienced testifies to their capacity and determination to take advantage of the opportunities presented by their suburban communities.

The experiences of Gautreaux children in their white suburban schools were complex and varied. Suburban schools differed dramatically from inner-city schools in several respects, including greater educational resources, as reflected in superior physical facilities, new textbooks, a greater range of curricular and extracurricular programming, and smaller class sizes. The suburban schools also provided a safer environment and higher educational standards.

Some of the positive aspects of the suburban schools, however, had a negative side. For example, while women recognized the benefits of higher academic standards, the reassessment of children's achievement vis-à-vis those standards was often distressing. Many children were placed in special education. Although the children in special education received extra attention, some women worried that the placements resulted from racial bias.

An examination of teachers' treatment of Gautreaux children reveals a similarly complex picture. Retrospectively and in comparison with city movers, suburban women felt that suburban teachers were significantly more helpful and responsive to their children's needs. Through the frequency and quality of the school-parent communication, women became partners in their children's education. Yet many of the same women who expressed general satisfaction with schools and teachers reported that their children also experienced racial discrimination by teachers and others in the school setting. Some women reported incidents of name-calling, harassment, humiliation in front of the class, favoritism towards white students, isolation, and a tone that sanctioned discriminatory behavior by other children.

The early effects of the suburban move on students' behavior and achievement were difficult to gauge. Most of the children had significant problems in the months following their moves as they adjusted to virtually all-white schools, as well as to higher academic and disciplinary standards. After children were settled in their new schools, both those who had moved to the suburbs and those who had moved elsewhere in the city showed similar rates of behavior problems, grades, and class rank. However, since the suburban schools made stronger behavioral and achievement demands, suburban children had to adapt to higher standards and thus may have had to perform at a higher level to achieve academic standing comparable to that of their city counterparts.

A follow-up study of Gautreaux youth seven years after the initial study showed that suburban and city students continued to receive similar grades. The follow-up study also found that despite the poor quality of their pre-move education and the higher academic standards in the suburbs, suburban youth were significantly more likely than their city counterparts to be in high school, in college-track classes, in four-year colleges, employed, in jobs with higher pay and with benefits, and either in school or working.

Suburban women credited the suburban environment with motivating their children to succeed and identified a number of factors that played a role. These included the higher expectations regarding academic achievement in the suburbs, the quality of suburban schools, the teachers' expectations and the extra help they provided, college counseling at the high school, positive role models, and peer pressure. For the suburban youth, the move to the suburbs provided better opportunities for education and employment—and perhaps greater prospects for the future—than they would have had if they had remained in the city.

While the Gautreaux program ended in 1998, it was destined to play a significant role in national housing policy well into the twenty-first century. Beginning in the 1980s, national housing policy began to move away from providing project-based subsidies to providing assistance to tenants in the form of vouchers and certificates which are used to lease housing in the private market. As contracts expire or HUD forecloses on existing subsidized developments, and deteriorating public housing units are demolished, vouchers have become the central strategy for providing replacement housing. While the emphasis on vouchers is driven by a desire to reduce the costs associated with housing subsidies, key objectives of the voucher strategy are to reduce concentrations of poverty and increase housing choice throughout metropolitan areas. Policy makers and program administrators can learn much from the Gautreaux program and the experiences of the families who participated in it regarding the issues that must be addressed and the conditions that will affect the success of the voucher program in providing housing for low-income families in neighborhoods that can offer them better opportunities.

Finally, the Gautreaux program gave rise to several similar programs through Gautreaux-like litigation, federal legislative initiatives like the Moving to Opportunity program, and voluntary local initiatives. These mobility programs became part of the legacy of Chicago's Gautreaux program. The contextual and programmatic factors that shaped the implementation of the Gautreaux program also influenced these initiatives, providing a framework for assessing their effectiveness. None of these later efforts exceeded the scale or pace of mobility moves achieved in the Gautreaux program, and the Gautreaux program remains the preeminent example for understanding the possibilities and the limitations of mobility programs and the families who participate in them.

This book is divided into two parts and a concluding chapter. Part 1, "Getting There: From the Inner City to the Suburbs," examines the remedial initiatives in the Gautreaux case, especially the metropolitan-wide Gautreaux program, in terms of the factors affecting the implementation of mobility programs. Chapter 2 discusses the contextual and programmatic factors operating in the scattered site program, the initial remedial effort in the Gautreaux case. Chapters 3 and 4 focus on the larger, more prominent Gautreaux program, examining its purposes, structure, and implementation in terms of the contextual and programmatic factors. Chapter 3 looks at the program's origins in the 1976 landmark Supreme Court decision and its design pursuant to the principles laid out in the Court's opinion. Chapter 4 considers the factors affecting the ability of the Gautreaux program to achieve racial and economic integration over its twenty years of assisting low-income Black families to relocate from the inner city.

Part 2, "Moving Experiences: For the Sake of the Children," looks at the experiences of Gautreaux program participants as a way of assessing one aspect of the sustainability of mobility-based residential racial and economic integration: the ability of programs to attract and keep low-income participants. This part, consisting of Chapters 5 through 9, examines that question by considering the experience of more than one hundred families who moved to Chicago's predominantly white, middle-income suburbs in the first six years of the Gautreaux program. Rarely had poor Black and middle-class white families lived as neighbors for any length of time, so the suburban movers' accounts provide a rare glimpse into the sustainability of such arrangements from their perspective. For comparative purposes, these chapters also consider the experiences of about fifty families who relocated through the Gautreaux program to predominantly Black Chicago neighborhoods.

Chapter 5 sets the stage for the examination of participants' experiences. It introduces the women whose accounts shed light on their families' experiences in the Gautreaux program. The women who had relocated to the suburbs had a rare vantage point, having lived in both the largely Black inner city and in mostly white, middle-class suburbia. Those who relocated through the program to city neighborhoods that were more similar to those from which they departed provide an important comparison to the suburban movers' experience. Chapter 5 also discusses the multiple methodologies used to explore the pre- and post-move experiences of suburban movers and to compare the suburban movers' experiences with those of city movers.

Chapters 6, 7, and 8–9 examine three interrelated aspects of these families' experiences: the safety of the children and their mothers, their social interaction with other community residents, and the children's schooling, respectively. In each chapter, the focus is on the city and suburban environments, the community responses to these families, and the families' methods of dealing with each of their worlds.

Chapter 10, in conclusion, considers the relevance of the Gautreaux program for housing policy and programs at the turn of the century, as demand-side programs using certificates and vouchers have become the centerpiece of federal housing policy. The chapter examines demand-side programs—especially those fostered by Gautreaux—in terms of the factors that affect the implementation of those programs. In doing so, the chapter explores the potential of mobility-based programs to achieve and sustain residential racial and economic integration.

PART I

GETTING THERE
FROM THE INNER CITY TO THE SUBURBS

TWO

Desegregation Within the City's Limits: The Scattered Site Program

THE GROWTH OF A SEGREGATED METROPOLIS: CREATING THE COLOR AND CLASS LINES

In the late 1700s, Jean Baptiste Point du Sable established a fur trading post in what is now Chicago.[1] Du Sable was the first nonindigenous settler in the area, and he was also Black. Although the accounts are sketchy and contradictory, he apparently lived well and accumulated substantial property during his tenure.[2]

In 1833, a half century after Du Sable's arrival, Chicago was incorporated and began a rapid growth from two hundred to about thirty thousand by 1850.[3] The population increase included hundreds of Blacks who arrived through the Underground Railroad, taking advantage of the city's reputation as a stronghold of abolitionist sentiment.[4] Different classes and races lived in the same areas, in part because transportation was not advanced enough to allow people to live far from their work. Blacks, who made up 1 percent of the population, lived interspersed with whites.

Chicago continued its explosive growth during the second half of the nineteenth century. The Black population grew steadily and proportionately to the city's mushrooming growth, but Blacks remained less than 2 percent of the city's population throughout the nineteenth century. While Blacks often encountered discrimination in housing, employment, city services, and public accommodations, their limited numbers kept biased whites from viewing them as a major threat to their neighborhoods.[5] Most Blacks lived in pockets on the city's South Side, but they continued to be interspersed with whites, and their children went to school together.[6] Thus, until the late nineteenth century, Chicago experienced a substantial amount of racial and economic integration, as employers and employees lived in relatively close proximity to each other and to the workplace.

While that early history shows that there was nothing natural or inevitable about racial or economic segregation, Chicago's residential patterns began to change as suburbanization took hold in the late 1800s. Like most major American cities, Chicago grew from the central core out to the periphery.[7] The separation of work and home created by the movement to outlying areas of the city and independent suburbs facilitated the segregation of people by race and class.[8] Suburban local governments and private developers planned for racially and economically homogeneous communities, thus excluding both Blacks and people of modest means.[9]

While the city's overall population tripled between 1890 and 1930, reaching 3.4 million, its Black population, fueled by the first "Great Migration" from the South, increased more than sixteen times, to 233,903, or 6.9 percent of the city. As Chicago's Black population grew, it also became increasingly concentrated. Most Blacks arriving from the South left the train or bus directly for the emerging South Side Black Belt, a narrow strip that housed most of the city's Blacks until a West Side Black community began to develop in the early 1900s.[10] The belt expanded as Black newcomers filled in formerly racially mixed neighborhoods as whites moved out. Although the Black areas also expanded into adjacent white neighborhoods at times—especially during the boom years of the 1920s—much of the growth of the Black population was within the city's already heavily Black areas, which became more Black and more crowded.[11] Meanwhile, the Black suburban population grew to just 2.1 percent during the twentieth century's first four decades, while the overall population of Chicago's suburbs tripled, growing from 386,175 to 1,172,835.

A substantial measure of economic integration characterized South and West side Black neighborhoods. Business owners and lawyers and doctors lived alongside factory workers and laborers, service and domestic workers, and unemployed residents.[12] In contrast to white immigrants and their descendants, who were free to move to areas with better material conditions as their fortunes improved, Blacks had great difficulty entering the wider urban world, no matter how successful they were.

These Black communities were contained and constrained by public and private devices of exclusion and confinement. White institutions, organizations, and individuals who were hostile to the growing Black presence used a variety of means to ensure that Blacks stayed within narrow confines, including imposing restrictive covenants forbidding owners in other areas from selling their property to Blacks, filing lawsuits to enforce those agreements, and demanding that real estate agents sell or rent only to whites.[13] Whites also resorted to threats, fights, and bombings to protect what they viewed as their turf. In the summer of 1919, the tensions over territory boiled over into a race riot. It started when a Black teenager swimming in Lake Michigan drowned after a white man standing on a nearby breakwater hit him with a rock. The five-day conflict that ensued killed 23 Blacks and 15 whites, injured 342 Blacks and 195 whites, made 1,000 people homeless and destitute, and forced out blocks of Blacks permanently.[14]

The 1919 riot and other racial confrontations grew out of a pervasive system of race and class constraints designed literally to keep Blacks "in their place." Nevertheless, whites were not always successful in preventing Black entry into their neighborhoods. Increasingly after 1900, and especially after World War I, real estate brokers took advantage of the disparity between the supply of, and demand for, housing for Blacks. Through "blockbusting" or "panic peddling," they profited by facilitating the conversion of neighborhoods from white to Black, or resegregating. Some sold homes to a few Blacks and then circulated rumors about a Black invasion. White "flight" then resulted in the area's becoming all Black, as other whites refused to buy in the neighborhood.

During the Depression of the 1930s, public housing became part of Chicago's system of residential segregation. In 1937, Congress passed the United States Housing Act, which allowed localities to establish public housing authorities to construct, own, and manage low-rent public housing. Federal money covered construction costs, and tenants' rent paid for maintenance.

The Illinois legislature created the Chicago Housing Authority (CHA) to run Chicago's public housing program. The CHA had authority to initiate proposals and develop public housing on its own, without city council approval. While the CHA was legally independent of city government, the mayor appointed the commissioners who set the agency's policies.[15] The CHA began to build apartments, but they did not nearly meet the need. More than ten applications arrived for each of the 2400 apartments that opened in 1938.[16] The CHA built most of these units as small, walk-up developments in predominantly white neighborhoods, often on the city's outskirts. Black families gained access to only 60 of the units, even though they were most in need of this housing.[17]

In the quarter century from the end of World War II through the mid-1960s, the face of the Chicago region changed dramatically. While the second "Great Migration" brought large numbers of Blacks to the city, the postwar suburban boom led to a similarly large exodus of middle-class whites to the region's burgeoning suburbs. Between 1944 and 1960, Chicago's Black population increased by almost thirty thousand per year.[18] As the six-county metropolitan area population exploded, the city's population started falling by the 1950s. The decline occurred despite the arrival of other racial and ethnic groups, especially Latinos and Asian-Americans, in increasing numbers.

Although these dramatic postwar population shifts provided another chance to expand housing opportunities for Blacks, both public and private actors instead used both new and old means to continue to confine Blacks. At the same time, most suburban development was characterized by racial and economic exclusion, both intended and structural. The region's color and class lines were reinforced.

Congress also substantially increased funding for public housing, enabling the CHA to undertake a huge public housing construction program in the 1950s and 1960s. In planning for major additions, the CHA addressed controversial questions about the location and size of developments. While the site selection debate often focused on the advantages and disadvantages of "slum" and "outlying" locations, the underlying issue was whether to build public housing in predominantly white areas or locate developments exclusively in Black neighborhoods to serve the increasingly Black tenancy. Ethnic whites, many of whom took great pride in having built their own neighborhoods and in having risen from poverty to the middle class, were especially hostile to the construction of public housing in their neighborhoods.[19] The CHA, led by Robert Taylor, its first Black chairperson, and Executive Director Elizabeth Wood, a reformer, favored a mixed strategy of building developments both in outlying, predominantly white areas and in the inner city.[20]

The controversies also involved tenant assignment. From the start of Chicago's public housing program, most complexes housed only one race.[21] The few exceptions usually segregated the races within developments and maintained strict quotas of each.[22] In the late 1940s and 1950s, when most of Chicago's racial disturbances involved housing conflicts, some of the worst violence occurred when CHA assigned to the few developments in white areas small numbers of "model" Black families—two-parent families with one parent employed.[23]

The CHA's position on site selection and its efforts to move Blacks into white developments led many city council members to conclude that the CHA, left to its own devices, would build housing in predominantly white areas and assign Blacks there.[24] Consequently, in 1949, the state legislature gave the Chicago City Council—alone among Illinois cities—veto power over proposed public housing sites. Public housing would henceforth be built mainly in Black neighborhoods because council members from majority white wards would try to exclude CHA developments.[25]

While site selection questions elicited the greatest controversy, the scale of developments was also a crucial issue. Earlier public housing consisted mostly of row houses and low-rise buildings, so the much larger scale of the post–World War II program dictated a rethinking of the design question. Some thought that massive high-rise developments, which offered significant open space for recreation, could replace slums and create positive new communities at a reasonable cost. Critics thought they were recipes for social disaster.

Between 1957 and 1968, the CHA built 14,895 high-rise public housing units—more than 1,200 apartments per year. They included Robert Taylor Homes, the largest public housing complex in the world—a South Side development with 28 identical 16-story buildings, 4,415 apartments, and 27,000 residents; the 1,684-unit Stateway Gardens, which combined with Robert Taylor Homes to form a 6,000-apartment unbroken strip two miles long and one-quarter mile wide; Cabrini-Green, with 3,021 units on the city's Near North Side; and the 1,656-unit Henry Horner Homes, on the Near West Side.[26]

The CHA emphasized large apartments for large families—those who were least well served by the private market. Three-fourths of the apartments built from 1957 through 1968 had three, four, or five bedrooms. Robert Taylor Homes was designed especially for large families, with 3,500 three- and four-bedroom units, and 1,000 units with an oversized bedroom that could accommodate three or four people. At the end of 1968, the CHA's family housing averaged four children per unit; half the families had five or more children; and more than 2,500 families had nine or more members.[27] While many white families and increasing numbers of Latinos and Asian-Americans were income-eligible, Chicago's public housing became increasingly identified as a program for Blacks.

In the private market, continuing racial exclusion from predominantly white areas led to overcrowding and deterioration of Blacks' housing, as well as acceleration of the neighborhood transition dynamic of earlier decades. With large parts of the city remaining virtually all white, the average square mile of the Black Belt in 1950 housed as many Blacks—75,000—as lived in the entire city less than forty years earlier.[28] As a result, many Blacks paid high prices and risked harassment and violence to move into white neighborhoods. Real estate brokers' "blockbusting" tactics induced large numbers of whites to leave and others not to move in. Racial succession, or resegregation, proceeded quickly, so few neighborhoods stayed racially mixed very long. In the 1950s, an estimated 74,500 units, or three and a half blocks per week, changed hands from white to Black.[29]

Meanwhile, Chicago's suburbs burgeoned, and the balkanization of the region into increasing numbers of local units accelerated. Far more housing was built in the suburbs than in the city following World War II.[30] Most were single-family homes occupied by whites.[31] Federal, state, and local governmental policies and practices, as well as private discriminatory actions, excluded most Blacks and other people of color and low-income people from relocating in the suburbs. Until the late 1960s, most residential racial discrimination was legal in most Chicago-area communities. By the time federal, state, and local fair housing laws were enacted, systemic and structural barriers had firmly entrenched racial and class residential separation in both public housing and the private market throughout the Chicago metropolitan area.

Despite the constraints, growing numbers of Blacks moved to the suburbs as their incomes grew after World War II. Middle-class Blacks increasingly left deteriorating inner-city neighborhoods, resulting in increasing class segregation among Blacks. Still, racial patterns in the suburbs replicated those in the city, with Black areas hemmed inside mostly white suburbs. Even suburban Cook County's public housing program largely mirrored the city's racially segregated pattern.

As illustrated by the small size of suburban Cook County's public housing program, housing opportunities beyond the city limits remained very limited for families with low and moderate income. As of 1970, when Chicago's public housing program had 42,687 apartments, only 5,235 housing units in the suburbs were subsidized under *all* federal programs. The majority of those, moreover, were reserved for the elderly. Large areas of the suburbs, including all of DuPage and McHenry counties, had no public housing at all.[32] In fact, the DuPage County Housing Authority was formed in order to ensure that there would be no public housing built in the county.[33]

THE GAUTREAUX CASE: CHALLENGING THE SEGREGATED SYSTEM

In the summer of 1966, American Civil Liberties Union (ACLU) lawyers went into federal court to challenge one aspect of the racially and economically segregated metropolis: racial discrimination in Chicago's public housing program. They argued that the CHA's past practices and proposed projects—nine more developments in Black neighborhoods, four of them high-rises, and six next to existing public housing complexes—violated Title VI of the 1964 Civil Rights Act, prohibiting racial discrimination in federally funded activities, and the U.S. Constitution's equal protection guarantee.[34] Dorothy Gautreaux, a civil rights and public housing tenant activist, lent her name to two class action lawsuits on behalf of all public housing residents and applicants—one against the CHA and the other against the United States Department of Housing and Urban Development (HUD), challenging racial policies and practices.[35] The HUD case was held in abeyance while the CHA case proceeded.

Federal Judge Richard B. Austin, a one-time Democratic candidate for governor, was skeptical when first assigned the case: "Where do you want them to put 'em (public housing developments)? On Lake Shore Drive?"[36] (Lake Shore Drive, which runs along Lake Michigan, included some of the city's most valuable real estate.) However, Austin's initial skepticism toward the plaintiffs' case turned to strong criticism of the CHA as the agency's covert policies and practices were revealed.

Early in 1969, Judge Austin concluded that the CHA had discriminated intentionally in selecting sites for public housing and in assigning tenants to its developments.[37] No state or local law required operating the public housing program on a racially segregated basis. Nor had the CHA adopted a formal policy of segregation. Instead, his finding of a site-selection violation was based on the CHA's having built most of its family housing in predominantly Black neighborhoods. From 1954 through 1966, 99.4 percent of the CHA's 10,256 family units—all but 63—were placed in largely Black neighborhoods. Austin determined that only intentional racial discrimination could explain such a pattern. CHA officials' admissions about their race-conscious processes added more proof of their discriminatory purpose.

The judge rejected the CHA's defense that it proposed sites throughout the city but that the City Council rejected most sites outside Black neighborhoods. He concluded that the CHA's willingness to abide by the council's segregated approval patterns violated the plaintiffs' civil rights, even if the agency would have proceeded differently on its own. Consequently, public housing was deeply embedded and implicated in the city's segregated residential patterns. The CHA's site selection practices reflected the private market patterns, while reinforcing and perpetuating them as well.

The judge also found the CHA's tenant-assignment practices illegal because the agency used separate waiting lists for Blacks and whites and "steered" Blacks to developments in Black neighborhoods in order to maintain a segregated system. Moreover, the four developments in predominantly white areas remained well over 90 percent white as a result of racial quotas, while the other CHA family developments had a 99 percent Black occupancy.[38] The CHA argued that separation of the races was justified to avoid the racial tension and violence that occurred when the CHA tried to move Black families into white-area developments. Judge Austin concluded that a history of tension and violence could not justify denying Black families their civil rights.[39]

THE DESIGN OF THE SCATTERED SITE PROGRAM

The Gautreaux decision dramatically changed the legal context, declaring the whole system under which the CHA had operated for a decade and a half illegal. But the remedy for such a violation did not follow by some logical process. Relief had to be constructed or created when it involved correcting the system prospectively as well as addressing the continuing effects of the years of operating illegally.[40]

Judge Austin ordered the parties to work together to develop a proposed remedial order, and if they could not agree, for each to submit its own proposal. The CHA resisted working together, so the parties proceeded largely independently. They operated in largely uncharted territory, since there was so little prior experience on which to base a public housing desegregation plan. While plaintiffs' counsel developed a detailed plan, the CHA proposed simply that it be ordered not to consider race in seeking locations for public housing.[41] After a five-month planning process, the judge largely adopted the plaintiffs' counsel's proposal as his remedial order in July of 1969.[42]

The order was designed with an eye toward implementation. It took into account the context in which the remedy would operate—the city's housing patterns and dynamics and the area's governmental structure. It also focused on programmatic factors that could affect its operation, including supply and demand aspects, administration, and community response. It did not address the resources needed for implementation.

The order incorporated a "mobility" assumption—that desegregation was to be achieved by low-income Blacks moving to mostly white areas. The centerpiece of the court's order, the scattered site program, relied primarily on a supply-side approach to desegregation. It required the CHA to provide additional public housing under a racial formula stressing predominantly white areas from which public housing had been systematically excluded during the construction heyday. The first seven hundred apartments were to be in predominantly white neighborhoods, known as the "general public housing area," as were three out of every four additional units. The "general" area excluded any census tract with 30 percent or more Blacks, as well as a one-mile "buffer zone" surrounding such tracts—referred to as the "limited area."[43] While racial integration was the focus, the program could also produce some economic integration because many white neighborhoods were largely middle-class as well.

The CHA still had to secure the City Council's approval of proposed public housing sites, as state law required. In addition, the CHA had the option of providing up to one-third of the white-area housing in suburban Cook County, with the agreement of suburban officials, as state law also required. While the court order specified that the CHA was to make additional housing available "as rapidly as possible," it did not include a timetable.[44] Nor did it quantify the total numbers of families to be housed or apartments to be provided.

The order also incorporated the recently enacted federal "Section 23" leasing program, under which the CHA leased apartments from private developers, rented them to public housing applicants, and paid rent subsidies on tenants' behalf. This was a small program that the CHA used mostly to help elderly tenants secure low-rent accommodations in the private market. Because of the Section 23 program's small size and emphasis on the elderly, it was not expected to play a significant role in remedying the violation.

The CHA also had to adopt a nondiscriminatory tenant-assignment plan for its existing public housing complexes; but it could continue to use quotas—albeit at perhaps a higher percentage—at developments in mostly white neighborhoods, in order to attract Latinos, because the CHA believed they would not move into majority Black developments.[45] Moreover, the court order did not emphasize integrating existing developments in Black neighborhoods. It did not require public housing residents to move from one development to another in order to achieve integration, so it left the pattern of thousands of racially segregated apartments largely intact. This was an implicit recognition of the intractability of the deeply entrenched racial occupancy patterns in public housing. Even though many white families—both Anglos and Latinos— were eligible for public housing, there was little chance of attracting enough of them to predominantly Black neighborhoods to produce a stable racial balance.[46]

In order to promote interest in the new program, the order required the CHA to inform public housing residents and applicants about its plans and allow them to sign up on a new waiting list. Also, features such as small-scale developments in neighborhoods not dominated by public housing were designed in part to attract families.

As defendant, the CHA had to administer the scattered site program. While the initial order did not grant the CHA any authority it did not already have under state law, the court offered the agency the opportunity to use its full range of powers. Not only was the CHA to build in predominantly white city neighborhoods, contingent on City Council approval, but it could also develop some of the mandated housing in Cook County suburbs, with local officials' agreement. The order also reflected the judge's doubts about the CHA's commitment and competence, incorporating a racial formula for locating new public housing rather than leaving it to the local agency's good-faith efforts to build in predominantly white neighborhoods.

Given the history of white neighborhoods' hostility to public housing, the scattered site program also included features designed to minimize expected community resistance. The racial formula, with its strong majority of whites and a buffer zone, was designed to accommodate the definition in the white receiving communities of an acceptable racial mix. Also, instead of the concentrations of high-rise complexes that characterized much of the CHA's housing, future housing was to consist of low-rise, small buildings on scattered sites. Generally, developments could not house more than 120 people, nor could they be located in neighborhoods that already had a substantial amount of public housing. This dispersal of public housing on both a racial and class basis was also designed to accommodate white middle-class communities' residential preferences and ensure their continued neighborhood dominance.[47] In fact, the level of dispersal in the Gautreaux order was far greater than what was characterized as "scattered site" development in other large cities. In the Forest Hills section of New York City, a "scattered site" public housing development featured three twelve-story buildings on one site.[48] In addition, half of the units in any CHA scattered site development were to be reserved for low-income families already living in the neighborhood—presumably white families in predominantly white neighborhoods.

Thus, the program sought to maximize peaceful and stable integration and minimize white "fight and flight." The small-scale and scattered nature of the developments was designed to calm whites' fears as to the entry of large numbers of Blacks and to combat the negative images of public housing "projects." Reserving units for neighborhood residents sought both to integrate buildings and send a reassuring message about the developments to the community.

The order was silent on the amount and source of funding for the scattered site program. Since the remedy emphasized the public housing program, it assumed that HUD would fund the CHA's program as it had in the past.

IMPLEMENTATION: THE CHA ERA

For almost two decades, implementation of the scattered site program was virtually nonexistent: only several hundred units had been provided by 1987 compared to the thousands of apartments that the CHA built in the preceding comparable period. Judge Austin, who recognized from the outset the level of opposition to his order and the ability of the city and the CHA to resist it, speculated that the case could mean the end of public housing construction in Chicago. In 1987, years after Austin's death, Judge Marvin Aspen, who had the case by then, was so frustrated with the lack of progress that he took responsibility away from CHA and appointed a receiver—an agent of the court charged with implementing the judge's orders—to carry out the stalled program.

The lack of progress was not for lack of demand. Thousands of eligible families expressed interest in scattered site housing. They needed rent subsidies and anticipated that the housing and the city neighborhoods where it was to be located would be an improvement over their deteriorating public housing developments.

The problem was not lack of resources, either—at least not in the early years. HUD initially set aside funding for CHA to develop 1,500 family public housing units. While that was a substantial scaling back of CHA's request for ten thousand apartments for families and the elderly, it far exceeded the program's initial needs. Moreover, HUD assumed that this allocation would last a few years, and then the agency would make available additional funding as needed.

Instead, administrative failings, combined with community resistance, stymied the scattered site program. Even with several provisions in the order designed to accommodate white community concerns and minimize opposition, there was a great deal of resistance to scattered site housing. Those impediments were compounded by the program's supply-side housing strategy, which relied on new construction and rehabilitation. That approach resulted in high visibility, which made development an easy target for opponents. Public procedures and local government approvals were frequently required, thus opening opportunities for opposition by public officials and private citizens.

The initial response of the CHA and the community—both top down from political leaders and bottom up from organized residents— served as a sign that implementation would be very difficult. Race- and class-based concerns, as well as the taint of public housing in general and the CHA in particular, led quickly to widespread resistance. The CHA, Mayor Daley, the City Council, and organized residents combined to prevent the program from getting started on a timely basis, thus establishing a pattern that plagued the program for many years.

The CHA was a reluctant desegregation program administrator, as foreshadowed by its previous practices and its resistance at the planning stage. The question about the CHA was not so much whether it was committed to the court's objectives, but whether it would comply with the court's orders. The CHA's intransigence and incompetence emerged early and persisted. The organization both reflected and shaped the community's response to the program.

The CHA was very slow to locate white neighborhood sites. Moreover, its initial list of proposed sites included, in addition to a number of appropriate ones, a newly built school, an operating factory, and a nonexistent address. There was also delay as the CHA sought suburban sites on the grounds that housing was a problem in the entire metropolitan area that called for regional solutions. The CHA invited suburban public housing officials to join in the scattered site program, but none accepted, even though the new program promised far different physical and social arrangements than in the past.

Once the CHA compiled a list of apparently appropriate sites, it decided not to submit them to the City Council until after the 1971 mayoral election, because of the anticipated political fallout. Frustrated by the delays, the district judge ordered the agency to submit sites to the council well before the election. After appeals that necessitated establishing a new deadline, the housing authority waited until two weeks before the 1971 mayoral election before submitting the sites to the City Council—thus thrusting the issue squarely into the political arena.

With one of Mayor Richard J. Daley's closest political allies serving as CHA chairman, the agency's and the city's responses to the judge's order were closely coordinated. Mayor Daley, along with the City Council that he controlled, vigorously opposed the scattered site program when the sites were announced. Both the proposed sites and Daley's response were front page stories in the local newspapers. Daley objected to the federal court's dictating where poor people should live; instead, the mayor said, the housing should be provided "where people want it."[49]

Events between 1966 and 1969 help explain why Daley resisted the desegregation order so strongly. In the summer of 1966, Dr. Martin Luther King and a coalition of local civil rights groups—the Chicago Freedom Movement—marched into white neighborhoods to dramatize Blacks' exclusion from much of the area's housing market. The marchers encountered large, hostile crowds, who assaulted them verbally and physically, and damaged or destroyed many of their cars. The open-housing marches alienated two of Mayor Daley's most important constituencies—white ethnic groups because the mayor permitted the marches and sent police to protect the marchers, and Black activists because the mayor failed to protect them adequately or open up housing opportunities. While Daley emerged largely victorious in negotiations that ended the marches, these demonstrations cost him a degree of control and laid bare the city's deep racial divisions.

The spring and summer of 1968 witnessed two more events that challenged Daley's authority. In April, Blacks took to the streets in frustration and anger after Dr. King's assassination. As Blacks burned buildings in their West Side communities, Daley's inability to control the neighborhoods was apparent. A few months later, when the Democratic convention came to Chicago, thousands of antiwar protesters demonstrated against the country's involvement in Vietnam. Daley's control of the city was once again threatened, as protesters massed in Grant Park throughout the night and demonstrated in front of the convention's major hotel.

In 1969, Mayor Daley viewed a federal court's mandate of public housing desegregation as still another threat to his grip on the city. Building public housing in white neighborhoods would once again have pitted the Democratic machine's major constituencies against each other and risked alienating both of them. Construction could also have led to renewed violence, challenging Daley's ability to maintain public order.[50] Once again, outsiders were trying to tell Chicagoans how to run their city—this time it was the federal government in the form of an unelected and unaccountable judge. Daley's plea for local control found a responsive audience among white residents and their elected representatives.

The Chicago City Council followed the mayor's lead, repeated its own pre-Gautreaux pattern, and took no action on most of the sites the CHA proposed. Even HUD's withholding of $38 million in urban development funds because of the lack of progress did not overcome the council's resistance.

In the meantime, the CHA abandoned the elaborate public education program that it had paid to have developed, even before unveiling it. This initiative was designed to inform communities slated for scattered site public housing about the dramatic changes in the program, and to create a new image for public housing in the city. Once political leaders opposed the program, the CHA canceled the effort and warehoused the materials. As a result, the program faced a hostile environment resulting from its high visibility combined with misinformation that was not countered by the accurate information that the CHA had prepared.

As of 1974, no new public housing had been built in the five years since the original order. The district judge, citing the City Council's continuing failure to approve sites as frustrating relief without good reason, granted the CHA additional authority by ordering it to ignore the state law mandating council approval and proceed with development.[51] While that removed an important legal barrier, and ground was finally broken on housing for approximately sixty-five families in predominantly white neighborhoods in 1975, both administrative problems and community opposition persisted.

Although the CHA was obligated under the court order to use its "best efforts" to increase the supply "as rapidly as possible," inaction continued to characterize its response. The agency assigned almost no staff to the effort, and it failed to take steps necessary to acquire sites and buildings for the program. It did not keep current on available sites, use its power of eminent domain to secure sites, package proposals to overcome HUD's cost limits, or otherwise use its initiative to advance the program.

The agency sometimes secured neighborhood acquiescence in its plans to acquire and rehabilitate apartment buildings; but then it allowed buildings to remain vacant for years, creating a blighting influence as the boarded-up properties deteriorated further. It also failed to make needed repairs in completed scattered site units or used contractors that did shoddy work. The result was that the limited good will dissipated and was replaced by a sense of betrayal, with greater hostility than ever to the scattered site program.

After Richard Daley's death in 1976, a succession of Chicago mayors expressed greater receptivity to the scattered site program, but those rhetorical changes did not have much effect on the program's progress. Mayor Jane Byrne expressed support for scattered site housing as part of a 1979 arrangement with the court that eliminated the requirement of placing the first seven hundred apartments in predominantly white areas and changed the formula from three-to-one in "general" and "limited" areas, respectively, to one-to-one. However, Mayor Byrne subsequently backed off from her support of the program, even attempting unsuccessfully to obtain the court's permission to terminate the scattered site program and use the funds instead to maintain existing housing. On another occasion, in response to white community opposition to two proposed sites in a southwest side neighborhood, Byrne asked the CHA to sell the sites. While the court blocked this effort, Byrne's obstructionist tactics contributed to the continued glacial progress.

In his 1983 mayoral campaign, Harold Washington expressed support for the scattered site program. He argued that it was important to comply with the law, and that scattered site housing could help address the city's pressing need for affordable housing. Nevertheless, the program continued to stagnate, as the CHA still lacked the capacity to carry it out. Moreover, white community opposition did not diminish with Washington's encouragement to move forward.

There was little organized community support for scattered site housing from the outset, and many private citizens worked to frustrate its implementation. As in the past, overt racial prejudice combined with residents' race and class-based fears about property values, crime, school quality, and physical and social deterioration. The resulting opposition manifested itself in many ways. When proposed sites were announced, many lobbied their alderpersons to block the sites.[52] On the city's Southwest Side, where whites had long resisted Blacks moving in from the Black Belt, fifteen hundred homeowners hanged Judge Austin in effigy.[53] In a more covert strategy, private builders purchased and developed proposed sites before the CHA could gain control of them. Any delays, including the city council's inaction, made possible this private attrition of proposed sites.

A coalition of community organizations and individuals filed a lawsuit to block construction, arguing that public housing tenants were likely to engage in criminal and other antisocial activities. It invoked the law and the courts to assert competing rights, making a class-based argument that low-income people constituted an environmental hazard.[54] The judge rejected the claim.

Resistance generally diminished after families moved into scattered site housing, partly because the CHA contracted out the management to local nonprofit organizations and management firms. Competent management of these units and strict screening of tenants helped to alleviate community hostility once the units were rented.[55]

Resistance from public and private actors met little counterpressure from the Black community.[56] Black organizations focused increasingly on gaining political power and developing their own communities rather than on desegregation. In fact, several local Black organizations and civil rights groups sought modification of the court order to permit leasing or new construction in Black neighborhoods.[57]

While funding limitations did not impede the program at the outset, they played a role later. Delay resulted from the Nixon administration's 1973 nationwide moratorium on the public housing program. The president impounded appropriated funds in order to undertake a comprehensive review of federal subsidy programs and develop alternative housing policies. In order to implement relief in Gautreaux, HUD lifted the moratorium for Chicago, but not until more than a year later.[58]

More generally, HUD's development-cost restrictions made it difficult to purchase scarce, suitable, vacant land in the "general area" and to build the low-density developments that the program contemplated. While the agency raised its limits to take into account the shortage of vacant land in the "general area," its delays slowed the program. HUD's temporary reduction of funds for administrative expenses also impeded progress.

IMPLEMENTATION: THE ERA OF THE RECEIVER

Plaintiffs' counsel made three requests over almost a decade to have the intransigent and incompetent CHA displaced in favor of a court-appointed receiver to administer scattered site development. In each instance, the judge found serious deficiencies in performance and leveled harsh criticism at the CHA. The first two times, however, the judge exhorted the CHA to make marked improvement or face additional judicial intervention, but refused to take the program out of the agency's hands. Finally, in 1987, after almost two decades of persistent administrative failings and scant progress, the judge took the highly unusual step of appointing a receiver. He selected the Habitat Company, a Chicago-based developer of middle-income and luxury housing, to take over the development program. (The company is unrelated to Habitat for Humanity, known for its association with President Jimmy Carter.)

Unlike the CHA, Habitat actively sought the opportunity to develop scattered site public housing. While there was a potential for profits, this task was likely to be more difficult and less profitable than Habitat's market-rate developments. (Habitat earned about three million dollars in fees in its first decade as receiver.) Consequently, Habitat's economic motivation seemed less important than its desire to make a contribution to the community.

Moreover, while Habitat had not developed housing for low-income families, it had extensive experience and a solid reputation in housing development. The company's background in land acquisition, financing, architectural work, and construction indicated that it had the capacity to operate the scattered site program more effectively than the CHA. Habitat's resources enabled it to staff the program with experienced housing professionals and to engage well-regarded architects.

With its appointment as receiver, Habitat stepped into the shoes of the CHA, except that Habitat reported to the judge rather than the CHA board. Consequently, Habitat had a degree of political independence that the CHA staff lacked. Unlike the CHA, Habitat carried out an extensive public education effort, preparing materials and visual presentations, and meeting with community residents in neighborhoods slated for public housing.

With greater commitment, capacity, and authority than the CHA, Habitat picked up the pace of the scattered site program. By the end of its first decade as receiver, Habitat had built or acquired and rehabilitated 1,846 scattered site units in three-fourths of the city's "community areas."[59] This included 1,161 units in the "general area" and 685 units in the "limited area"—in neighborhoods designated as undergoing economic revitalization. This was far more than the CHA had accomplished in almost two decades.

However, while improved administration was necessary for the program's progress, it was not sufficient to make a breakthrough because other constraints continued to beset the program. The continued emphasis on new construction made affordable land an essential element; but there was little vacant land available in mostly white neighborhoods within HUD's cost ceilings. In addition, Habitat's efforts to build and acquire housing ran up against legal constraints, including delays in securing zoning and construction approvals. Habitat also encountered federal regulations that often impeded progress.

Moreover, as Habitat continued the highly visible supply-side strategy, building public housing and purchasing housing for the CHA, the program continued to encounter community resistance to public housing and its residents. White (Anglo), Latino, and even Black groups all organized at various times to block scattered site housing in their respective neighborhoods. While the opposition did not stop the program, it reduced its scale and pace. Habitat used a variety of strategies to overcome community resistance. It engaged in public education through presentations and discussions with residents in neighborhoods slated for scattered site housing. It also negotiated with community groups to find development plans that were acceptable to residents. At times, it simply used its legal authority to build or buy housing in the face of community opposition—anticipating that things would settle down as tenants moved in and neighborhood fears were not realized.

One of the most dramatic examples of such hostility was the well-organized 1996 attempt by hundreds of working- and middle-class white residents of a far northwest side neighborhood to prevent Habitat's acquisition and rehabilitation of a three-flat building there, even though at least one of the units in this small building would go to neighborhood residents. Community protests based on fears of lost property values and a drug influx were angry and persistent, some of the most intense opposition in three decades. Habitat and the CHA had a series of meetings with neighbors to discuss their concerns about public housing and about not being consulted. Ultimately, Habitat acquired the building for CHA ownership in spite of the neighbors' objections. However, none of the three initial tenant families were African-American, perhaps because of fears of reprisals. Two households were from the community, and the other was on the CHA's waiting list. One was Latino, one Anglo, and one Arab-American. The level of opposition to this small building, the first public housing in this virtually all-white area, illustrated the continuing white resistance to scattered site housing in spite of the change in administration.

Resistance also emerged in Latino neighborhoods, which were part of the "general housing area" under the 1969 racial formula. Latinos comprised less than 2 percent of the city's population in 1970, but by 1990 they had become a substantial presence in the city both numerically and geographically. These neighborhoods became important locations for Habitat's development plans as other white areas shrank due to continuing resegregation and white suburban migration. In addition, land in those other areas was developed, and the scarce vacant parcels became increasingly unaffordable.

In the early 1990s, Latino organizations objected to what they considered undue concentrations of public housing in their communities, especially since their neighborhoods already had substantial amounts of privately owned subsidized housing. Persistent and effective opposition in white neighborhoods made less politically powerful Latino communities prime candidates for scattered site housing.[60] While census tracts with high-rise public housing complexes were only 1.3 percent Latino, scattered site tracts averaged over fifty percent Latino.[61] Ultimately, Latino community organizations and the receiver negotiated a reduction in the size and number of scattered site developments in Latino neighborhoods.

Community opposition spread to Black neighborhoods when the judge permitted additional public housing construction in predominantly Black neighborhoods in order to redevelop inner-city neighborhoods on a mixed-income basis. In effect, this was a decision to forego racial integration, at least in the short run, in favor of class integration. That expanded Habitat's authority geographically, permitting an increased pace of development, while generating additional community opposition.

Habitat encountered resistance from working- and middle-class West and South side residents as it sought to build public housing in their predominantly Black neighborhoods. A scattered site proposal on the South Side sparked opposition from Black homeowners trying to revitalize the neighborhood.[62] They argued that the proposal for more than two hundred public housing apartments on multiple sites would threaten the neighborhood's viability. With some modifications and many delays, development proceeded.

By the end of Habitat's first decade as receiver, it was clear that the future prospects for developing scattered site housing in predominantly white neighborhoods were quite limited. Scarce vacant land and limited federal funds, coupled with continued community opposition, made new construction in those areas an increasingly difficult task.

THREE

Inventing the Metropolitan-Wide Gautreaux Program

THE HUD CASE

The case against HUD moved along a separate and distinct track from the CHA litigation. After the judge held the HUD lawsuit in abeyance while he decided against CHA, proceedings began against HUD in 1970. The HUD case, which derived from the CHA one, reflected the structure of the public housing program. The federal government paid the capital cost of local developments. While local agencies had significant autonomy in administering their public housing programs, HUD also approved construction sites and tenant assignment plans. The plaintiffs claimed that HUD acquiesced in CHA's illegal activities by approving housing sites and the agency's tenant assignment plan and by funding the discriminatory program with over $350 million between 1950 and 1966.

Judge Austin dismissed the case against HUD, portraying the federal agency as facing a dilemma. Having tried in good faith but unsuccessfully to get CHA to operate on a nondiscriminatory basis, HUD had to continue funding the discriminatory program or deprive low-income families of much-needed housing.[1] The court of appeals reversed, finding that HUD's approval and funding of a program that it knew to be discriminatory fully implicated federal officials in the local agency's illegal conduct.[2] Plaintiffs' counsel argued that the remedy against HUD should encompass the six-county Chicago metropolitan area, in order to provide housing opportunities for the more than forty thousand plaintiff-class families. He further suggested that an approach encompassing the metropolitan area would have educational, employment, and other benefits for the families involved.[3]

However, the district judge ruled that because HUD's violation—like CHA's—took place within Chicago and the plaintiffs were city residents, he did not have the authority to grant relief beyond the city limits.[4] Once again, the court of appeals disagreed, deciding that metropolitan-wide relief was permissible. The U.S. Supreme Court affirmed that view, even though two years earlier it had rejected a proposed metropolitan-wide remedy in a school desegregation case. In *Milliken v. Bradley*, the Court held that school desegregation measures could not extend into Detroit's suburbs because the violation and its effects were limited to the central city.[5]

However, the Supreme Court took a different tack in the *Gautreaux* case. In the landmark 1976 decision, the justices agreed 8–0 that a metropolitan-wide housing desegregation remedy was permissible.[6] The Court's opinion distinguished *Gautreaux* from school desegregation cases because HUD's own definition of the appropriate geographical area for its program's operations was the Chicago "housing market area"—the six-county metropolitan area within which homeseekers compete for housing units. In addition, the justices concluded that it was possible to design a regional remedy that did not impermissibly interfere with the traditional powers and functions of innocent governmental bodies. The authority of suburban governments and public housing agencies would remain intact, including zoning and other land use controls. Moreover, local housing officials would not have to initiate housing proposals to accommodate Chicago residents.[7]

The Supreme Court left the district court to decide, in light of the facts of the case, whether to extend the remedy beyond the central city. However, it noted the great difficulties encountered in providing relief in Chicago and discussed possible metropolitan approaches. The opinion emphasized the changes in federal housing programs since the initial *Gautreaux* decision in 1969, focusing on the Section 8 program Congress enacted in 1974.[8] The program provided rent subsidies for low-income families to live in private housing, making up the difference between the market rent and a specified percentage of tenants' income.[9]

The Supreme Court also referred to another aspect of the 1974 Housing Act, in which Congress stated as a goal the deconcentration of low-income people.[10] Thus, even though the *Gautreaux* case was based on racial discrimination, it had class implications as well. The plaintiff class consisted of low-income families, so suburban relief would likely entail class mixing as well as racial integration.

With that, the Supreme Court sent the case back to the trial court, leaving the judge with a great deal of discretion on the threshold question of whether to mandate metropolitan-wide relief as well as the content of the remedy. At the same time, the Court placed substantial limitations on the trial court's remedial powers.

Both the process of designing a HUD remedy and its content reflected the lessons learned from the frustrating experience with the scattered site program. The parties sought ways to overcome the obstacles that had beset that program's seven lean years.

THE PROCESS OF INVENTION

Although the Supreme Court's opinion contemplated further trial court proceedings to decide about metropolitan-wide relief, the lawyers for the plaintiff class and HUD preempted that process by negotiating a temporary remedial arrangement. They agreed to a one-year experimental metropolitan program, with both sides retaining the option to return to court to pursue a more favorable resolution.

Both sides had compelling reasons for avoiding further litigation. The CHA scattered site remedy designed by plaintiffs' representatives, adopted by the Court, and imposed on local housing officials who had opted out of the planning process had produced only token amounts of housing and demonstrated the limits of judicial coercion. Instead, if the remedial initiative was a product of co-operative efforts between the parties, HUD would have a stake in carrying it out rather than resisting it. Although HUD had appealed the case to the Supreme Court to prevent a metropolitan-wide order, it too stood to gain from a negotiated agreement by escaping the court's coercive power. Moreover, the agency had statutory affirmative fair housing and "deconcentration" responsibilities and administered many of its programs on a metropolitan-wide basis.[11]

After counsel for HUD and the plaintiff class sketched out the broad outlines of a metropolitan program on a napkin at a downtown Chicago restaurant, plaintiffs' lawyers and a team of housing experts developed the rest of the structure.[12] The Chicago Housing Authority, which had no formal role in this part of the litigation and had demonstrated neither the commitment nor the capacity to address these issues, was not involved in the process. Also absent from the process were the public housing tenants and applicants, because their lawyers believed that it was not possible to represent the views of forty thousand plaintiff-class families.[13] While leaving them out risked reducing demand for the program because of a lack of awareness and credibility among public housing residents and applicants, poor people have regularly participated in programs in which they had little input, so it was unlikely that families would reject the program en masse on that account.[14]

By early June 1976, the lawyers agreed on the steps that HUD would take to carry out a one-year experimental program, which came to be called the Gautreaux Assisted Housing Program, or simply the Gautreaux program, and agreed as well on the efforts both sides would make to reach an ultimate resolution of the case. A series of short-term agreements continued the initial program until, in 1981, the district judge adopted a consent decree that the parties proposed in order to institutionalize the metropolitan-wide approach.[15] The program remained in place until 1998, when it reached the stipulated goal of assisting 7,100 families to secure housing.

THE STRUCTURE OF THE GAUTREAUX PROGRAM

The Gautreaux program might be thought of as a metropolitan reinvention of the scattered site program—continuing its objectives, making major changes to alleviate the constraints that impeded its implementation, and accommodating changes in the spatial and legal context. The new program retained the objective of facilitating the movement of low-income Black families into predominantly white areas—a mobility program with integrationist goals. It also continued some of the earlier initiative's tactics, such as dispersing families.

At the same time, the program's structure applied the lessons learned from the scattered site program. It made significant modifications in order to address impediments to implementation such as administrative failings and community opposition.

Moreover, the new initiative took into account the changed context. The legal context changed with the addition of the suburbs as permissible destinations, the assignment to HUD of remedial obligations, and the incorporation of the Section 8 subsidy program that Congress had created two years earlier. With the new emphasis on suburban movement, the Gautreaux program faced different demographic and development patterns than the scattered site effort. While racial and economic residential separation were common to both the city and suburbs, the suburbs had much larger portions that were predominantly white and middle-class. With the exception of some southern and western suburbs that were either predominantly Black or racially integrated, the bulk of suburbia represented possible destinations under the Gautreaux program's racial formula. The residential patterns also ensured that participants would often cross class lines as well as racial ones.

While the law of the *Gautreaux* case applied to both the city and the suburbs, local law differed between the city and many of the suburbs. Suburban land-use laws limited apartment development and escalated development costs, thus presenting the program with a very different housing stock than the city's. Because the new program relied heavily on renting existing units, those differences were a potentially important part of the context.

Finally, operating in the suburbs meant the possibility of families moving to more than two hundred municipalities rather than within one, and the potential involvement of more than a dozen public housing agencies, rather than one. Multiple jurisdictions added to the complexity of the administrative challenge but opened up much greater opportunities spatially.

The 1976 agreement contemplated mobility-based integration on a metropolitan-wide basis.[16] The Gautreaux program, which would assist families to move into existing private housing, specified that at least 75 percent of the families must locate in the suburbs. It even identified tentative goals for suburban Cook County and the five other counties in the area.[17] Like the scattered site program, the agreement used a racial formula:

> Not more than 25% of the families to be housed under this demonstration may locate in any portion of the City of Chicago or in minority areas (to be designated by agreement between HUD and the plaintiffs) of the Chicago SMSA outside of the City of Chicago.[18]

Subsequently, the earlier definition of "limited areas" as having 30 percent or more Black residents was incorporated into the Gautreaux program. The agreement also provided for dispersing families within each of the region's six counties, leaving the task of defining and implementing this requirement to program administrators.[19] In addition to the Gautreaux program, the agreement said that HUD would try to give plaintiff-class families access to new HUD-assisted developments in the six-county region, regardless of the area's racial composition.

ADMINISTERING THE PROGRAM

In the regular Section 8 program, eligible participants secured certificates from the local public housing agency, and the market operated in quite traditional ways after that. Although the public agency paid part of the rent and ensured that units met minimum standards, prospective tenants and landlords made their own matches. The Gautreaux program, however, included additional administrative functions because the market alone was unlikely to achieve the program's metropolitan integrationist objectives.

Several concerns motivated not leaving the program entirely to the vagaries of the marketplace. Significant information gaps existed among both plaintiff-class families and area landlords, and efficient operation of markets requires that both sides have adequate information. The families had little, if any, direct experience with the suburbs and few networks that provided information about Chicago's numerous and varied suburban communities. They also lacked information about the experience of residential integration. Through counseling of families, the program aimed to overcome these barriers. Counseling was to serve as a support mechanism—including sometimes accompanying families on site visits to affirm their ability to make the move, and to help them adapt to their new surroundings.

Landlords might also have lacked adequate information about the families involved in the Gautreaux program. Many had limited experience renting to Blacks or low-income families, and may have had negative views based on stereotypes of inner-city or public housing residents. Absent provisions to overcome these information barriers, landlords might not volunteer in sufficient numbers.

While defendants ordinarily shoulder primary if not sole responsibility for carrying out remedial initiatives, neither CHA nor HUD were likely candidates in this case. The scattered site program experience showed the importance of having administrators who were both committed to the enterprise and capable of carrying it out. The CHA had shown neither, nor did it have the legal authority to operate throughout the six-county area. HUD, on the other hand, operated throughout the region; but as the public housing program illustrated, HUD traditionally funded and regulated, while local, regional, state, and private entities administered the programs. HUD lacked the authority and expertise needed to carry out day- to-day Section 8 responsibilities.

An administrator was needed with sufficient geographical and programmatic authority, as well as the commitment and competence to carry out a metropolitan-wide mobility effort. Because of the innovative character of the Gautreaux program, no organization had the precise experience or the demonstrated capacity to implement it. However, the parties agreed that the Leadership Council for Metropolitan Open

Communities was the best choice for a lead agency. While the Leadership Council had its shortcomings, the parties concluded that it was not only more qualified than the CHA and HUD, but that it also surpassed actual or potential competitors. Most other entities lacked either the authority to operate throughout the metropolitan area or the capacity to perform the necessary functions. The agreement stipulated that HUD was to contract with the Leadership Council to perform the key administrative functions—to "locate, counsel, and assist members of the plaintiff class to find existing units, and locate owners of housing willing to participate in the program."[20]

The Leadership Council was a nonprofit fair housing agency created a decade earlier as the result of negotiations surrounding the Chicago Freedom Movement's open housing marches that Dr. King led into white neighborhoods. The city's political, business, and civic leadership, and the civil rights activists agreed that there should be an ongoing organization that would monitor and implement steps to end discrimination and open up housing opportunities throughout the metropolitan area.

In the ten years since its founding, the Leadership Council had established itself as one of the preeminent fair housing agencies in the country. It had a staff of housing professionals and lawyers, and a board comprised of influential members of Chicago's business, civic, and civil rights leadership.[21] The agency had a wide range of experience in fair housing, including legal action, public education and advocacy, and counseling of Black homeseekers.

The Leadership Council's mission closely matched that of the Gautreaux program. The Leadership Council operated on a metropolitan-wide scale, with a strong emphasis on the suburbs. In the early 1970s, the Leadership Council worked with a group of suburban mayors through the Regional Housing Coalition, promoting affordable housing in the suburbs. The agency also focused on the real estate industry, developing relationships with like-minded landlords and property managers. It had secured voluntary cooperation of the real estate industry in accepting Black families in nearly all-white areas; but it had also sued industry members and suburban public bodies for discrimination.

Moreover, the Leadership Council had already begun an initiative similar to the Gautreaux program. Earlier in 1976, the agency had contracted with the Illinois Housing Development Authority (IHDA), the state housing finance agency, to locate, counsel, and assist *Gautreaux* plaintiff families to move into state-financed rental housing. Based on an agreement with the Gautreaux lawyers, the IHDA required developers it assisted to set aside a small percentage of their apartments for those families. Although the program was new, small-scale, and did not require the Leadership Council to locate willing landlords, it put the agency in touch with plaintiff-class families and provided helpful experience for carrying out the Gautreaux program. Finally, Leadership Council staff helped design the Gautreaux program and was thus in a good position to implement it.

At the same time, the Leadership Council lacked some important assets for the task. Rather than operating as a grassroots organization with a neighborhood-based constituency, it was a "downtown" civic organization with an elite governing board. While the agency had worked with many Black families, most were working and middle-class people seeking housing in the unsubsidized private market. It had not worked extensively with public housing residents or other poor Blacks and thus had not had the opportunity to gain needed experience, relationships, or trust. The agency also lacked hands-on experience with the Section 8 program, so it had limited familiarity with the program's mechanics and few ongoing contacts with the suburban public housing agencies administering that program.[22]

The Leadership Council's dual role relative to the real estate industry presented problems as well as opportunities. While the Council's highly regarded fair housing litigation unit had challenged many landlords' and property managers' policies and practices in court, other staff had worked cooperatively to educate industry members about their responsibilities under fair housing laws. This ambiguous agency-industry relationship added uncertainty to the Leadership Council's prospects in the Gautreaux program because success depended so heavily on landlords' voluntary participation.

The Leadership Council's qualifications for running the program far outweighed its limitations. Its closest competitor was the Home Investment Fund (HIF), another Chicago-based, nonprofit, fair housing agency, which also vied for the opportunity to administer the new program. Founded in 1968, the HIF counseled and otherwise assisted minority families seeking to relocate in predominantly white Chicago area communities. The HIF and the Leadership Council had an affiliation agreement, overlapping boards, and had secured funding and worked cooperatively to achieve common objectives. But the HIF argued that its service orientation and experience helping Blacks find housing in white areas put it in a better position to run the Gautreaux program.

While the HIF had more recent and extensive counseling experience than the Leadership Council, it lacked the resources and stature of its older and larger affiliate. It also shared some of the same shortcomings, including a lack of grassroots connections and experience working with low-income Black families, since it primarily counseled middle-class homebuyers. HIF later merged with the Leadership Council.

Most other potential candidates—suburban public housing agencies, the state housing agency, and other private groups—lacked the authority to operate throughout the metropolitan area or to perform the necessary tasks. Most of the Chicago region's local public housing agencies administered their own Section 8 programs, but they had limited geographical jurisdiction, ranging from a single municipality to a suburban county. Numerous agencies lacking experience with joint ventures would have had to be enlisted to carry out a coordinated regionwide program.[23]

In addition, none of the agencies had counseled families or solicited landlords. Nor had they shown any inclination to help Chicago residents move to the suburbs when the CHA invited them to participate in the scattered site program. With their jurisdiction limited and their commitment and capacity in doubt, public housing agencies were not likely candidates for lead agencies in this new initiative.

The Illinois Housing Development Authority (IHDA) qualified geographically but not programmatically. It operated throughout the metropolitan area, but it mainly financed private housing development, rather than counseling families or working with owners other than the ones it assisted. Finally, no private profit-making organization, like a real estate firm, was prepared to administer the program.

DEMAND

The Gautreaux program offered families rent subsidies and an opportunity to move out of the inner city—mostly to suburban locations. Chicago's subsidized housing initiatives had always had long lines of people waiting to get in—even the problem-plagued public housing program. The CHA also had an extremely long waiting list for its own Section 8 program. But it was not clear how many low-income Black families were willing, ready, and able to cross race, class, and city boundary lines to middle-class white suburbia. While there were potential benefits such as better schools, safer streets, and expanded job opportunities, those moves could put relocatees at a substantial risk of racist encounters and a substantial distance from extended family, friends, churches, and other networks.[24]

The dispersal provision added to the uncertainty about interest in the program. Participants' locational options could be constrained by earlier movers' choices. Moreover, dispersing movers risked facing social isolation in their new suburban homes by limiting their opportunities to live near one another.

HOUSING

Metropolitanization dramatically expanded the geographical area within which families could secure housing. Rather than being limited to the city of Chicago, with 3.4 million people, 1.2 million housing units, and 228 square miles, they potentially had access to 214 municipalities in six counties, with nearly 7 million residents, 2.3 million housing units, and 3,690 square miles—an area larger than Delaware. While the metropolitan scope added dramatically to the rental stock potentially available to the program, it was uncertain how much of that housing would fit the program's size, cost, and quality requirements, and how many housing providers would participate in the program. The Gautreaux program emphasized Section 8 subsidies and the private housing market, in sharp contrast to the scattered site program. Placing families in private housing seemed most promising for several reasons. Congress had begun to phase out funding for new public housing in favor of the Section 8 program. Experience in the *Gautreaux* case suggested that suburban officials would not voluntarily seek federal funds for public housing that would include Chicago residents. Moreover, the frustrating and unproductive experience with the scattered site program did not bode well for using public housing as a remedial vehicle.

The Section 8 program allowed for both "supply" strategies—rent subsidies tied to new construction and rehabilitated housing—and "demand" strategies—providing families with certificates that landlords would accept as partial rent. The Gautreaux program was primarily a demand program, as families received subsidies to use in existing private housing throughout the Chicago metropolitan area. The parties focused on tenant-based certificates for existing housing for several reasons. First, this avoided the delays inherent in new construction, often resulting from community resistance or bureaucratic complications. The scattered site program offered a memorable example of the severe obstacles in new construction. Further, even the normal processes of planning and building multifamily housing would delay any new construction for several years. Gaining access to the existing stock thus became a key to the agreement.

The agreement also included a new construction component—a "supply-side" strategy. HUD was to encourage private developers it assisted through various programs in the Chicago metropolitan area to accept plaintiff-class families as tenants.[25] In the 1977 extension of the agreement, HUD agreed to require those developers to set aside a percentage of their Section 8 apartments for those families.[26] New construction had one distinct advantage over the existing housing program in that HUD could offer a financial incentive for developers to participate in the Gautreaux remedy. However, the new construction provision initially applied throughout the region, including Black neighborhoods, so it did not necessarily achieve integration objectives. That changed with the 1981 consent decree, which applied the racial formula to all remedial initiatives.

COMMUNITY RESPONSE

Suburban communities showed both receptivity and hostility to the in-migration of low-income families. The federal Community Development Block Grant program (CDBG), which began a year before the Gautreaux program, required recipients to develop plans for accommodating low-income households—including nonresidents who would be likely to reside there if affordable housing was available. Most of the Chicago area's eligible municipalities, as well as all four of the region's eligible counties, applied for CDBG funds and developed the required housing plans.[27] However, five Chicago suburbs turned down CDBG funds so they would not have to accommodate low-income minorities as residents.[28] Arlington Heights, in northwest Cook County—a subregion that the Leadership Council focused on initially—was one of the suburbs that turned down CDBG funds in 1975. It was also the defendant in a racial discrimination lawsuit by the Leadership Council's development arm because of the community's refusal to rezone a parcel of land to permit construction of 190 racially and economically integrated townhouses.[29]

The deeply embedded suburban patterns of racial and economic segregation, as well as recent acts of suburban and city resistance, provided impetus for structuring the program to minimize community hostility. A number of features were intended to increase the chances that suburban communities would accept the Gautreaux program. The expected scale and pace, along with the regionwide scope and dispersal provision, ensured that there would be no significant influx of families into any single community. Hundreds—or perhaps thousands of people, ultimately—were to be spread among several million suburbanites. Many more communities were available in which to seek the program's acceptance. Moreover, many of the areas were so far from the city that they had no reason to expect much migration through the program or of Blacks, generally. In many areas, there was little chance of resegregation occurring as it had in the city and some inner ring suburbs.

In addition, the program's privatization thrust, with its emphasis on existing housing, avoided both the stigma of public housing and the visibility of new construction. The demand-side approach did not lend itself as easily to organized opposition as did the new construction stressed by the scattered site program.

RESOURCES

The program was to use Section 8 rent subsidy funds to help families move into dispersed, private rental housing throughout the six-county Chicago metropolitan area, primarily in predominantly white areas. HUD's commitment consisted of providing funding for the new initiatives beyond the regular Section 8 subsidies available to the Chicago metropolitan area. HUD further agreed to pay the administrative costs associated with the program, including a staff of six professionals and three clerical employees initially.

The initial agreement specified a goal of accommodating approximately four hundred families in the first, experimental year.[30] Subsequent agreements also specified numbers of families to be assisted, which quantified roughly the Section 8 subsidies that HUD would provide. Because the program was designed to be a legal remedy, the funding commitment was linked to that purpose. While there was no termination date, resources for subsidies and administration would flow only until HUD fulfilled its legal obligations.

Although the initial agreement and subsequent arrangements specified numbers of families to be assisted in moving, they did not state how long participating families could receive Section 8 subsidies once they moved. That was to be governed by the general rules of the Section 8 program, which provided for five-year renewable contracts with landlords. Nor did the agreements provide guidelines about rent ceilings in apartments rented for the program. HUD's "fair market rents" regulations applied, thus setting the limit on subsidy levels for families and units.

The June 1976 agreement envisioned a start-up period of a few months, after which the program would assist about forty families to move each month, with a goal for the year of approximately four hundred families.[31] Like the Supreme Court opinion earlier in the year, the consummation of the agreement marked the end of one important chapter of the *Gautreaux* saga and the beginning of another. The parties had avoided another protracted stage of litigation, instead designing an innovative approach to provide metropolitan-wide housing opportunities. In doing so, however, they once again entered uncharted waters with great uncertainty about the future, especially in light of such a problematic past.

FOUR

Implementing the Gautreaux Program:
Two Decades of Moving Out

Implementing the Gautreaux program entailed moving from theory to practice, with all the attendant challenges and uncertainties. During its life, the Gautreaux program easily surpassed the scattered site program and became by far the country's largest and best known mobility program. At the same time, it never reached the forty family moves per month rate projected in the initial agreement. Moreover, the program took more than two decades to reach its goal of assisting 7,100 home-seekers to relocate. In the heyday of public housing construction in the 1950s and 1960s, CHA built housing for twice that number of families in half that time. Thus, the Gautreaux program exemplified both the possibilities and the limitations of mobility-based strategies.

Families moving through the Gautreaux program settled in more than one hundred suburban communities as well as the city of Chicago. In many of those places, they were "pioneers"—among the first African-Americans living and going to school there. At the same time, some suburban movers, preferring familiar faces and places, returned to the city to live.

Contextual factors posed great challenges, especially the region's entrenched racial and economic segregation; they also provided important opportunities, especially the legal change permitting a metropolitan approach, and created substantial uncertainties, including those arising out of the region's political fragmentation. Likewise, programmatic factors worked in different directions. In spite of initial uncertainties, demand burgeoned and remained high throughout the program's life. Plenty of eligible families were willing, ready, and able to move to the designated destinations. Community responses did not serve as a bar because, unlike the scattered site program, the Gautreaux program met little organized opposition. In addition, the Leadership Council demonstrated great commitment, performed very capably, and weathered some controversies along the way. While there were changes in demand, housing availability, and the pace of moves, the program was characterized by substantial continuity in structure and operation over more than two decades.

At the same time, while HUD provided resources throughout the life of the program, limitations on subsidy levels and administrative support sometimes impeded progress. Rent ceilings set maximum subsidies for individual units, thus excluding a portion of the rental housing stock, and limitations on administrative funds precluded providing services that could have facilitated the transition, such as job training. More important, while changes in the program's operation produced incremental progress in gaining access to housing that met the program's needs, there were no breakthroughs in this area.

With the first family moving on November 1, 1976, the Gautreaux program began a more than two-decade run. In its initial fifteen months, the Gautreaux program helped relocate 168 families, well short of the one-year goal of 400 families.[1] Still, the parties considered the start sufficient to warrant continuation. The program continued for five years through a series of informal agreements between the parties. In 1981, the court approved a consent decree that the parties proposed, which institutionalized the Gautreaux program.[2] Citing the extraordinary delays that limited the CHA's scattered site city program to only token relief in more than a decade, the judge decided that the HUD-funded metropolitan remedy should continue until the agreed-upon number of 7,100 families had relocated.[3]

ADMINISTRATION

The Leadership Council administered the Gautreaux program throughout its more than twenty years. While the original agreement designated the Leadership Council as administrator, objections to the lack of opportunity for others led HUD to use a competitive bidding process for continuing the program. HUD selected the Leadership Council again, and when the consent decree was adopted in 1981, it specified the Council as administrator for the duration of the program.

The Leadership Council's major responsibilities included counseling families, recruiting landlords, and working with public housing agencies as they carried out procedures and made subsidy payments under the Section 8 program. The Council created a full-time position for a Gautreaux program director and added several housing counselors to help families move and real estate specialists to locate landlords who would accept the families.

The agency developed an extensive counseling role because families might not successfully make integrationist moves, especially to the suburbs, without considerable information, preparation, and persuasion. Counseling included group briefings, individual counseling, home visits, site visits to suburban housing, and after the first few years, an increasing amount of training that helped families to conduct their own housing searches. The Council tried to enroll only families capable of adjusting to dramatically different environments. Families that were interested and eligible thus received counseling designed both to assist them and to determine their ability to move. A credit check, for example, might demonstrate that a family probably could not afford the move until the Council helped it get its financial house in order.

Initially, the Council engaged its own real estate staff, rather than having families search for landlords on their own. The Council expected that only intensive education and advocacy would engage landlords in the program, and concluded that real estate professionals could perform those tasks better than the families.

Finding landlords willing to participate was one of the Gautreaux program's major challenges. The Leadership Council employed a variety of strategies to gain access, using its influence with individual property owners, firms, and industry organizations. The Council added new approaches over the program's life, at various points using board members, staff, other fair housing agencies, outside real estate experts, and participating families to engage housing providers in the program.

The Council's initial landlord recruitment efforts had a geographically targeted search, tactics tailored to different segments of the market, and assistance from suburban fair housing centers. In light of the Leadership Council's limited resources, the program's racial provisions, and the large size of the region, the agency concentrated its initial search in areas with relatively high vacancy rates, apartments within HUD's Section 8 rent ceilings, and access to services such as schools, shopping, and public transportation: rapidly growing northwest suburban Cook County, surrounding O'Hare Airport, and DuPage County, a mostly white, affluent area west of Chicago. The Council also searched for housing in inner-ring suburbs, because many eligible families did not own cars, and more-distant areas lacked public transportation. Moreover, inner-ring communities were closer to potential participants' old neighborhoods, near families, friends, and churches. However, the Council later placed families in more than 120 communities throughout the six-county area.

The landlord recruitment strategy took into account the bifurcated structure of Chicago's real estate industry, which had a small number of very large firms and many small ones. The agency tried to gain access to the developments of large owners and management firms in the hope of getting substantial commitments and help in enlisting other industry leaders. A few firms allowed the program to access some units, but contacts with large firms yielded limited initial results. One owner even changed management firms because the firm inquired about his interest in the Gautreaux program.[4] Fifteen years later, the Council enlisted a real estate management firm to interest high-level officials of major management firms in the program. The agency hoped industry leaders' peers would garner more credibility than a social agency, but this approach also produced only modest results.[5]

The Leadership Council called and visited as many small landlords as this labor-intensive process would permit.[6] It also made presentations to real estate organizations and circulated information to their memberships. Finally, the Leadership Council contracted with several suburban fair housing centers to solicit landlords in their local areas. In recognition of the program's need for larger apartments, the subcontracts included a goal that more than half the units obtained would have at least three bedrooms.

HUD assisted the effort to secure housing for Gautreaux families by giving them preference for vacancies in financially struggling developments it assisted. In addition, HUD encouraged all sponsors of new, federally insured, multifamily housing to accept Gautreaux families.

In addition to counseling and landlord solicitation, administrative responsibilities included the regular Section 8 operations. Fourteen Chicago-area public housing agencies (PHAs) already administered their own Section 8 programs, including inspecting apartments, entering into subsidy contracts with landlords, and paying monthly subsidies on behalf of tenants. HUD asked these agencies to perform those functions for Gautreaux families moving into their jurisdictions.[7]

These agencies' participation was important because any substitutes would have less experience and sensitivity to local concerns, and would require recruiting, selecting, and training. In addition, if PHAs declined to join, already skeptical landlords might have been even more leery about participating. Increased community resistance might also have greeted outside entities administering the program.

HUD's request posed political, practical, and public relations dilemmas for suburban public housing agencies, in part because many operated largely in middle-class, predominantly white areas. The Gautreaux program involved PHAs in the politically unpopular process of assisting low-income, Black Chicago families to compete with local residents for scarce affordable rental units in their communities. Also, some agencies already administered substantial public housing and Section 8 programs, so they might have strained their administrative capacities by adding Gautreaux program responsibilities.[8]

Some PHAs agreed to HUD's request promptly, including the CHA, the Housing Authority of Cook County, and the Elgin agency. Others wanted to limit the number of families moving into their locality and to ensure that communities without subsidized housing shared responsibility fairly. Several insisted that families be dispersed within their community as well as among suburban municipalities. One racially mixed suburb wanted families to move to predominantly white neighborhoods, so as not to disturb the community's racial balance.[9] Several agencies wanted to start their own Section 8 programs—to take care of "their own"—before Chicago families moved in. One declined, without giving a reason, and several did not respond to HUD's repeated requests.[10]

Overall, however, the suburban housing agencies were far more receptive than they had been to the CHA's request to join the scattered site program—none had accepted that invitation. The Gautreaux program's modest scale, use of existing housing, and its dispersal provisions reassured housing officials. Also, the PHAs' responsibilities were more limited than they might have been under a suburban scattered-site program. Finally, HUD accommodated their concerns about timing and other matters.[11]

DEMAND FOR THE PROGRAM

At first, the Gautreaux program elicited skepticism as well as interest among potential participants. Many had lived their entire lives in the inner city and could not envision moving to the suburbs—the program's favored destination.[12] Some replied to the Leadership Council suggestion that they move to mostly white, middle-class suburbs with "Are you crazy?"[13] Moreover, relatively few people knew about the program in its early stages. The Council's original notification system—sending postcards to selected eligible families—largely failed to reach the intended recipients.

Although initial response to the program was modest, interest burgeoned quickly and remained high. Many people learned about the program through the Council's continuing outreach efforts, as well as through informal networks of families and friends.[14] By the early 1980s, so many families applied on their own that the Council dropped its formal notification procedure. The agency began an annual two-thousand-family, in-person registration process at its downtown office. Initially, several days passed before two thousand families were registered. But in 1984, thousands of people arrived at the Leadership Council's office on the specified day, filled the building's elevators and corridors and blocked the streets outside.[15] The Council canceled that day's registration at the request of the police, who felt that they could not control the crowd.[16]

Consequently, the Leadership Council changed its registration process to a one-day-a-year telephone call-in system, which it staffed with twenty telephone operators. The lines became so clogged and the percentage of successful callers was so small that some suspected the Council was not answering the phone but was instead selecting its favorite families.[17] By the early 1990s, the telephone company estimated that the Council received at least ten thousand calls on registration day.[18] It was not possible to determine how many different callers tried to get through, but by that time all doubts about the demand for the program had long since disappeared.[19]

The Gautreaux program generated great interest because many families wanted better housing in better, safer places.[20] The program's housing subsidies also served as a powerful draw for eligible families. Finally, counseling and other incentives reduced housing search costs and the risks of a hostile reception.

Program participants were motivated to move for their families' safety, their children's schooling and social relations, and their own job opportunities.[21] Chicago's inner city was in decline, both absolutely and relative to other parts of the metropolitan area.[22] Many public housing complexes had deteriorated dramatically from the 1950s and early 1960s, when low-income people often saw them as a significant step up and considered them desirable residences.[23] Many people had witnessed the decline over the years and saw little evidence that their public housing complexes or other inner-city neighborhoods were going to be rebuilt, physically, socially, economically, or institutionally. For many residents, CHA developments had become places to escape from by whatever means possible—as illustrated by the 17,000 calls that the Leadership Council received on registration day 1993.[24] Registration that year came just months after a sniper's bullet killed seven-year old Dantrell Davis at the Cabrini-Green public housing complex as he walked to school with his mother.

Word of mouth and television and newspaper accounts about movers' experiences also generated demand.[25] Thus, applicants' motivations probably reflected the experiences of earlier movers who found increased safety, better schools, more job opportunities, and less risk of gang activity among children. Some families viewed opportunities for racial integration as an additional draw. Some wanted to expose their children to whites in order to prepare them to live and work in a predominantly white society.[26] On the other hand, families' willingness to move to white middle-class suburbs did not necessarily indicate their preference for those destinations. In fact, many families that moved to the suburbs would have preferred to move within the city; but they adapted to the opportunities offered them.

The Gautreaux program also offered desperately needed housing subsidies that became an increasingly powerful attraction for low-income families.[27] Program participants received rent subsidies for at least five years, as long as they remained in the program and were not evicted, and subsidies were very likely to continue beyond that time.

During the program's twenty years, housing options for low-income Chicago-area families worsened significantly. The shortage of affordable rental units—the number of low-income renters minus the number of low-cost housing units—increased from 75,000 in 1975 to 149,000 a dozen years later.[28] Increasing numbers of low-income Chicagoans paid a high percentage of their income for rent—far more than the 30 percent HUD considered the appropriate maximum.[29] The value of the average renter's income declined while rents increased; decent housing thus became increasingly less affordable.[30] The decline in the value of welfare benefits and wages particularly reduced income.[31] A dwindling supply of affordable housing for low-income people brought rent increases in the remaining stock.[32] Moreover, the 1980s witnessed a dramatic cutback in federal housing subsidies. From fiscal years 1981 to 1991, annual commitments for rental assistance nationally averaged 78,000 new low-income households, down almost 75 percent from the 1977–80 average of 290,000.[33]

The so-called housing-renter income gap led many low-income families to seek housing subsidies wherever they could among the few avenues available. The CHA's public housing waiting list was thousands of families and many years long. Similarly, the regular Section 8 program was so oversubscribed that the CHA stopped taking applications for years at a time.[34]

Thus, the Gautreaux program was the last best hope for many low-income families. The Leadership Council's registration process produced a new waiting list and another shot at subsidies each year. Those able to register could, in effect, leapfrog the CHA's Section 8 waiting list and begin their housing search within weeks or months, rather than the years they would have to wait even if they could get on the regular Section 8 waiting list.

In addition to offering mobility and housing subsidies, the Gautreaux program provided other incentives for participation. People interested in the program could attend group briefing sessions that served as reinforcement for prospective participants. The Leadership Council informed homeseekers about available rental housing and the communities where it was located. Initially, counselors even accompanied families to the sites. As the program evolved, the Council increasingly trained families to search for housing on their own because hundreds of families searching in the market could find housing more effectively than a few counselors, reducing both families' housing search costs and their risk of failing to find a place in the allotted time.[35]

The Council's help saved families' time and money.[36] Many families had little experience in searching for housing in the private market, a market in which racial discrimination often made the process longer and more costly.[37] Searches in outlying areas of the city and the suburbs imposed especially high search costs, since few families were familiar with suburban areas or had easy ways of obtaining information about them. Counselors who accompanied applicants on site visits helped them overcome skepticism and fears about moving into predominantly white suburbs and helped them represent themselves with landlords.

The Council's post-move counseling and support services—which helped families gain access to community services, resolve disputes with landlords, and develop support networks—further reduced moving risks. In keeping with the overall strategy of minimizing the program's and the families' visibility, the Leadership Council assured families that it would not disclose their identities to the media or the public, in order to protect them from the hostility sometimes directed at participants in subsidized housing programs.

Finally, some families may have found the idea of relocating manageable because migration has been a central element of the African-American experience, from the Underground Railroad through the two "Great Migrations" of the twentieth century, when hundreds of thousands of southern Blacks migrated to the urban centers of the North. More generally, relocating in search of a better life reflected an American ethos.[38]

At the same time, eligible families had reasons to avoid the Gautreaux program, above all the potential for harassment and other forms of racial discrimination or isolation. Black families moving into predominantly white areas of Chicago or the suburbs risked hostile reactions, including physical violence, property damage, and other forms of harassment.[39] Moreover, some feared the loss of their children's racial and cultural identity.[40] Most surveys of Blacks indicated that they defined desirable integration as a 50–50 ratio, a very different formula than the Gautreaux program used.[41]

Some friends and families of those planning moves to white communities raised these objections.[42] Fifteen years into the program, a landlord in Cicero, one of several notoriously racially exclusionary suburbs, agreed to accept a family through the program.[43] The family ultimately decided not to move, after friends and family members predicted that they would encounter racial hostility there.

For some, staying in the Black community represented an ideological, political, or social commitment to rebuilding their neighborhood and its institutions. Some criticized the Gautreaux program for draining resources, attention, commitment, and people that might otherwise help to meet the Black community's pressing needs. Other families did not apply for the Gautreaux program for more personal reasons, such as remaining involved in their churches.[44] Still others simply had more confidence in their ability to negotiate the known terrain of the inner city than the uncertain circumstances of the places the program emphasized.

HOUSING FOR THE PROGRAM

The high level of family interest shifted the challenge to securing housing for the program. The program needed access to rental units that met the program's objectives, which depended on the supply and cost of housing and the willingness of providers to rent to participating families. Although enough housing became available to permit the program to proceed at a steady pace, no breakthrough occurred to match the surge of family interest.

With the Gautreaux program's strong emphasis on existing housing, the available housing stock was a crucial starting point. The dramatic postwar growth of suburban rental housing gave the program a large supply of potential units.[45] However, of the approximately 1.1 million rental units in the Chicago metropolitan area in 1975, many did not meet the program's locational objectives, size needs, or Section 8 quality and cost requirements.[46] Moreover, housing providers' willingness to participate in the program was critical. While there were some incentives for their voluntary involvement, many landlords had strong—if sometimes illegal—motivations for declining this invitation. Thus, while the Chicago region's rental housing market held promise for this privatization strategy, the program's access to that market was substantially constrained.

The program's initial and increasing emphasis on predominantly white areas and the suburbs excluded increasingly large portions of that housing stock. Most participants could move only to predominantly white areas, especially in the suburbs. The Council initially deemphasized and later excluded the large portions of the city and parts of the southern and western suburbs where significant numbers of Blacks lived. Those areas contained a disproportionate amount of the area's affordable rental housing—and many landlords there accepted Section 8 tenants. After the early years, the Leadership Council discouraged relocation into the southern suburbs, many of which had substantial amounts of Section 8 housing and significant numbers of Black residents.[47] After 1982, fewer than 5 percent of Gautreaux placements were in South Cook County.

In order to maintain racial integration in communities where it existed, and to minimize visibility that could lead to community resistance, the Leadership Council also imposed moratoria on Gautreaux placements in integrated places. Thus, within predominantly white areas, some neighborhoods, developments, and buildings were off-limits to the program, or the number of families permitted to move to those locations was limited. Moreover, in its last five years, the program excluded Chicago entirely.

There was also a size mismatch. The Leadership Council's initial notification procedures quickly produced a backlog of families needing three-bedroom or larger places. The Council therefore limited applicants to smaller families, eliminating half of the households in CHA family housing.[48] Thus, a large number of eligible families could not be served by the program because the private market did not have available the three-, four-, and five-bedroom apartments that those families needed.

In addition, the Gautreaux program could use only housing with actual rents within HUD's established ceilings—"fair market rents."[49] The higher-priced housing typical of many white suburban areas, however, was often too costly for the program. Moreover, HUD sometimes established fair market rents at levels below actual private rents.[50] In addition, fair market rents often did not adequately reflect the widely varying market conditions across the Chicago region.[51] HUD's delays and failure to make subregional adjustments helped make fair market rents one of the Gautreaux program's major constraints.

Public housing officials in DuPage County, an affluent, rapidly developing area west of Chicago, exacerbated the fair market rent problem by their inaction.[52] The Leadership Council repeatedly urged them to request HUD to increase the Section 8 fair market rents for its submarket because of the high market rents there. A local request was a prerequisite for HUD to make such a change, but the county agency declined to make the request, which significantly limited the number of Gautreaux families who could relocate there.[53]

The Gautreaux program also depended crucially on the willingness of housing providers in predominantly white areas to accept participating families as tenants. Owners receiving HUD assistance were first encouraged and later obligated to participate through the "set-aside" arrangements the parties negotiated,[54] but the vast majority of landlords had a choice whether to become involved in the Gautreaux program.

The primary incentives for their participation were economic, coming from both the Section 8 program and the Leadership Council's efforts to reduce landlords' costs and risks. Section 8 subsidies provided landlords a stable stream of revenue by paying the part of the market rent that exceeded the tenant's share. HUD guaranteed funding for five years, with the likelihood of two five-year extensions.[55] The importance of these subsidies to low-income families increased tenants' incentives to maintain good relationships with landlords, which in turn made the program more attractive to landlords.

These incentives were most effective when the rental market was "soft" in predominantly white, middle-class communities. Some small landlords in predominantly white areas found the program's financial arrangements especially attractive. Some individual investors purchased single-family homes in order to rent them to Section 8 tenants, thereby providing most of the program's few opportunities for large families.[56]

The Leadership Council also tried to make the program attractive by saving landlords much of the cost of evaluating potential tenants and reducing their risks of encountering problems in renting to Gautreaux tenants. The Council screened applicant families to ensure that they would meet landlords' criteria. It obtained credit checks and made home visits to assess families' housekeeping and confirm the number of people in the household. Further, the Council assured landlords that their involvement with the program would remain confidential, thus reducing the risk of negative community reactions.[57] The Council's policy of dispersing families further reassured landlords by avoiding concentrations of low-income Black families in their areas.[58]

Several landlords who shared the program's social goals participated in the program for ideological reasons. Some of those tried to persuade others to follow suit. Occasionally, a housing provider agreed to accept Gautreaux families in order to settle a Leadership Council discrimination lawsuit.

Many landlords, however, declined to participate in the Gautreaux program. While it was difficult to determine their motivations, the main reason seemed to be the race, class, and composition of the prospective tenant families. In addition, some owners objected to the Section 8 substantive and procedural requirements that were incorporated in the Gautreaux program.

Most landlords in predominantly white suburban areas were accustomed to renting to white middle-class families, often with two parents. Participating in the Gautreaux program was a drastic departure from their customary practices because it meant accepting low-income Blacks, many of them female-headed, single-parent families who lived in public housing or elsewhere in the inner city.[59] The combination of the program participants' race, class, gender, family composition, and inner-city origins tapped into landlords' stereotyped fears that gangs, drugs, and violence would accompany them. The families' attributes were probably the decisive factor for many landlords who opted out of the Gautreaux program.[60]

Race was probably a consideration for many landlords who declined to participate in the Gautreaux program or rejected individual families as tenants, even though that violated federal and state law and local ordinances in many communities.[61] Only rarely did landlords acknowledge racial bias. However, some families reported incidents of discrimination in their housing search. The Chicago area's documented patterns of housing discrimination suggested that these incidents constituted only the tip of the iceberg. Discrimination may have been so subtle that Leadership Council staff or families searching for housing were not even aware of it.[62] Moreover, landlords did not have to provide an explanation for not participating, because the program was entirely voluntary.

Resistance to Gautreaux families was sometimes based merely on personal taste, but economic considerations often played a role as well. Landlords were concerned about alienating existing or prospective middle-class white tenants, whose racial biases or lifestyle preferences— such as taste in music or cars—might have caused them to object to Gautreaux families.[63] Even landlords who had not rented to Gautreaux families believed that they were "nothing but trouble."[64] "Horror stories" about suburban landlords' experiences with Gautreaux tenants, such as tales of damaged apartments and nonpayment of rent, contributed to that image.[65] They also doubted whether low-income tenants could afford to pay for repairs for which they were liable.

Nevertheless, the Leadership Council and the media reported quite positive landlord-tenant experiences. To counter distortions circulating among landlords, the Council asked satisfied participating landlords to spread the word about their experiences. However, landlords often had little incentive to seek systematic information about other landlords' experiences. Suburban Section 8 residents and Gautreaux families competed for the same housing. Suburban landlords interested in the Section 8 program preferred suburban tenants, who were more likely to be white, two-parent families, and who could locate vacancies first because of their greater familiarity with the local housing market.

In addition to family characteristics, the Section 8 program requirements deterred landlords. From 1987 to 1995, Congress prohibited landlords who accepted any Section 8 tenants from discriminating against other Section 8 applicants.[66] Suburban landlords worried that they would not be able to limit access of low-income families. Also, many landlords viewed the HUD-specified form lease and eviction procedures as intruding inappropriately on their discretion in selecting and removing tenants.[67] Other landlords complained that public housing officials sometimes sent them Section 8 monthly rent subsidies late—an especially serious problem for small landlords.[68] Also, while housing had to meet federal quality standards, this requirement had little effect on landlords in middle-class suburbs because the market required maintaining high standards.[69] Finally, some landlords avoided government programs on principle, to guard their prerogatives in an increasingly regulated housing market.

COMMUNITY RESPONSE

Implementing the Gautreaux program also required a threshold level of receiving community acquiescence. Widespread resistance in the predominantly white, middle-class communities that dominated the metropolitan landscape might have seriously impeded the program, as it had thwarted the scattered site program. However, while opposition to the scattered site program was persistent over decades, often intense, and quite pervasive geographically, the Gautreaux program encountered only sporadic, moderate, and relatively isolated adverse public reactions. The newer initiative was able to distinguish itself thoroughly enough from the scattered site program to avoid widespread resistance. The initial community response to the Gautreaux program was quite moderate and muted, and it remained that way over time.

At the outset, HUD determined that it had to tell elected municipal and county officials about the program before it began and invite their comments.[70] But HUD waited while a small group of suburban mayors already active in promoting affordable housing wrote to other regional mayors seeking their acceptance of the program. Their letter explained the Gautreaux program as a modest undertaking that would disperse participating families and noted that it could be their last opportunity to address these issues voluntarily.[71]

HUD then asked the region's more than 250 mayors and village presidents, as well as the six county board presidents, to comment on the Gautreaux program's consistency with their local housing plans. HUD aimed to dispel local officials' fears by stressing the program's dispersal goals, suggesting that some communities would not receive any families, and noting that the Gautreaux program just modified the Section 8 program, which already operated in their communities.

The concerns about widespread initial opposition to the program turned out to be unfounded. Most local officials did not comment to HUD. Even Cicero and Berwyn, which had histories of racial exclusion and had rejected the federal block grant funds that required accepting low-income nonresidents, remained silent. Moreover, none of the region's six county board presidents responded to HUD's letter. Comments came only from Chicago officials and six mayors whose communities spanned the diverse range of the region's suburbs. Furthermore, although the respondents viewed Gautreaux families as a burden that should be distributed fairly across the region, none objected to the program in principle.[72] None replied further when HUD informed them of its intention to proceed with the program.

The Gautreaux program's small scale and dispersal provisions may have made it nonthreatening even to suburban officials who wanted to maintain racial and class dominance in their communities.[73] They had little reason to anticipate an influx of new residents from Chicago's inner city. Moreover, outlying suburbs, especially those not yet served by public transportation, were too inconvenient for most Gautreaux families. Similarly, communities with little or no rental housing, or whose rental housing was at the high end of the market, offered them few opportunities. Furthermore, if a problem developed, the market could take care of it. Strong local opposition could lead landlords to exclude the program by declining to participate in it.[74]

Finally, mayors who might have considered joining forces to oppose the Gautreaux program would likely have been constrained by information and coordination problems. With communities potentially vying with each other to avoid the impact of the program, concerted opposition might have been difficult to orchestrate.

The limited and restrained response set the pattern for the next two decades. In Chicago, there was little community reaction to the Gautreaux program even though homeseekers' destinations included predominantly white neighborhoods. In the suburbs, there were scattered and sporadic concerns. Residents of one largely white area expressed concerns about the program's potentially harmful effects, as did residents of a few integrated communities who feared that the program would concentrate Black families and threaten their racial diversity.[75]

The first public sign of community concerns appeared during the first year when a suburban newspaper reported that HUD planned to require developers it assisted to set aside units for Gautreaux families. A city councilman in the far northwestern suburb of Crystal Lake organized a meeting of public officials with Kale Williams, the Leadership Council's executive director, to object to both the plan and the secrecy surrounding it. But Williams reassured the officials by explaining the program's limited scale and dispersal policies.

Several years later, in Bolingbrook, a racially and economically mixed suburb southwest of Chicago, residents' fears of racial resegregation or an influx of poor people prompted their objection to numerous Gautreaux families moving into the community. Leadership Council staff met with Bolingbrook residents to reassure them that only a few Gautreaux families had moved there and that the policy was to disperse families throughout the region. Following the controversy, no additional Gautreaux families moved to Bolingbrook in the next decade.

In Oak Park, a racially mixed community on Chicago's western border, a nonprofit housing center dedicated to maintaining the community's racial diversity objected when a Gautreaux family moved into an integrated building. The Council and the housing center agreed to coordinate their activities more closely in the future.

This general acceptance of the Gautreaux program was attributable to its very limited local impact, the use of a privatized, demand-side housing strategy, the quality of the Leadership Council's administration, the media treatment of the program, and local governments' incentives for acquiescence. Those factors produced a low-visibility program that received little public attention until it was well established, at which point it received positive notice that may have blunted any latent organized opposition.

The program's metropolitan scope was fundamental to limiting its impact on the region's more than two hundred localities. The program's modest scale and dispersal policy ensured that Gautreaux families were scattered widely across many communities—only a few participants lived in any one development, neighborhood, or municipality. An average of about two families per year entered each of the receiving communities, and some did not stay—instead moving to other suburbs, back to the city, or out of the region.

Middle-class suburban communities a long distance from Black areas also had little reason to anticipate significant Black or low-income in-migration across the physical, psychological, and economic distance from the inner city. At most, they could expect a small number of Chicago families arriving through this program. Even in Chicago, the impact was limited, and the small number of Gautreaux program city movers also kept visibility to a minimum. As of late 1994, the CHA had more than thirteen thousand outstanding regular Section 8 certificates and vouchers, while fewer than one-fifth as many families had moved within the city through the Gautreaux program.[76]

Relying primarily on private existing housing rather than new construction—especially of public housing—also helped mute potential resistance. The demand-side strategy, along with privatization, contrasted sharply with the scattered-site program's emphasis on the highly visible and contentious supply-side approach of building public housing.

The Leadership Council also adopted a low-visibility strategy, in part because of the intense opposition following media coverage of the CHA's scattered site program. HUD and the Leadership Council did not publicly announce their contract signing. The Council informed only those whose participation they sought—landlords, eligible families, and public housing agencies—and discussed the program with local officials and community residents only as the need arose. The agency protected the anonymity of participating families and landlords, and avoided publicity until the program was well established. The resulting general lack of information reduced opportunities for coordinated resistance across the fragmented metropolitan area.

A more general public education campaign might have built support and blunted opposition to the program, but it would also have risked provoking the intense community resistance that program administrators feared. It also might have dissuaded landlords concerned about their standing in the community from joining the program.

The Leadership Council's performance stood in marked contrast to the CHA's—whose history tainted even the far more effective efforts of the Habitat Company when it took over the scattered site program. The Leadership Council had worked with suburban officials, and it had a generally positive reputation even among those who disagreed with its goals.

Moreover, media coverage, which included local and national print media and national network news, a CBS *60 Minutes* segment, and a Donahue show, generally portrayed the program, its participants, and their experiences quite favorably.[77] Also, most media coverage did not identify the communities where families relocated. One article that did name the place actually helped reduce racial tensions. The article described racial conflicts that arose in a suburban community when a white and a Black teenager—a Gautreaux participant—became friends. The piece created a good deal of community support for both teenagers.[78]

Finally, there were financial and other incentives for communities not to oppose the Gautreaux program. Many Chicago-area communities had economic incentives in the form of federal Community Development Block Grants that were contingent on addressing housing needs, including those of low-income nonresidents interested in moving into the community.[79] Moreover, residents of integrated communities who had concerns about the program's impact faced a dilemma because protest against it could have harmed the community's reputation and ability to sustain the desired diversity.

RESOURCES

While housing and resource availability constrained the Gautreaux program throughout its life, federal funding was the ultimate limiting factor.

Even though the program's duration was indefinite and its life spanned more than two decades, it was designed to be a finite legal remedy rather than an ongoing publicly funded program like Social Security or Medicaid. That was demonstrated concretely in 1998, when the program reached the agreed-upon 7,100 family moves, and funding for relocation ceased.

Resource flows also had direct and indirect effects on implementation throughout the life of the program. Most directly, the several hundred Section 8 certificates HUD made available for the program determined the ceiling on possible moves.[80] Less directly, the fair market rents that HUD established also affected moves through the Gautreaux program. They placed a cap on the subsidy funds available on behalf of individual families, thus limiting the program's access to housing by defining the portion of the housing stock that was potentially available and the landlords who could be recruited. Actual market rents that exceeded HUD's fair market rents prevented some families from using their Section 8 certificates.

In addition, administrative funding affected the amount of counseling, landlord recruiting, and other activities the Leadership Council could undertake to assist families in relocating. At the program's peak, the Leadership Council received something under $400,000 annually from HUD for administrative costs. That supported a staff of ten.

The level of administrative funding was a matter of debate between HUD and the Leadership Council, with the federal agency pressing for reducing costs per placement and the Council seeking to provide additional services, including more post-move support. The result was a compromise, in effect.

The Leadership Council did not achieve the cost reductions that HUD sought. This highly labor-intensive program enjoyed few economies of scale and did not seem very susceptible to such cost savings. HUD sought to reduce administrative costs to $550 per family placed, from the first-year rate of $750. Instead, costs gradually increased with inflation. Expenditures for the three years ending September 30, 1993, were $1.1 million, or $985 per household placement. In 1996, the average cost per family placed increased to $1,430, with the average cost per family counseled at $555. At the same time, post-move services remained limited in scope and duration, as HUD proposed initially.

It is not clear what would have happened if HUD had substantially increased the annual allocation of subsidy and administrative funds for the program.[81] While the scale of the program might have increased proportionately, it is also likely that constraints such as limited access to housing would have remained and perhaps increased with added pressure on vacancies and landlords. Moreover, efforts to increase the scale might have made the program more visible and jeopardized the community acquiescence that the program enjoyed. Administration might also have been more difficult, resulting in less efficient use of the additional resources.

MOVES AND MOVERS

After the program was institutionalized by the consent decree in the early 1980s, annual placements averaged around 300 families.[82] The rate jumped for the first time in the early 1990s, with placements going from 279 families in 1991 to 467 the following year and remaining at a similar level (440) in 1993.

About 20 percent of the eligible families who enrolled each year actually used their Section 8 certificates and moved.[83] Between 1988 and 1992, an average of 1,700 of the 2,000 families who signed up each year were found to be eligible for the program; an average of 325 families moved—a rate of 19 percent.[84] While there is no systematic information on why most eligible families who were the right size and expressed interest in the program *did not actually move*, this attrition seems to be attributable to Leadership Council screening, self-selection, and families' inability to secure a unit in the time allotted.

Self-selection and housing availability probably explain the lion's share of the pre-move attrition, especially since the Council moved from excluding to counseling applicants with credit and other problems. Many families probably opted out because they did not want to leave the city, especially for almost all-white suburban communities. That seems particularly likely in light of the program's "pioneer" emphasis, the history of suburban racial and class exclusion, and families' clearly and consistently stated preference for the city.

Lack of housing availability was also an important explanation for pre-move attrition—with families being screened out by the market. Many families ran out of time as they tried to secure a unit. Some families opted out of the process before their certificate expired, out of frustration with trying to find a suitable unit that the landlord would rent to them.

By early 1998, when the Leadership Council enrolled its last families, about 6,000 families had moved through the Gautreaux program. (The rest of the 7,100 families specified in the consent decree were assisted through other initiatives.) More than half the families moved to the suburbs, mostly to predominantly white, middle-class communities. Over 4,000 Gautreaux families moved to about half of Chicago's 232 suburbs. The program focused increasingly on the suburbs, culminating with the Leadership Council placing Chicago off-limits in 1991.[85]

While the locational formula stressed the racial composition of destinations, families' new communities were also substantially more affluent and middle-class in character than their points of origin.[86] Families—especially suburban movers—went to places with higher income levels, lower unemployment rates, and higher educational levels than the places they left. In 1993, families moved to census tracts with an average poverty rate of 6.7 percent—less than one-fifth the average rate of their old tracts—and a median household income of $43,507.[87] In the origin tracts, 11.4 percent of those twenty-five years old or over had a college degree, while in the destination tracts the figure was 23.1 percent.

While the program took more than two decades to reach its goal, it was far more productive than the scattered site program. Even though the Gautreaux program began seven years later, by 1998 it had housed more than three times as many families as the earlier effort. The lack of community opposition to the Gautreaux program explains much of this difference, as do the factors underlying local acquiescence—limited demographic impacts, the use of existing private housing, competent administration with a low-visibility strategy, and timely and positive media coverage. While landlords' attitudes and rent ceilings constrained this market-oriented program, families' movement into existing housing did not have the visibility or present the same opportunities for opposition as new construction.

In addition, with the scattered site program effectively limited to the central city, the availability and cost of suitable vacant land presented a major obstacle that the demand-side Gautreaux program did not have to face. While the scattered site program played a role in inner city redevelopment after Habitat became receiver, the company had a difficult time finding appropriate sites on which to build in predominantly white neighborhoods. Also, the complexities of the construction process, including securing local and HUD approvals at various stages, produced additional delays. Even with housing acquisition or rehabilitation, regulatory requirements affected the pace of the scattered site program.

Moreover, the Leadership Council had more authority, including the crucial metropolitan reach, commitment, and competence, than the CHA. That helped with all elements of the program—tapping demand, locating housing, and muting communities' responses. The Leadership Council also had HUD funding for administrative responsibilities that were new to the Gautreaux program. On the other hand, the CHA's fiscal problems were so severe that at one point it sought the judge's approval to suspend scattered site development in order to avoid bankruptcy. With Habitat taking over as receiver, the administrative picture changed significantly and the pace increased; but the Gautreaux program's assets permitted it to continue outpacing the scattered site program.

STAYING AND LEAVING

About 70 percent of the families who moved to the suburbs before 1990 were still in the suburbs in 1997, either at their original destination or in a new location. Some relocated within the suburbs, often to escape problems in the first development, school, or community. The first move to the suburbs gave families additional information on which to base judgments and thus enabled them to find new residences more easily. Some moved back to the city, either remaining in the program or leaving it. Others left the metropolitan area. Still others may have increased their income beyond the eligibility limits for Section 8 and left the Gautreaux program—staying in the suburbs, moving back to the city, or leaving the metropolitan area. Many moved voluntarily, while others faced evictions or nonrenewal of leases.

Much of the post-move attrition probably involved a return to the city. Many eligible families had a strong preference for living in the city. Moreover, many families reported racial problems in the suburbs. Some families who were most affected by those encounters might have returned to the city.[88] Families were free to move and take their Section 8 certificate with them anywhere in the metropolitan area, including Black areas of the city, after one year. Some entered the program with the purpose of staying in the suburbs for a year and then moving back to the city. This gave them a way to get a Section 8 certificate long before they could otherwise, but still end up in the city where they wanted to be in the first place.

Some families left the program because their household income increased beyond Section 8 eligibility, enabling them to stay in the suburbs without subsidies. Suburban movers had a higher rate of post-move employment than city movers. With the greater job access that the suburbs provided, some may also have increased their income and remained in the suburbs, within reach of their jobs. At least one suburban family bought a home, and another woman put all of her children through college.

CONCLUSION

The Gautreaux program finished enrolling families more than thirty years after the litigation began. There were no major breakthroughs in the scale and pace of the program's operation over its two decades; but perhaps there were none to be had, in light of the constraints the program faced—funding limits, rent ceilings, and especially the private market's cautious response to this initiative. While there is no systematic study of the Leadership Council's performance in administering the program, its leadership contrasted sharply with the CHA's bungling of the scattered site program. The Council's administrative problems in finding and retaining staff, working with families, and recruiting landlords paled in comparison to the CHA's difficulties.

The agency demonstrated both persistence and flexibility in addressing challenges it encountered. As it tapped into the growing demand, it adjusted its procedures to accommodate the increased interest. As landlords remained skeptical, the Council tried innovative approaches to enlist them, including training clients to search for their own housing. Moreover, the agency worked effectively with communities to maintain low visibility and to convey a positive image of the program when it did become public. While it was not always successful, the Leadership Council also worked with PHAs and HUD to overcome impediments in the Section 8 program, such as rent ceilings and slow subsidy payments to landlords.

The Leadership Council managed to retain some key staff throughout much of the program's life, thus building and applying accumulated substantive and programmatic expertise. At the same time, as with most programs requiring high levels of commitment and offering low pay, there was considerable staff turnover—including five directors.[89] That posed transition problems and created some unevenness in leadership and staff capacity over the life of the program. Through the Leadership Council's efforts, the Gautreaux program became the largest mobility program in the country by a large margin, and it served about one-sixth of the plaintiff class. The question of how well it served them is addressed in part 2.

MOVING EXPERIENCES
FOR THE SAKE OF THE CHILDREN

FIVE

Families on the Move

Part 2 examines the Gautreaux program through the experiences and perspectives of some of its participants. Their accounts are central to understanding the program's impact and identifying the potential and limitations of mobility programs in general.

Almost all participants (97 percent) left neighborhoods that were over 90 percent Black. While those who relocated within the city moved to areas similar to those they left (averaging 99 percent Black), those who moved to the suburbs entered middle-class communities that averaged 96 percent white. These families were often pioneers—among the first Black people in those communities and perhaps the only low-income Black residents. These chapters focus on families' safety, social interactions, and schooling, in both their suburban and city neighborhoods, with primary emphasis on the experiences of their school-age children.

The chapters are largely based on two sets of interviews at the beginning and end of the 1980s with Gautreaux participants who moved to the suburbs and a comparison group who moved within the city in the early years of the program (1976–81). Their firsthand experiences gave them insights into their communities and their communities' responses to them. The two groups interviewed are referred to as "suburban movers" and "city movers."

PARTICIPANTS' PERSPECTIVES

Participating families' views are critical to assessing the Gautreaux program as a remedy in a landmark lawsuit, for their constitutional rights were at stake, and the program was intended to vindicate those rights. The Gautreaux program was the first and largest undertaking of its kind—a racial and economic integration initiative that included an entire metropolitan area.

Part 2 emphasizes the firsthand accounts of participant families. The discussion focuses primarily on the suburban movers' experiences and compares them to the experiences of the city movers. The importance of the former accounts is enhanced by the unique perspective of these new residents of suburbs where people like them have seldom lived.[1] While racially and economically homogeneous neighborhoods and communities dominate America's metropolitan landscape, the discussion here emphasizes the very atypical experiences of those who are living among people whose race and economic status are different from their own.[2] Suburban movers offer the unusual perspective of having lived both in the inner city and in predominantly white, middle-class suburbs.[3] Through these experiences, they came to know both of these places in a way, and with a depth and richness, that few people can claim.

Their stories are those of "strangers in a strange land" whose race and class distinguished them from most of the residents of their communities. Their perceptions of these communities and their experiences there are quite different from those of more typical residents—even other Black residents. Like members of immigrant groups who have made similar journeys, most Blacks who have moved to middle-class suburbs achieved middle-class status first and then left the city. But the suburban movers left without any prior change in economic status. Thus, their different perspectives on suburbia may result, in part, from not sharing the middle-class status of their suburban neighbors.

The suburban movers also gained dramatically different bases of comparison. Inner-city residents rarely have an opportunity to compare their surroundings to middle-class suburbia. In addition, suburban movers' perceptions of the inner city changed with the perspective they gained from relocating. Their accounts are about straddling two different, often opposing worlds. They reflect the families' challenge to maintain "multiple consciousness"—to retain aspects of their racial identity and urban Black culture while trying to assimilate into mostly middle-class white suburbia.[4]

METHODOLOGY

The analysis compares the participants' accounts of their experiences in predominantly middle-class white suburbs and Black inner-city neighborhoods in three ways. The first compares suburban movers' experiences in their new suburban communities with those in their all-Black, inner-city neighborhoods. Second, the discussions compare suburban movers' experiences with those of participants who moved to predominantly Black city neighborhoods. Third, the analysis provides comparisons over time by looking at both suburban and city families' experiences at two stages seven years apart.

All three comparisons emphasize the impact of the program on the children. The importance of the children's immediate opportunities and long-term life chances loomed so large in the program—especially for suburban movers—that the children's experiences are central to an understanding of what happened to the families.

REVIEWING THE SUBURBS AND RECALLING THE INNER CITY

The following chapters focus primarily on the stories of families who moved to predominantly white, middle-class suburbs during the first six years of the Gautreaux program. Participants had to have moved more than one year before the time of the interview (1982), so that they could talk about experiences in the suburbs, and had to have at least one child who had attended a city school, so that they could compare city and suburban schools.

They first discussed their experiences with interviewers in 1982, after having lived in the suburbs for from one to six years (average of thirty-two months). The women in these families described their experiences in their suburban communities and recalled many facets of life in their inner-city neighborhoods. As requested, when they talked about their children, they focused primarily on the experiences of one randomly selected child who was between six and sixteen in 1982 and who had lived and attended school both in the inner-city neighborhood and in the suburban community. In addition, sixty-one of those children were interviewed; however, their youth and reticence about talking to strangers made their responses difficult to use, and so this report mostly relies upon mothers' accounts.

Under the Gautreaux program's integrationist provisions, the suburban families had to move to areas that were more than 70 percent white, but few suburbs ranged from 70 to 90 percent white, so they actually moved to suburbs that were more than 90 percent white, with an average of 96 percent. Most of these areas were virtually entirely white and middle-class. The few exceptions were older, relatively self-contained "satellite cities" on the periphery of the metropolitan area. To offer support to movers, the Leadership Council tried to move two or three families to each area, but they also sought to avoid concentrating families, so they rarely moved more than three families to any area in any year. As a result, the 114 families were scattered across many buildings, developments, and more than one hundred communities.

Seven years after the initial contacts, in 1989, a follow-up study located 68 of the original 114 families. Of these, 53 were still in the suburbs; 13 had returned to the city, and 2 had moved out of state. Low-income families are generally difficult to locate because they are highly mobile and often are not listed on standard sources (telephone listings, drivers licenses, credit report agencies). Once contacted, less than 7 percent of families refused to be interviewed.

By 1989, the children were eighteen years old on average. The questions focused on the children's employment and educational attainment as well as their social interaction and self-esteem.[5] Most were interviewed in their homes; the two families who had moved out of state were interviewed by telephone.

This format provided two snapshots of the families' experiences, seven years apart. Both the families and the communities changed during that period, in reaction to each other as well as in response to other forces. These families' accounts illuminate important themes and provide unique insights into these unusual odysseys.

COMPARING SUBURBAN AND CITY MOVERS

Secondly, the analysis compares the experiences of the 114 suburban movers with those of 48 city movers who relocated through the Gautreaux program to sharply contrasting destinations—city neighborhoods with populations averaging 99 percent Black, based on 1980 Census tract data. Families who moved to city census tracts with less than 7 percent unemployment rate, less than 7 percent below poverty level, or more than 25 percent college graduates were eliminated to reduce heterogeneity in the city sample and make a clearer contrast to suburbs. The follow-up study in 1989 included 68 suburban and 39 city movers—63 percent of the mothers and 93 percent of the children interviewed originally. Due to the small number of city families, the 1989 study added an additional 10 city families who were comparable to the original city families in tenure in the program, proportion of female-headed families, age of mothers and children, and post-move census tract attributes.

To the extent that the two groups of families—the suburban movers and the city movers—were comparable, the differences between their experiences could be related to differences between the places they lived rather than the people. As a threshold matter, the families in both groups shared important characteristics that made them members of the plaintiff class in the Gautreaux lawsuit—Black, low-income, and residents of (or wait-listed for) Chicago's public housing program. The suburban and city movers also went through the same selection processes and met the same selection criteria to enter the Gautreaux program.

Moreover, the program allocated families to neighborhoods in a quasi-random fashion, so the program took on the form of an experimental design. Families were assigned to housing units on a first-come, first-served basis, and since suburban and city units became available in a random way, and family sequence for qualification was random, the matches were virtually random. While families could choose to reject an offer, they rarely did, since they would have had to go to the bottom of the queue and might not get another chance during the six months they were eligible for placements. As a result, the program took on the character of a social experiment, and the city and suburban groups were highly comparable.

The two groups were very similar on a number of attributes. All moved within the first six years of the program, and had lived in their neighborhoods from one to six years at the time of the initial interviews. The children selected were similar in average age and gender. The mothers in the two groups had comparable levels of education: 32 percent of both groups were high school graduates, 17 and 18 percent of the two groups had some college but no degree, and 8 percent of suburban movers and 4 percent of city movers had college degrees, rates highly similar to those for eligible nonparticipants and regular Section 8 participants.[6] Virtually the same proportion were female-headed (86 percent and 88 percent)—rates which are similar to the 86 percent estimated by an earlier HUD study of Gautreaux and to the 89 percent for eligible nonparticipants and the 90 percent for regular Section 8 participants.[7] Nearly the same proportion were satisfied with their pre-move neighborhoods (85 percent suburban, 89 percent city).

Some observers have worried that neighborhood assignments were not random because of the "finders-keepers" program, which allowed families to find apartments on their own.[8] However, the finders-keepers strategy did not begin until 1985, so it did not affect the sample selected in 1982. Moreover, the finders-keepers program did not involve large numbers of families until after 1990. While this is a good reason to doubt the randomness of the program *after* 1990, it had little effect prior to that time. Indeed, an analysis of the complete program records for the 3400 families moving before 1990 found no correlation between family attributes and neighborhood placement.[9]

The program's procedures did not preclude the possibility of systematic differences between the suburban and city movers. For example, children who moved to the suburbs might have been doing better in their city schools, on average, than the children whose families stayed in the city. If such differences did exist, they could explain, at least in part, differences in post-move academic outcomes that would otherwise seem to be attributable to differences in the places to which the families moved. However, the available information suggests that the suburban movers were not different from the city movers. Indeed, the two groups showed minimal differences in pre-move characteristics.

Moves back to the city could also be a potential source of bias. Those who returned to the city might have had more negative experiences in the suburbs. In the 1989 study, eight suburban movers had moved back to the city (and are not included in the 1989 analysis because of their ambiguous status). These families had chosen to move back to the city because of the same kinds of discomforts that other suburban movers reported—distance from old friends, daily harassment, difficulty of using Medicaid in suburban hospitals, children's social and achievement difficulties in the first year in school. Their accounts did not seem to differ in kind or severity from those of other suburban movers. Moreover, by the time of the 1989 interview, six of these families reported that they were sorry they had returned. While it is not clear how representative these returnees were, the results did not suggest that those who returned to the city had any different suburban experiences than other suburban movers. They seemed to have the same unpleasant experiences that others had, and in the time of discomfort, they chose to leave. How people make such crucial existential decisions is very hard to say.

Attrition could also be a potential source of bias. If the families that this study could not find in the suburbs had lower outcomes than the ones that were found, then the observed outcomes would have an upward bias. However, the suburban children had so much higher outcomes than the city movers that even if one attributed the city levels of performance to the suburban youth who were not found, the suburban outcomes would still remain significantly higher than the city outcomes. Thus, attrition probably would not eliminate the better outcomes in the suburbs.

Table 5.1 Characteristics of the Sample: City-Suburban Comparison

	City N = 112	Suburb N = 230	t	Significance
Years on Gautreaux	6.04	5.34	1.92	n.s.
Years at address	3.37	2.76	2.04	*
Age	37.47	35.39	1.90	n.s.
Age of youngest child	9.95	7.75	2.89	**
Number of children	2.47	2.54	0.38	n.s.
Years of education pre-move	11.56	11.90	1.69	n.s.
Years of education post-move	12.35	12.33	0.10	n.s.
Marital status				
Married now (percent)	9.82	7.39	0.59	n.s.
Never married (percent)	42.90	43.90	0.03	n.s.
Getting AFDC (percent)	53.60	48.30	0.85	n.s.
Second-generation AFDC (percent)	50.90	51.30	0.01	n.s.
Disabled person in household (percent)	22.20	21.40	1.02	n.s.

$*p < .05; **p < .01; ***p < .001.$

SURVEY OF A RANDOM SAMPLE OF 342 FAMILIES

Another survey was conducted to get information on a large sample. While the larger study was done primarily to study suburban effects on mothers' employment outcomes, it included questions about family social interaction, and the results are reported in chapter 7.[10] Because of its size and the absence of constraints on children's age, this survey probably provides the best information on the attributes of Gautreaux families.

In the fall of 1988, a random sample of Gautreaux participants was surveyed. The response rate for the survey was 67 percent, yielding a final sample of 230 suburban movers and 112 city movers. This sample matches the distribution of participants in the Gautreaux program.[11] To understand respondents' experiences, in-depth interviews were conducted with 95 participants in their homes (52 suburban movers and 43 city movers).

Since participants had little latitude for choosing where they would move, city and suburban movers were expected to be highly comparable. The results confirm that expectation. Few differences existed between the demographic characteristics of city and suburban movers (see table 5.1). City movers were two years older on average than suburban movers, as were their children, and they had been at their present addresses an additional seven months. However, the two groups were very similar in other ways. Both groups had been in the program about six years and had between two and three children. Just over one-fifth of respondents in both groups reported someone in the household with a disability. About half of both samples were receiving AFDC payments. Just under 10 percent of city movers and 8 percent of suburban movers were married at the time of the interview, and about 43 percent of both groups had never been married. Both groups had similar education: about 20 percent of both groups lacked a high school diploma, and about 35 percent had some college education. Since the two groups were highly similar, the city movers were a good comparison group for the suburban movers.

Generalizing to the larger universe of low-income Blacks is more difficult. In the second year of the program, HUD conducted a study of the participants, and found that they were highly similar to eligible nonparticipants and to regular Section 8 participants.[12] Some of the specific findings are reported above.

Despite these similarities, it is important to understand the program's selection criteria. The program had three kinds of criteria, which were intended to select participants who would be good tenants. Placing families would be worse than pointless if they turned out to be poor tenants and were evicted. The aim of these criteria was to select families who could meet the ordinary expectations of a good tenant—to fit into the units without overcrowding, to pay their portion of rent, and to avoid causing property damage.

First, because there are few large apartments in the suburbs, the Gautreaux program tended to select families with four or fewer children. Anecdotal evidence suggests that this was an important constraint. However, research indicates that 95 percent of AFDC families had four or fewer children, and 90 percent had three or fewer.[13] This suggests that the sample would not be very different than the pool of AFDC families.[14] Second, as in the Section 8 program, Gautreaux applicants were screened to make sure that they regularly paid their rent and that they had some source of income (usually AFDC). The Leadership Council estimated that about 12 percent were rejected by the credit check or rental record. Third, counselors visited applicants' homes to determine which people were such bad housekeepers that they would be undesirable tenants. Housekeeping inspections were not concerned about neatness or dust; families failed if their homes showed significant property damage. About 13 percent of families were rejected on housekeeping criteria. Therefore, Gautreaux participants were probably not typical of public housing residents in general; they were in some respects among the "better" public housing residents. They had smaller families, they had good rent-paying records, and they met housekeeping standards, at least on the day of the counselor's appointment.

However, the requirements of the Gautreaux program were not so stringent as to make participants totally atypical. Program experience indicates that the three criteria sequentially eliminated 5 percent, 13 percent, and 12 percent of applicants, so together they reduce the eligible pool of applicants by less than 30 percent. Self-selection may further reduce generalizability, but self-selection is likely to be correlated with these three criteria, so its additional impact may be quite small. With more than forty thousand families in Chicago housing developments, the program participants were likely to represent a large number of people.[15]

In sum, although this is an above-average group of housing project residents, they are by no means an elite or "highly creamed" group. All were very low-income, current or former welfare recipients who had lived most of their lives in impoverished inner-city neighborhoods, and many were second-generation welfare recipients.

THE INTERVIEWS

Through a wide range of questions, the interviews focused on the places people lived in order to understand their experiences before and after moving. The questions emphasized women's perceptions and their subjective reactions, focusing particularly on the experiences of the randomly chosen school-aged child. The interviews included both open-ended questions that invited wide-ranging and elaborate accounts and closed-ended questions with specific sets of possible responses. There were general inquiries about positive and negative aspects of living in the city and the suburbs, and about how people treated the women and their children in each place they lived. The second interviews, in the late 1980s, also included questions about the children's advanced education and employment experiences, since most of them were beyond high school age by that time.

The first interviews (1982) avoided direct questions about racial discrimination; the initiative in raising that subject was left with the women and children themselves. This approach reduced the risk of appearing to solicit particular kinds of responses, which could inadvertently elicit overstatements. It also ensured that the incidents described were ones the women viewed as significant. While this strategy may have led to under-reporting of discrimination, women were not reluctant to discuss the discriminatory experiences they had.

All interviewers in the first study were Black women. Since 87 percent of the families were female-headed, the study focused only on mothers' responses, for comparability. Having Black female interviewers helped to make the women more comfortable about discussing their experiences. Many appeared eager to talk. They seemed to speak quite openly, frankly, and extensively about their families' experiences before and after their moves. The original suburban in-person interviews averaged more than two hours in length and ranged from one to five hours. Follow-up interviews ranged from forty-five to ninety minutes. Many of the initial and subsequent interviews contained a considerable amount of detail and specificity, including personal comments and revelations. Some of the accounts were complex and richly textured, with a mix of positive and negative reactions to the places families lived.[16] The variety of accounts suggests that no "party line" developed among participants concerning what to say about inner-city or suburban experiences.

Almost all of the women contacted agreed to speak with the interviewers. In the first round, they received no compensation; in the follow-up process, they were paid ten dollars for their time.[17]

Each of the next four chapters discusses a major element of families' experiences before and after their entry into the Gautreaux program: safety, social interaction, and schooling. All chapters emphasize the children's experiences, mostly as described by their mothers.

The adaptation of these families to the suburbs suggests considerable strengths and survival skills, and seems quite at variance with the "culture of poverty" hypothesis, which predicts that people who lived in poverty would have great difficulty adjusting to a middle-class environment. Similarly, these accounts cast doubt on the analyses that define Black, single-parent families as pathological and deviant, unable to function effectively, in part because of the absence of husbands and fathers. In both the city and the suburbs, the women demonstrated their commitment to raising their children as well as they could, with strength and dignity, in very trying and challenging circumstances. They also projected a future orientation, a focus on their children's opportunities and life chances, rather than the drive for immediate gratification that is sometimes attributed to low-income people.[18]

SIX

Safety First

When these Black, inner-city families moved to predominantly white, middle-class suburbs, they traded one set of disadvantages for another. Their inner-city neighborhoods were rife with crime, gangs, and random violence, which drastically restricted their daily lives. Although these families moved to suburbs that were far safer, they faced new risks of racial incidents that they had not experienced in the city. These events were sometimes frightening, and potentially life-threatening. Yet even the worst racial incidents, which may have been intended to drive these families out of the suburbs, rarely approached the level of danger from the daily threats of the inner city.

THE PERVASIVENESS OF INNER-CITY CRIME
In the late 1970s and the 1980s, Chicago's rates for violent crimes—murder, forcible rape, robbery, and aggravated assaults—were among the highest in the country.[1] Crime rates soared even higher in Chicago's inner city, subjecting residents to great risks from the crime and violence that surrounded them.[2] For example, in 1980, residents of Robert Taylor Homes, the nation's largest public housing development, constituted less than 1 percent of Chicago's population, but accounted for approximately 10 percent of the city's murders, aggravated assaults, and rapes.[3] A decade later, Robert Taylor Homes and Stateway Gardens public housing complexes had the highest rates of homicides, sexual assaults, robberies, and serious assaults in the city.[4]

The pre-move experiences of suburban Gautreaux families are reflected in these patterns. Almost half of the participants told of dangerous and frightening incidents that occurred regularly on the streets of their inner-city neighborhoods, in front of their homes, and even in their buildings. The pervasiveness of the crime and violence crossed several dimensions. No time or place offered respite.[5] As Alesa Butler recalled, "It was not safe to walk through my neighborhood at night and sometimes even during the day." Crime occurred daily, at any time of the day or night.

Crime threatened both persons and their property. Women described a constant barrage of criminal acts, ranging from violent crimes to serious and petty property crimes. Crime permeated every aspect of their lives. Alesa Butler recalled, "They snatch your bag, rob your house, mug you on the elevator." Delores Gore suggested that becoming a victim of crime was almost unavoidable: "They steal too much in Chicago. They'll steal your tires. They'll steal your hubcaps. They'll snatch your purse. I had my chain snatched off my neck in a restaurant. They're just too roguish. You have more of a concentrated area of desperate people."

The actual incidence of crime in Chicago, especially in the inner city, is probably much higher even than official figures suggest. Police do not record all reported incidents.[6] Moreover, many victims—as high as 50 percent—do not report crimes to the police, in part because of a perception that the criminal justice system is ineffective in apprehending and prosecuting offenders.[7] Alesa Butler described her frustration with this situation:

> Everybody knows what's going on. Some people would tell me after I was broken into, "I knew they were going to break in but I didn't know it was you." Some people knew who did it but they wouldn't [testify], they would just tell me who did it, so I had no proof. And the ones who did it would brag about it. But there's no proof. Last time they got caught, and I don't know what happened; we went back and forth to court, but I just don't think the system works fast enough, so you lose your property. . . . The police won't come fast enough.

Underreporting crime is particularly prevalent in inner-city neighborhoods, where residents often fear retaliation.[8] As Annie Winters pointed out, "The older boys were breaking into people's houses, and you would see them, and they'd tell you you didn't see anything."

Women's accounts suggested a sense of helplessness in preventing and solving crimes, as well as obtaining redress. Women believed they were abandoned by the system and especially by those they knew in the community, whom they could not trust. Their feelings of isolation and helplessness may have further intensified their sense of the overwhelming magnitude of the crime in their midst.

FEAR OF CRIME

The likelihood of crime and violence, as well as its unpredictability, made women fearful and anxious that they would be victimized.[9] Many Gautreaux participants described this chronic fear and anxiety for their own safety and the safety and well-being of their children; as Dianne Cotton recalled, "I would be afraid all of the time in the city. Every time you went out, you'd have to be looking over your shoulder. This is not some time. This is all the time. Looking over your shoulder."[10]

Poor Blacks, and particularly women, have consistently higher levels of fear of crime.[11] Mothers not only feared for their own safety, but for their children's ability to protect themselves. Nia McFar emphasized her chronic anxiety about her daughter's safety amidst the rampant crime and violence: "It was not comfortable enough living for anyone with children. . . . I didn't care too much for letting my daughter go out for fear of her life. I was always afraid that a fight would break out when she was down the street. One time it did happen, and there was a crowd, and I couldn't find her."

Women also regarded neighborhood disorder and decline as particularly threatening.[12] Several women feared harm from the drug addicts and drunks "hanging around" in their decaying urban communities. Aretha Smith described the "beer cans, wine bottles, and paper everywhere" in her Chicago neighborhood, and she recalled her terror of the drug addicts:

> Now I had started to get paranoid. The area I was living in was a heavy drug area. Drug addicts would terrify me. I was afraid of them. It was obvious they were on something. They were hanging around all day up and down the streets. Walking backwards and forwards. That kind of scared me. They didn't have anything to do with their time. I can imagine they were just messing around and got bored one day and said, "Hey, I'm going to have a little fun. Pop this chick up the side of the head and see if I can bring me some joy."

Women's accounts emphasized not only the expectedness and certainty of crime, but its unpredictability. The frequent use of alcohol and drugs in their neighborhoods heightened women's feelings that many of the crimes were random and irrational acts. Aretha Smith feared that one day drug addicts might not "have anything to do with their time" and kill her out of boredom.

GANGS

Participants seemed to share the police department's view that gangs dominated the inner city and public housing complexes and accounted for many of the crimes and much of the fear among inner-city residents.[13] Inner-city residents were at high risk of becoming victims of gang crime, as well as of being injured or killed as innocent bystanders by stray bullets during gang shootouts. Nia McFar said she was afraid "that a stray bullet would come from one of the higher floors, and you would never know who shot you."

As general levels of crime escalated in the inner city, so did random violence. By 1990, police reported that innocent bystanders were shot in Chicago public housing developments almost daily.[14] Much of this random violence was attributable to gang activity and disputes over drug-dealing or more traditional turf battles.[15] The presence of gangs made it extremely difficult to stay out of harm's way.

Some families told of having been caught in gang cross fire, even in their own homes. The magnitude of the inner-city violence prompted many women to describe their experiences with the graphic phrases and terminology of war.[16] Lenore Sowell recounted the great dangers involved in being caught between rival gangs and the "warfare" that invaded her home. Nia McFar recalled "people shooting at people." As in war, women spoke of the victims, and many were children. Dorothy Martin noted that "every time you look around somebody was killed—children and grown people."

Women's greatest fears about gang encounters focused on their children rather than themselves. Children were more exposed and vulnerable to gang crimes and random gang violence in traveling to and from school and spending time on the streets. Mothers feared that their children would get shot. Lenore Sowell expressed her fear for her daughter June's safety: "It was unsafe for [June] to go outside. There were gangs all around the area where we lived. We lived in a bad area. Children were getting shot all around there." Carolyn Ellis also feared for her son Jeremy's safety amidst the gang violence: "The gangs were always fighting, shooting, stabbing each other. It didn't bother me. I just didn't want my son there."

As Carolyn Ellis noted, some women appeared resigned to the situation and their inability to protect their children. They could only hope that their children would be fortunate enough not to be shot in gang warfare. Monica Bates decried the "way [the gangs] do things so openly" in her Chicago neighborhood. She discussed her daughter Mayana's fear of gang fights and shootouts, which occurred even as children played in the playground: "You'll just be sitting on the porch. . . . You knew this was going to happen anyway. We just accepted it."

The mothers' focus on their children may have reflected their confidence in their own ability to negotiate the dangerous terrain because of their experience and greater maturity. They may also have been accorded a degree of respect as mothers, especially because they were often the sole parent present and the head of the household.[17]

The gangs presented both physical and psychological threats to children, who were more vulnerable to these dangers. They could be randomly caught in the cross fire of a gang shootout while they were outside playing or even in their own homes. They might also be specifically targeted as victims. Children faced harassment by gang members for no apparent reason, even between home and school. Mothers, teachers, and the children themselves could do little more than hope that the children could run fast enough to protect themselves. Alesa Butler described her son Russell's fears and his efforts to avoid the reach of gang members: "Mostly he was afraid to come home from school, so the teachers would let him leave a little early or a little late. Most of the time the teachers would tell him to run home. He was afraid of the gangs."

The psychological dangers also threatened the children's well-being. Mothers worried that children were influenced by the negative role models and violent gang ethics. As Monica Bates recalled, "It's hard for the children. Plus some children think that's what they're supposed to grow up and do. That was sad."

Women also feared "losing their children" to the gangs.[18] Many inner-city children became involved in gang activities and subjected themselves to an even more dangerous world of drugs, guns, and violence. Young people were often attracted to the gangs and joined in hopes of reaping financial benefits or for honor and security.[19] In some communities, gang membership was "expected and desirable," and youths were drawn to gangs in order to fulfill a variety of psychological needs that were not otherwise satisfied.[20]

Gangs also put pressure on children to join.[21] Gang members threatened physical harm or stole possessions and money from children in order to pressure them to join. Refusal to join a gang could mark someone as an enemy. Avoidance was one of the only possible options for a young boy trying to resist gang pressure or recruitment. Russell Butler "was afraid of the gangs" and tried to run home after school, so he wouldn't be confronted by gang members: "When they ask you to run with them and you don't want to, they pick with you. They would take your cap and glove, money, anything else they wanted, and beat you."

The pressure to join gangs appeared substantially gendered. Mothers and children focused on male gangs and their recruitment of young males. In spite of the presence of females in male gangs and female-only gangs, the women and children did not talk about them.

VICTIMIZATION

Chicago's public housing tenants were twice as likely as other city residents to become victims of violent crime.[22] More than a dozen suburban movers described having been crime victims before moving from the city. That probably understates the actual number of crime victims in this group because participants were not asked specifically about victimization but only about generally positive and negative aspects of life in their former neighborhoods. Also, some people who were victims may not have wanted to reveal that fact.

The pattern of women's victimization tracked the overall pattern of crime fairly closely. Women spoke of physical violence, such as attacks and attempted rapes, as well as property crime. Their victimizations also reflected the same time and locational dimensions. Women were victimized at all times of the day and night, in their neighborhoods, and even in their homes. Their accounts emphasized the toll that victimization took, undermining their sense of safety and restricting their movements and daily routines. As Dianne Cotton recalled, "In the city. . . . I got stuck up a couple of times. And I got attacked one time. You always had to live in fear."

Hazel Tucker remembered that she was afraid of "people on the street. Period." A robbery exacerbated these feelings:

> Anything could happen. I was coming home from school one day and this boy was walking behind me and my sister. And he spoke to us and everything, and we didn't think anything of it. We were just talking. . . .
> He spoke: "Hi, how are you doing?" And we figured he was going the same way we were. But he dropped behind us. And all of a sudden we had stopped right in front of the door, right in front of the building. And he pulls the gun out and says: "Give me your purse." And I looked at him and said, "Huh?" And he said: "Give me your purse." I said,

"Well, here take it. There's nothing in it anyway." And he took her bus tokens and her bus pass and that. Well, everything happened so fast, it just didn't register. It didn't register until we got in the house. We called the police, and they came over.

Some participants were repeatedly robbed and even attacked in their own homes. Jenny Moseley recalled the horrors: "I was attacked many times in Chicago. A guy came into my apartment while I was asleep. My house was broken into; two attempted rapes; was robbed standing at the bus stop. A guy tried to snatch me one night when I was getting out of my car."

Women also feared the rash of break-ins that plagued their inner-city neighborhoods. Anita Higgins constantly worried that her possessions would be missing when she returned home:

You'd be afraid they would be breaking in. You always had to leave somebody at your house. You'd be wondering if you'd have your TV when you got home. You'd always worry about it if you didn't have any-body there. Especially if you lived on the first floor. . . . Cause where I was living at the time somebody tried to break in on me twice. I was on the third floor. And they broke my window.

Diane Cotton recalled that she was "afraid all of the time in the city." Rebecca Owens "never felt safe, even inside my home. I was often afraid in the daytime." Carolyn Ellis "was afraid of everything." Their fear caused them to look over their shoulders, rush into their homes, and sometimes try not to leave—except to leave for good, through the Gautreaux program.

INDIVIDUAL RESPONSES TO CRIME AND FEAR OF CRIME

The fear of crime had substantial practical and psychological effects on people's daily lives and routines. People who fear for their safety engage in risk-avoidance behaviors to reduce their chances of becoming victims.[23] In their pre-move neighborhoods, participants treated coming and going as matters of conscious and calculated risk-taking rather than simple daily routines. Efforts to avoid danger constrained their world and limited where they and their children went, and when.[24] Evora Fleming described how the dangers affected her life:

I never went any place. I was scared to go out of my apartment. I worried that if I went out, something would happen. I would get downstairs and think, "I hope this elevator is working when we come back." Often it wouldn't. I had to walk those stairs seven or eight times when I was pregnant, because the elevator didn't work, carrying groceries and laundry up the stairs.

Fearing for their children's safety, women exercised strong control. They restricted their children's activities and supervised them closely, often prohibiting them from playing outside or with other children. Gautreaux participants also described precautions they took to feel safer.

The structural and design features of the public housing developments exacerbated women's fears. Elevators and windows, for example, make high-rise housing appealing to residents in some communities and frightening for inner-city residents. Elevators are essential in most high-rise buildings, but they pose a significant source of danger in inner-city neighborhoods. In these enclosed public spaces, women and children were particularly vulnerable to rape and other assaults. Elevators also made flight or escape from an attacker difficult and allowed no way to seek assistance. They also broke down frequently, leaving the generally darkened and isolated stairwells as the only alternative for exit and entry.

Residents of public housing could not avoid the elevators, stairwells, and other public spaces that jeopardized their safety. Just entering or leaving their apartments subjected residents to dangerous risks. Evora Flemming feared that her daughter would be seriously harmed in the elevator or walking down the stairs of her own building:

> We lived in the projects, and I didn't allow her to be out of my sight too long. We lived on the twelfth floor, and it was dangerous going in and out of those elevators. Sometimes I let her go to her girlfriend's house that lived on the eleventh floor, but I was really scared for her to get on the elevator or walk down the steps then. I didn't want her to be raped, killed, or worse.

Windows also had very different and negative implications in the inner city than in safer communities. While a welcome source of natural light and air, they provided a literal "window" to the crimes and violence on the streets. As Joyce Robinson recalled, "You could look out your window and see someone get cut up. . . . It was so real. I was right in the middle. I was living it."

Windows also allowed crime and violence to invade families' homes. Bullets entered their homes through windows, endangering their families.

Windows also provided easy access for intruders, especially in low-rise buildings and on the lower floors of high-rises.

The very structures and features that were intended to provide safe and convenient high-rise living may have actually imprisoned women and their children. Still, some people responded aggressively in spite of the risks that this entailed. Children frequently fought to protect themselves; as Joyce Robinson recalled, her son had to "fight a lot in the city." Some women, like Carolyn Ellis, took aggressive actions although they could not eliminate the risks entirely: "I was afraid of everything. My mother and I just came out of the house one day, and we were walking down the street, and these two guys were behind us, and they said, 'Give me your purse.' These were punk kids, eleven or twelve years old. I swatted him one, and they took off."

Crime and the fear it generates have significant psychological effects on people who live in dangerous neighborhoods. Crime victims often become fearful and anxious about their safety and are afraid of becoming victimized again.[25] They may feel helpless, and their feelings of vulnerability may be generalized to other areas of their lives, causing apathy and depression.[26] Crime may exacerbate the fear and anxiety many inner-city residents already experience. Faced also with poverty and high unemployment, they may experience even greater difficulty in coping with victimization.[27]

COMMUNITY RESPONSES

The pervasive danger in the inner city not only disrupts individual lives and psyches, but also tears at the fabric of the community. Community residents tend to withdraw and have less contact with their neighbors.[28] Their fear of crime also promotes passivity and may prevent neighbors from helping each other.[29] As neighbors become more fearful and suspicious of each other, the community becomes more vulnerable to criminal activity, informal social controls are weakened, and community support systems may fail.[30]

Gautreaux participants lived in communities plagued by suspicions and passivity. Hazel Tucker described how neighbors distanced themselves from each other: "They had a lot of break-ins. They didn't really stick together. When something really went wrong, they wouldn't really stick together. They wouldn't help each other. Stuff like that." Annie Winters, in turn, believed that if she "opened [her] mouth" against the neighborhood boys who were breaking into peoples' homes, "my house would've gotten set afire or something like that." Women could not trust the police to protect them, nor could they rely on their neighbors.

As a result, women distanced themselves from each other, and some perceived each other as threats.[31] Claire Clinton even feared that her "friends" would victimize her. This reflected an ironic twist on the concept of friendship, which implies trust at its core: "I've found that I can't have too many friends in the neighborhood because if you start letting people come into your house, they see what you've got, and when you go to work or away from home for any reason, they break in. I've had that happen before."

People in high-crime areas tended to feel more isolated than people in safer communities.[32] This feeling was most intense when a crisis created an obvious need for assistance and neighbors or bystanders saw the need and had the opportunity to help, but took no action. Diane Cotton recalled her helplessness when neighbors failed to come to her aid: "Nobody will come to your rescue. I got stuck up [robbed], and the boy came back up at me again, and me and him were fighting, and nobody came to my rescue, and people were standing all around. It was in the summertime, and nobody tried to help me but this boy out of the service."

Fear may inhibit people from intervening, including calling the police, when they come upon a crime in progress.[33] These threatening and dangerous encounters were exceptionally frustrating and frightening for the people involved. They reveal the levels of fear that permeated these neighborhoods and the devastating isolation women experienced even in the midst of others. Marie Jones described how her neighbors repeatedly refused to help: "They broke into our house and a lot of more people's houses where I lived, and nobody ever called for help. . . . I've heard people saying that they've seen people getting beat up on the street and people won't even call for help. It's like they're afraid to even go to the phone and call."

MOVING AS A RESPONSE

Previous studies have found that Black families express their dissatisfaction with their neighborhoods and their desire to move more than other groups.[34] Many residents, particularly middle-class ones, leave as communities become unsafe.[35] The Gautreaux program offered the same opportunity to some low-income Black residents who normally would not have been able to afford such a move. Marguerite Jones wanted to "find a better place" for her children after her child was mugged in her front yard, and her children came home from school afraid. Families hoped that places outside the inner city would provide relief from the chronic fear and anxiety with which they lived. Annie Winters echoed the thoughts of other participants when she spoke about her desire to leave her inner-city neighborhood in order to feel safe:

> I didn't like anything about [my city neighborhood]. That's the reason I moved. Because the older boys were breaking into people's houses, and you would see them, and they'd tell you you didn't see anything. I just got tired of that "You didn't see." I'd rather go someplace where my life was more safe than throwing a bomb or something through your house. So I just moved out of the neighborhood.

Many suburban movers had grown up in inner-city communities and experienced these dangers as children.[36] Raised in Robert Taylor Homes, the nation's largest public housing complex, Carol Hughes wanted her daughter to be free from the violence of her own childhood:

> And those years that I was there were not so much terrifying but for a child to have to run for her life half of the time because you've got a gang there . . . a girl has to fend for herself. I can remember many a day going just for a sporting event—baseball, softball with the girls. We would go from Ida B. [Wells] to Stateway [Gardens], and I'd have to run for my life to get home. Piece by piece. I could not see my child growing up in no area like that.

Safety was generally not the only factor that precipitated families' moves, but the overwhelming crime and violence in the inner city may have played an important role in some women's decisions.

SAFETY IN THE SUBURBS

Moving to the suburbs provided most Gautreaux participants with a refuge from crime and violence. However, this pattern must be qualified in two ways. First, a few families moved to suburban communities that partly mirrored the city's age, heterogeneity, and social conditions, and that had significant and increasing crime problems of their own. Moreover, those who moved to predominantly middle-class suburbs encountered new risks in the form of actual or threatened racial violence.

Violent crime was significantly lower in suburban communities than in the city of Chicago.[37] In 1975, for example, Chicagoans were four times more likely to be victims of violent crime than suburban residents.[38] Suburban communities faced an increase in crime in the late

1980s and early 1990s.[39] Still, in the early 1990s, the rate of violent crime was ten times higher in Chicago than in the suburbs.[40]

SUBURBAN MOVERS' PERCEPTIONS OF SAFETY

Just as crime statistics suggest, the suburban movers viewed their new suburban neighborhoods as much safer than their former city neighborhoods—both during the day and at night. Respondents were asked if the streets within a few blocks of their home were dangerous. In the day, neighborhoods were said to be dangerous by few suburban movers (10 percent), but most city movers (67 percent) said their neighborhoods were dangerous in the day. Looking back on their pre-move neighborhoods, 75 percent of suburban movers said their former neighborhoods were dangerous in the day. When asked the same question about the night, only 31 percent of suburban movers said the suburban area was dangerous, while 71 percent of city movers said their neighborhoods were dangerous at night. Looking back, virtually all suburban movers (96 percent) said their former city neighborhood was dangerous at night. While it is possible that suburban movers' recollections exaggerate the danger, it is also possible that city movers may downplay the danger of the neighborhoods they must traverse every day.

Similarly, when asked how safe they felt being out alone in their neighborhood in day and night on a five-point scale from very safe (1) to very unsafe (5), both groups felt safe in the day, but at night, suburban women reported feeling "safe" (2.20), while city movers felt less than "in the middle" (3.30). Reflecting back, the suburban movers felt between "very unsafe" and "unsafe" (4.18) in the city at night. Approximately three-fourths believed that areas in their former Chicago neighborhoods were dangerous even during the day, including public transportation, the park nearest their homes, the streets near their homes, and the elevators and stairways in their buildings. They believed that there was a "good chance" that they would be victimized in the very areas they could not easily avoid, such as the streets near their homes and even within their buildings.

Even in their homes, suburban movers felt safer. Only 2 percent of the suburban movers believed their homes were dangerous during the day, while 44 percent recalled that being at home in the city during the day was dangerous. Twelve percent of the women who remained in the city still believed their homes to be dangerous in the day.

Women's accounts confirmed the stark contrast between violent inner-city environments and the safer, middle-class suburban communities. Nia McFar characterized the violence as "shocking and scary," and relished the relative tranquillity of her suburban environment: "It was nerve-wracking to me. I was always uneased. . . . Here in the suburbs, I don't have to worry about people shooting at people, seeing people chase people and shooting, fighting." Annie Winters also noted dramatic differences in the levels of safety:

> Because the older boys were breaking into people's houses. . . . The neighborhood out here [in suburbs], you don't have to worry about that stuff going on. You won't sit on your patio and see them stealing pocketbooks and stuff like that. Out there [in the city] I didn't like it because that [stealing pocketbooks] was happening and I couldn't do anything about it.

Peace and quiet characterized daily life in the suburbs. In sharp contrast with their frequent and graphic descriptions of inner-city violence, most women's observations reflected the absence of sounds such as gunshots. Arlene Moore recalled that she frequently heard "stray shots [in the inner city], and you don't hear that here."

Gangs were not seen as a threat in the suburbs. Mothers expressed significant relief over the absence of gang violence and gang recruitment in the suburbs. Dorothy Martin described the dramatic contrast between the gang violence in the inner city and its absence in her suburban neighborhood: "There is no violence here [in the suburbs], no gangs, no gangbanging. I'm used to all that gang-banging all night long, all day long. Every time you look around somebody was killed—children and grown people." Women consistently spoke about their children's increased safety and security in the suburbs. This confidence in their children's safety was central to a mother's ability to raise her children, as Margaret Hopper explained:

> It wasn't safe to live [in the city]. . . . Like now, it's this gang thing, you're surrounded by this mess with the gangs. If you have sons and daughters, it's really hard. . . . I feel safe, feel safe for my children [in the suburbs]. When I was in the city, I was worried about them. They weren't safe at all.

Mothers and children became accustomed to the safety in the suburbs. The dangers in the city, which were distressing when families lived there, became intolerable after they had lived in the suburbs for a while. Gwen Larson's son Jason feared returning to the city after he was robbed on a visit back to the city. Jason had become used to safety in the suburbs.

"He went to the city once last summer, and he was robbed. Some boys robbed him and a friend that was taking him to a concert. . . . But since he was robbed, whenever I say anything about moving back toward the city he says NO! He doesn't want it."

Despite the higher perception of neighborhood safety in the suburbs, some suburban movers perceived some dangers. The incidents of actual or threatened violence in the suburbs were usually race-based and sometimes very serious and frightening. Although few suburban movers received threats, the ones who did reported some frightening events. Anita Higgins received harassing letters when she first arrived. Gail Francis discovered that her car had been burned under suspicious circumstances. One of the most dramatic incidents happened when white teenagers nearly ran Claire Monroe off the road as she was driving home from work:

> Occasionally you will be met with racial slurs, from teenagers only in their cars. I've had a car full to chase me one night. I was driving, and they were chasing me with their cars. They had their windows down. First they were at the side of me, and they had their window down, and they yelled at me and asked me what I was doing there. I didn't belong out here. And I rolled my window up and they got behind me and just started to butt me; get along side of me and try to push me off the road. This went on for a long time. . . . I was coming home from work that night. . . . Teenagers are kind of mean.

Other women experienced similar assaults. Annamarie Palmer described having been "trail[ed] on the expressway, bumper-to-bumper." Claire Clinton recalled incidents where "young adults, adolescents, made . . . racial slurs, throwing rocks and things at my car." Alesa Butler was terrorized by a man and woman in a car who tried to, or pretended to, run her over when she was on her bicycle. Whites sometimes shouted insults from passing cars or walking on the streets. Yasmin Coleman described an incident that occurred in front of her home: "There were some teenagers sitting out in a car. They hollered a racial word. I went out and confronted them. They called me a nigger. I think they threw a beer can."

When Suzanne Franklin confronted a group of white teenagers whose name-calling had escalated into violent threats against her son, she turned things around so that some of the kids became friends:

About fifteen or twenty kids came last year, and my son had obviously
been in a fight with one of them and won. They had bats and sticks and
calling us "niggers" and come out of the house. I settled it by bringing
them all into the backyard and told them if they were going to fight, do
it one on one. They wound up all apologizing, and I told them to direct their energy elsewhere and form a baseball team or something. As
a whole it didn't turn into anything really big. They had come front
and back doors, vigilantes. They were getting ready to burst windows
out and [were saying] "Come out of there you niggers." I was home
alone so I had to handle it myself. I came out to protect my property
and my sons as well. It never continued. I was afraid of later on, maybe
the kids would be afraid to walk to school. But a lot of them have been
back at my house as friends of the kids. It was basically a kid thing.
There were no adults behind them or anything like that. They were
just angry. Some come in the house now and are friends.

Moreover, even when the hostility has not ended in violence, it can
lead people to worry. Viola Hodges described her terror on the streets at
night and the fear for her family's safety: "My greatest fear is at night.
They say "night has no eyes" and people can do things to you and nobody will see them. Nobody can identify them. . . . Somebody might
stop somebody from doing it if it was in the daytime. But truthfully, it
could happen day or night. I don't feel too safe."[41]

Perhaps none of the suburban attacks was more harrowing than that
experienced by April Jackson. She and her daughter Romana missed
their bus after returning from a festival in Chicago, and started walking
back a few blocks to their neighborhood. A group of white men ac-
costed them.

We walked past [these four white guys] . . . and they hollered, "KKK."
So we just kept walking. So we got a little farther, and he said, "KKK.
Niggers, what are you doing over here?" So, I didn't say anything, I just
kept walking. So finally we got to this little lounge, but it was
closed. . . . So I just went and picked up this beer bottle [and juice
bottle] out of this little trash can . . . and broke both of them. He said:
"Oh, we got a bad nigger." . . . So Romana said, "Mama, let's run." I
said, "No." I know I couldn't outrun them, and that's what they wanted
us to do. So the first thing that came to mind was that if they stopped
us, they probably would've raped Romana, and they would've beaten
her and anything. And I just knew I had to protect her. . . . We walked

on. They had gotten as close to me as this door here. . . . And she had picked up this rock and she was crying and she was just pulling on to my blouse.

I guess they saw the fear in her. I was scared in a way. I was scared afterwards. I wasn't afraid then. I think I was more hurt. So I just took my shoes off, and I turned around with these two bottles in my hand, and by this time there were three on the other side of the street that were okay. The other one he was on crutches. So when he saw them bothering us, he ran to the end of the street and started doing this. I thought he was going to say, "Man, leave them alone," or whatever. He took his crutches and threw them across the street to give to them I guess to beat us to death. When they got that close up on me, I decided I wasn't going to move again. I just took those two bottles and I said, "You all come on." You know I can't tell you all the words I did say. I bluffed my way through it. I said everything. I said, "I'm going to get one tonight. I don't know which one, but I'm getting one tonight."

Romana's just crying. She's just holding on to me just crying. They didn't take not one step, and I started walking towards them. I don't know what's wrong with me. I guess it was the fear. I was afraid and then I wasn't afraid, and I think I was protecting my child.

So then they stopped right dead in their tracks. They didn't say not another word. But I was stomping my foot and I was raving like a crazy woman. I was cursing. I was going to kill them. So finally the bus came. And you could see the expression on this bus driver's face. . . . I said "Romana, jump on that bus." She jumped on and I'm going to back in. They took bricks and bottles and those crutches and tried to tear that bus up. . . . [The bus driver] said this happens all of the time. It happens and they won't do anything about it. They don't do anything about it. Last summer. Summer of 1981.

Somebody must have heard me breaking those bottles. When we got off [the bus], the police were coming from each direction. Not a lot of them. One from that way and one from that way . . . here I am with two bottles in my hand and a brick, and Romana's got my shoes. The police just sat there and looked at me. I should have reported it, but I wasn't even thinking. I was just that upset. Nothing would have been done anyway. I could've reported it because the same thing happened to my girlfriend like that. . . .

I came home, and my son was here, and I was telling him about it. I was so upset and so nervous. Romana decided to sleep with me that night. And we woke up about two o'clock and she said: "Mama, were you scared tonight?" I said, "Romana, I was." And I started crying.

These attacks were serious, and they left psychological scars. No family that experienced such attacks felt comfortable in the suburbs, and some remained very anxious for a long time. Some women moved to other communities because of fear for their family's safety. Among the reasons mentioned for the moves, families sometimes cited incidents of racial hostility. Darlene Williams planned to move after repeated racial incidents involving her neighbors:

> I lack trust in the area. I don't really feel comfortable. . . . I've seen too much going on, as an adult, and I think the children see too much. . . . We had a group of whites that lived next door when I first came that used to throw firecrackers on the patio. They'd smoke reefer; they'd lay out on the lawn and fall asleep and get high and, you know, make "nigger" jokes.

However, while these incidents were shocking, inexcusable, and damaging, few incidents actually resulted in physical violence. Unlike the assaults, armed robberies, break-ins, and gunfire in the city, which posed clear risks to life and limb, the threats in the suburbs were more unclear in the danger they posed.

COMPARING THE THREATS IN THE CITY AND SUBURBS

While a few mothers were distressed by the threats in the suburbs as much as by those in the city, most indicated that the city threats were far more serious. While few women had experienced serious threats in the suburbs, many had been robbed, raped, assaulted, or shot at in the city, and because of the fear of gangs, no one would come to their defense. Florence Peterson reported the following incident:

> In my old neighborhood in the city, I would run from front door to back door, fearful about my kids' safety. I was mugged. I ran from the guy, but he caught me. . . . I was walking; it was in the summer on a Sunday night. He grabbed my mouth, so I bit him. . . . I didn't know him, so I ran, and he said, "If you scream, I'll beat you up!" And he meant it. Because I screamed and he beat me up. I screamed and screamed, and *no one came;* so I had to break away and run to my house.

I ran into the bushes and beat on my windows. . . . He was hitting me. Finally, my sister and brother came out and he ran. . . . After he ran and I was safe, the streets were full of people; they heard me!

Neighbors were ready to come out when the attack was over, but not while the attacker was present. This mother felt very nervous about the safety of her children in the city, and she felt much less worried about them in the suburbs: "In the suburbs [where I live] there are no gangs. I don't have to stand in the window and watch out for my kids. . . . They haven't had any problems. In the summer, most of the families in the complex look out for each other." Mothers felt there was a constant danger in the city. Lenore Sowell noted, "It was unsafe for [my daughter] to go outside [in the city]. There were gangs all around the area where we lived. We lived in a bad area. Children were getting shot all around there."

Even being at home in the city provided little security, as Ms. Sowell described:

It was a crime area, with gangs. We were between two different gangs, one on one side, one on the other. My windows got shot in several times; we had to *sleep on the floor.* At night you had to put your mattress on the floor because bullets would be coming through the windows. It was like Vietnam. [About the suburbs], there's no comparison.

Part of the reason was that the suburbs were more "controlled," which referred to school rules, to protection, and to kids who were more disciplined. Jolene Moss stated,

At [suburban] school, there is a closed campus. . . . They don't allow any outsiders on the playground or around the school unlike the [Chicago] school where there were "teenage boys" and "gang members" hanging around schools. They have policemen come around every so often and check.

Kama West commented that her suburban neighbors looked out for the children:

In the city, you worry about a child like Roberto. He would be easy prey for the gangs. . . . [But in the suburbs] I don't worry about things like that so much because out here you have more of *a community protection-type thing. You can know that [the neighbors] know that it's your child. . . .* "That's the West child." They'll tell you when they see something going wrong. They'll monitor him. . . . When we were in the city, our house was broken into like once every month regardless of whether or not we were home. They just come in.

In the context of these urban dangers, the suburban threats were shocking and disturbing, but they were much less threatening than the dangers in the city. Yasmin Coleman stated, "My mind is so at ease out here. I lived in fear [in the city]. It's kind of bad that you have to live like that. When I came in at night, I'd rush to get in the house. I was afraid that somebody standing there would knock me out to take my purse." Suzanne Franklin noted her son's fear:

> Dennis is afraid of it [the city]. He told me that the people in the city . . . will beat you up. . . . Out here the children are different. They're softer. I feel that if he went back to the city he'll be just like fresh meat. I'll never take him back there even if it did mean I'd have to work two jobs. He's very afraid of staying there permanently.

Lucretia Fletcher described how city gangs pressured children to join them:

> The schools here are quieter, but they still have the dope at noon. But you can choose, whereas in the city you were pressured and harassed. I used to meet my son at the bus stop every day because there were a bunch of teenage boys who would use guns and knives and everything to get him to join the gang.

Even the bad influences in the suburbs were a matter of choice. Drugs and gangs presented risks in the suburbs, but children were not coerced into participating.

CONCLUSION

These families left city environments where their lives and safety were threatened daily and moved to suburbs where gangs, muggings, and gunfire were very rare. The dangers that suburban movers reported were less life-threatening and less common than the ones experienced in the city.

Some of the suburban incidents were shocking, and the fact that they happened in the context of suburbs where such violence was rare made them all the more shocking. They were racially motivated actions directed against these mothers and children with deliberate malice. The peacefulness of the surroundings made this racial violence all the more jarring.

While suburban racial incidents were frightening, they were seldom as dangerous as incidents in the city. As Ms. Monroe reported, "Here, the fights are not physical; they are exchanges of words . . . there is no real damage."

The city dangers were also more pervasive, built into the fabric of the environment. Random gunfire, for example, from a passing car or through a window in a massive high-rise could not be confronted or stopped. In contrast, the suburban incidents were infrequent. In short, Gautreaux participants traded a much-reduced risk of violence for a much greater risk of racist encounters, which are discussed in the following chapters.

SEVEN

Social Interactions

A major concern about the underclass is that their increasing concentration in decaying urban neighborhoods deprives them of contact with more middle-class people or social institutions.[1] These inner-city residents are becoming increasingly isolated from mainstream society and live in a world where long-term unemployment, welfare dependence, and crime have become the norm. Although large numbers of young, affluent Blacks moved out of central cities and into surrounding suburbs during the 1970s, Blacks remained significantly more isolated than either Hispanics or Asians.[2] Of particular interest here, the location of this program—the Chicago metropolitan area—was consistently the most segregated large metropolitan area in the country.

Despite increasing concern about concentrated poverty, few policy initiatives have attempted to reduce the isolation of inner-city residents. Traditional poverty programs have focused on providing services (e.g., job training, Head Start, etc.) to give residents the skills to improve their status and move out. Most public housing projects tend to exacerbate the problem, concentrating low-income individuals in large, decaying apartment buildings in inner-city neighborhoods.

Thus, the social integration of these families is both important and problematic. The suburban movers in the Gautreaux program had the potential to break out of the environment of concentrated poverty that is the usual circumstance for other low-income Black families in the United States. The suburbs, however, are not always receptive to these families. As a result, even if families are living in the midst of middle-income white families, they may not be a part of their community, and they may not get the full benefits from it.

Some studies have looked at how Blacks and whites interact when they live near each other. This research generally shows that integration is most successful when Blacks and whites are of equal social status. It also finds that better educated, more affluent whites, exhibit the lowest levels of racial prejudice.[3] A survey of the neighbors of Blacks living in suburban communities found that affluent whites tended to have more positive attitudes toward Blacks than those who were less well-to-do, and that whites were more positive about Blacks when the Blacks were of the same social status.[4] A study of women living in integrated public housing developments in Lexington, Kentucky found that those who had the most interracial interaction were those whose previous interracial contacts had been with equal-status Blacks.

In a study of a city where a few Black families had moved into white suburban neighborhoods, the greatest levels of racial interaction occurred among people of approximately equal social status.[5] Whites in the neighborhoods studied were least likely to accept Black neighbors when homeowners feared effects on property values, and whites in well-mixed communities exhibited more tolerance than those living near a single Black family. In sum, research suggests that under certain circumstances, Blacks and whites can interact and form friendships.

Thus, one of the common threads of this research may be termed the "equal-status hypothesis": the greatest levels of racial interaction occur among people of equal social status. This hypothesis suggests that the Gautreaux approach would fail to lead to successful integration. Gautreaux adults were of lower socioeconomic status than their neighbors, and they could not afford to move to white suburbs without this unusual program. While the program made every attempt to avoid identifying participants as low-income people in a supported program, other tenants were likely to notice that the new tenants' cars, furniture, and clothes were less expensive than their own.

In addition, although most Gautreaux families moved into rental developments, making it less likely that worries about property values would arise, the sight of a less affluent family moving into their development might still have activated fears of neighborhood decline and deterioration. Finally, the Chicago area has a long history of racial tension and violence that threatens the success of any attempts at residential integration. Thus, a number of factors militated against the acceptance of Gautreaux adults in their new communities.

However, the distinctive features of the Gautreaux program made it hard to extrapolate predictions from past studies. Existing research generally examines the experiences of middle-class Blacks, so it may not apply to the experience of these low-income families. Although there are no other studies of low-income Blacks in middle-income white suburbs, previous research suggests some expectations. The "equal-status hypothesis" posits that suburban movers will be less socially integrated than city movers. These low-income Black women had very different experiences from their white middle-income neighbors, which might have limited neighbor support, friendliness, interaction, and friendships. In addition, their new environments were different from those they experienced in the city, and this unfamiliarity may have further limited their interaction and number of friends.

Moreover, since the equal-status hypothesis implies that individual attributes affect social integration, the best test of the suburbs' effects must involve control for individual attributes. These analyses help determine whether individuals with more middle-class attributes (such as more education, fewer children, and not receiving AFDC) were more integrated and had more friends.

The suburban movers left neighborhoods that were over 90 percent Black and entered areas that averaged 96 percent white. When they entered the suburbs, they wondered if they would be accepted. The answer turns out to be complex. Incidents of harassment experienced by the families had made newspaper headlines during the study, creating an expectation that suburban movers might be more isolated from neighbors than city movers.

This initial expectation was wrong. On a simple question of whether they had any contact with neighbors, suburban and city movers were *equally* likely to have some contact (85 percent for each group). Moreover, when asked about the frequency of contact on specific activities, the suburban mothers reported significantly *more* interaction with neighbors than the city group. Compared with reports by city movers, suburban movers reported more frequently visiting with neighbors, talking on the telephone with neighbors, sharing babysitting with neighbors, eating at a neighbor's home, and having a neighbor over to their homes for lunch or dinner. Retrospective versions of the last three items were also asked, and suburban mothers again reported more frequent interaction in the suburbs than in the city on two of the three items—eating at a neighbor's home, having a neighbor over to their homes for lunch or dinner, but no difference for sharing babysitting.[6]

In addition, many suburban movers reported that their neighbors were friendly. Indeed, 74 percent of suburban movers reported that at least one of their neighbors was friendly, and over 55 percent reported that five or more neighbors were friendly. Thus, interactions were often with several neighbors, not just one.

On the other hand, in the retrospective analysis, mothers reported that their new suburban neighbors were less friendly than their former city neighbors. Similarly, in comparison with city movers, the suburban movers reported that their neighbors were less friendly. On the five-point scale, the mean level of friendliness for suburban neighbors was said to be slightly less than "friendly," while the mean level for the city neighbors was midway between "friendly" and "very friendly."

In addition, negative incidents were more common in the suburbs. Suburban movers mentioned diverse incidents, including harassment, racial epithets, and exclusion. When asked if "there were any incidents where people treated you or a member of your family badly" in the first six months and in the past six months, significantly more suburban movers reported negative incidents in their first six months after moving than the city movers (36 percent versus 15 percent). While both groups indicated a strong, significant tendency for negative incidents to decline after that, significantly more suburban movers than city movers still reported such incidents in the six months preceding the 1982 interview (18 percent versus 2 percent). Subsequent interviews with these mothers found that this difference declined to insignificance by the time of the 1989 survey.

These findings appear contradictory. Compared with city movers, suburban movers had more interactions, but experienced less friendliness and more negative incidents. Apparently, neighborhood relations were more complicated than a single measure could capture. Indeed, although neighbor friendliness is negatively correlated with "incidents where people treated you or a member of your family badly," most (17 of the 26) suburban movers experiencing such negative incidents also reported that their neighbors were generally friendly (1 or 2 on the 5-point scale). Thus, even though they were being treated badly by *some* neighbors, these suburban movers simultaneously perceived that *most* neighbors were generally friendly. The antagonistic neighbors were not perceived as representing all neighbors; they were seen as a few isolated, unusual individuals. The same suburban movers who were being treated badly were also interacting with some of their neighbors in daily activities like talking in the hallway, baby sitting, and having a meal together.

Some of the negative incidents were indeed horrifying and distressing, which is why they made newspaper headlines. Newspapers sometimes portrayed such incidents as representing the views of a community, but they were generally perpetrated by one or a few individuals. Even mothers who experienced such incidents also reported considerable interactions with some neighbors, and many reported that their neighbors were generally friendly.

Thus, negative and positive interactions may be two different phenomena. High incidence of harassment does not predict low interaction or low acceptance. While harassments were perpetrated by one or a few hostile individuals, acceptance was offered by individuals at the other end of the spectrum. The existence of one group did not necessarily imply anything about the existence of the other. This account begins by describing the incidence of acceptance and its consequences. Besides a quantitatively large amount of interaction and friendliness, there was an abundance of qualitatively rich, warm, and accepting actions. Then we describe the avoidance, rejection, and harassment experienced. Unlike the outrageous threats and assaults, these events were less ominous, but their frequency may have had a serious psychological impact.

SUBURBAN SUPPORT AND ACCEPTANCE

Neighbors helping neighbors represented a recurring pattern in women's reports. Women described a community structure in which neighbors—both women and men—supported and assisted each other. Yasmin Coleman praised her neighbors' helpfulness and the cooperative environment in the community: "If my car breaks down, there is concern. If there is snow all around, there is help. They pitch in together."

Suburban women depicted a sense of connectedness among their neighbors. The greater amounts of interaction that women experienced in the suburbs suggest that suburban movers were less isolated in some ways than they were before they moved. As Denise Brown stated, "I like it here because everybody looks out for everyone." Alberta Geoffrey emphasized the interest that neighbors took in their community and in each other: "People care more about what happens to their community. They seem to slow down, find out what's happening around them, instead of always rushing around like they do in the city."

Twenty-one suburban mothers cited examples of neighbors' assistance, ranging from neighbors bringing food or household items to repairing each other's cars and caring for each other's children. Most of these accounts suggested that these acts were representative of a culture of cooperation in these communities.

Suburban movers' accounts about their neighbors' acts of kindness *were not isolated.* Seventy-four percent reported that at least one of their neighbors was friendly, and more than 55 percent reported that five or more neighbors were friendly. Hazel Tucker described her neighbors' commitment to helping each other, as well as their kindness towards her. Neighbors invited her "to do things with them" and loaned her their cars several times a week after her car broke down: "People are very friendly. I just about know everybody around here. They're helpful and participate. We help one another, it's just nice." Kama West also appreciated these acts of kindness:

> My neighbor right next door, she made me casserole the very first day I moved in. And her kids came over to talk to me and to try to help me get my house together. I didn't have a whole lot to put up. I just accumulated stuff. People would throw away stuff and would always remember to ask me if I wanted it. Or they gonna have a moving sale or a garage sale, and they always give me a deal on things. I've been very blessed.

There was no difference between city and suburban movers in terms of neighbor help. On the simple question, "When you first moved here, did any neighbors go out of their way to help you settle in?" suburban movers were just as likely to report that a neighbor helped as the city movers were (24 percent versus 25 percent). Suburban movers reported a variety of friendly behaviors by neighbors: "The neighbors are all white. They offered to help. They made a cake. Brought out coffee and wanted to chat." They offered reassurances: "The neighbors made me feel comfortable. They told me if I had a problem, I could use their phone. Just made me feel like 'You're not alone. We're in this boat together. Anything you don't know ask us. We'll help you.'" Neighbors also explained things and helped with children:

> I had one neighbor ask if there was anything she could help me with. She explained things in the building. She watched children for me. They welcomed me in, gave me things, showed me where the school was. They showed you where the grocery stores are, how to take the paths to them without walking on the streets. They babysat.

One mother mentioned that the maintenance man's wife brought presents for her children, and some landlords were also supportive: "My landlord did everything he could possibly do. He checked on us all the time, was always looking out for Tina. He found out my kids had never been in an airplane, so he took them and let them ride in his plane. Took them to his farm and let them ride his horses. Talked to me a lot."

Patricia Davis experienced a number of difficult situations, and each time her suburban neighbors stepped in to help care for her children. Shortly after she moved into the community,

> I didn't know anybody in the neighborhood . . . my girlfriend had got sick, and she asked me to take her to the doctor. . . . When I got home, [I saw a note telling me to call the police.] I . . . called the police. . . . They told me that when my kids had come home they found the door open so they called the police, and they are at your neighbor's house, and here is their phone number. . . . When my water pipes busted, we had to get water from the neighbors next door, who had just moved in, and they were always bringing things over. . . . If my kids are in trouble, my neighbors will help.

Patricia Davis's neighbors helped during other crises. The most dramatic was when her baby died. Her neighbors didn't know initially, "but when they found out, the phone was ringing, and they were offering all sorts of help."

Some women who moved to the suburbs reported finding *a sense of community* that they felt was lacking in their city neighborhoods. They had often felt isolated in the city, had withdrawn from the community, and had even become suspicious and fearful of their neighbors. Sometimes city neighbors ignored crime that they saw, and didn't try to stop it or report it to the police. In contrast, some described suburban neighbors who watched over each other's homes and property. Suburban movers believed that they could count on their neighbors' assistance, and some took active steps to protect others. Gwen Larson told how her neighbors intervened when things appeared wrong:

> If they see your lights on in your car, they'll come right up here to your door, or if they thought they see anybody tampering around, they kind of watch out. If they see your children participating in an activity and they figure you're the type of person that doesn't allow that, they'll come and tell you, or they will try to talk to your child about it.

This culture of cooperation enhanced women's peace of mind about their children's safety and well-being and provided yet another reason to ease up on the restrictions they had imposed in the city. Carolyn White gave her children much more freedom to play outside because neighbors watched over each other:

Kids running in and out, and I don't worry. 'Cause they're here, and if they see anything we're gonna all say something. We kind of look after one another. When she [a neighbor] goes away she comes and tells me "I'm going away. Look out for me." If I go away I'll ask her to look out for me. It's pretty much a working together area.

For many women, these acts of assistance provided important tangible benefits, such as transportation and babysitting. Just as significant for many women, however, was the psychological benefit of knowing that this support network existed. Carol Hughes described her relationship with her neighbors: "If I needed anything they were always there and vice versa, because with five babies you were always needing. And I let them know right off the bat that if there was anything that they needed they should feel free to come to me. And that's the relationship."

This mutual support and assistance that suburban neighbors offered each other gave the women a sense of security that often eluded them in the city. In contrast to her city experiences, Ruby Nelson felt more confident when she left her nine year-old-son at home babysitting his younger brother "because the neighbors out here, they kind of help watch too." Hazel Tucker described a male neighbor who regularly stood guard at 10:00 P.M. when she arrived home from work, to make sure she was safe walking through the dark parking lot.

Some women developed social relationships with their neighbors. Hazel Tucker found she could "communicate with [her suburban neighbors] better." In the inner city, she "argued a lot [with her neighbors]. Here we'll talk about it and solve it." She also joined her suburban neighbors for various holiday activities, such as Christmas shopping, baking, or sewing.

Women often attributed these positive relationships to their common interests in their children. Families' daily social interactions appeared to focus more on the activities of the nuclear family than in the inner city. Katie Hopson noted that she was "in closer touch" with her suburban neighbors:

We are on the same peer level. The same age groups. And our households are the same although I'm a single parent. Most of my neighbors have both parents in the home. We basically have the same things going for us. We have children who are in the same age groups, and many of us have the same lives and interests. We like to do a lot of the same things.

Not everyone wanted to be close to their neighbors. Diane Cotton appreciated the congenial, yet distant, relationships she shared with her suburban neighbors. "Everybody seems to mind their own business. The neighbors are friendly. I don't know any of them, but they will speak. I don't have any problems with the neighbors."

Like Ms. Cotton, several women expressed their own comfort with this distance. Lenore Sowell emphasized that she had no "problems with neighbors, in general. I didn't see them much, and they didn't see me, and that's the way it is here." They suggested that racial attitudes were not the primary factor. Marie Austin believed that neighbors rarely socialized, and she herself only spoke to one neighbor in her building: "I don't really have any contact with Blacks or white neighbors out here because they usually stick to themselves more. . . . I don't really visit them that often. And I kind of like it that way too, in a way. I don't want too many friends. Talking with a few is okay, but that's about it." Women often perceived their new environment as consistent with their own stated desire to be left alone. Jenny Moseley preferred to "keep to [her]self":

> I don't bother any of the neighbors because I don't want them both-
> ering me. Don't get in their affairs because I don't want them in mine.
> We see each other in the halls and chit chat, but we don't visit. I guess
> I'm the closest to the lady across the hall and don't see her very often.
> She will get my mail for me, and I do the same for her. She looks out
> for my house. I keep out of trouble keeping to myself.

Still, some women appreciated knowing that they could turn to their neighbors if they needed help. Florence Baker said that she thought such help was available and expressed an openness to having closer friendships under the right circumstances:

> In general, my neighbors are moderately friendly. I think if I needed
> something and went to them, it would be OK. For example, if my car
> broke down, or if I had a flat, if they had the time, they would help me
> with it. All of them know that I stay by myself. They see me coming in
> and out. It's not a real close friendliness. I like it that way. I prefer not
> to have it very friendly. That's just my personality. Of course, it de-
> pends on what neighbor it is. If it's somebody I think would be compat-
> ible, sure I'd like them as a close friend. But I haven't met anyone like
> that here. Some of the white neighbors are pretty nice, especially the
> housewives that are home all day.

SUBURBAN REJECTION

While 74 percent of the suburban families had one friendly neighbor, 26 percent reported not having any friendly neighbors. Many of these mothers experienced race-based social rejection in their daily activities. Shopping, for example, was a necessary activity that was unpleasant for some suburban movers. As Jacy Arnold stated, "[People are] . . . staring at you . . . in the grocery store, the neighborhood, in the office. They treat you different when you're Black."

Suburban movers reported a variety of ways that sales personnel and other shoppers stigmatized them. The very presence of these African-Americans appeared to elicit curious, suspicious, or even hostile reactions. Sonya Woodard eventually adjusted to the constant stares: "The whites look at you and watch you when you go in stores, but after a while you get used to it, you just look at them back when they stare you down. I don't mess with them, and they don't bother me."

A number of women complained of insults to their dignity. Store clerks were distant, and they avoided touching Black women. Monica Bates emphasized the disparate treatment:

> The only thing that's worse about the neighborhood is the racial over-tones here. You go to the store, and nobody says anything; but you can feel the tension, the stares. Not everybody, but sometimes. Like, when they give you your change back like this [without touching you]. You can see from the person ahead of you in the checkout line [that they don't treat everyone that way]. It's not everybody. I don't even think it's the majority.

Women also recounted having been ignored by store employees or the opposite—placed under constant surveillance. Angelique Dillon was most angered at having been followed by a store clerk who suspected her of stealing: "This lady working behind the counter started following me around, and I can't stand that." Sonya Woodard also resented the constant surveillance by store clerks: "In the stores they will follow you to make sure you don't steal something. That happens anywhere out here." Joyce Drummond recalled that a sales clerk prevented her from trying on clothes in a dressing room: "Everybody can try on things but me."

Women had few options, however, for avoiding these indignities. Katrina Anderson "more or less stopped shopping here" and boycotted three major chain stores because "they're real prejudiced there." Although a few women returned to city stores early in their suburban experiences, this was generally impractical since they were so far away.

Those who used food stamps were subjected to an additional stigma. As Joyce Drummond noted, store clerks looked at you as if "you had two heads if you produced food stamps." Suzanne Franklin described the deliberate humiliation she was subjected to by store clerks and other shoppers when she used food stamps:

> I'm on public aid and I have to shop with food stamps and the stamps are sometimes treated by the clerks in the stores as if you are really a lowly person. There was a person behind me in line, this old guy, he said, "They would have food stamps," meaning Black people. It was a big scene. . . . The clerks have a way of making your food stamps obvious . . . by yelling way across the store, "Do you have change for this $10 stamp?" It draws a lot of attention to you, can be very embarrassing. . . . I have several girlfriends who are white and have food stamps, and I don't see that they are being treated in that same way.

Hallie Stickney even shopped in the city for a time because she felt embarrassed using food stamps. As a new Black resident in the white community, she felt she had high visibility, which made her self-conscious:

> I have food stamps . . . and if nobody likes it, tough. But then we felt kind of strange since we were the new people in the neighborhood— Black and on display. It was my own self-consciousness. . . . Even now, if I look back in the line, I might see someone look at me with their nose turned up because I am using the stamps. But now . . . I'm used to it.

Silent Racism

Suburban neighbors also expressed racial hostility by their silence.[7] Some women saw that neighbors maintained a "social distance" from them and limited contacts from these neighbors. Suzanne Franklin described her sense of this distance:

> I believe there's a little bit of wariness in most of their being friendly. There's sort of a pulling back. There are smiles, but it's like a general wariness of those whom I'm not really close with. The smiles say one thing, but the eyes say "stay back, I don't really want to mingle with you. But since you moved next door to me, I'll be civil." It's that type of feeling.

Annie Winters portrayed her neighbors as "white and stuck up. . . . I guess they think they're better than you." Janice Vaughan attributed this to her neighbors' fear of Blacks: "They are very friendly. They're just afraid of Blacks. . . . I can just tell by the phony grin on their face."

Other women noted the absence of the welcoming symbols that normally greeted people moving into those communities.[8] An obvious example was the "welcome wagon," which some women believed passed by Black families' homes. As Erica Bennett stated, "They've got a welcome wagon out here, but no Black has ever seen it. I'll bet you no Black has ever been welcomed."

Of course, the process is complex, and it involves interpreting subtle signals. Observing the way their neighbors looked at them, some women believed their efforts towards friendship would not be welcomed, and so they did not take the initiative. Viola Hodges explained, "I haven't been so friendly myself because if a person puts up a wall between you as soon as you see them, even if you're outgoing—I am an outgoing sort of person—but you put your little wall down then. I don't go over it to make myself friendly."

For suburban movers who did not want to be close to their neighbors, social distance was desirable. Indeed, some reported that they had learned not to form friendships when they lived in public housing, because such friendships led to requests for loans (which weren't always repaid) or sometimes even led to thefts.

For others, however, the result was disappointing. Hallie Stickney described her disappointment:

> I wanted it to be like you see it in the movies, but it didn't turn out that way. I could see myself like a regular suburban housewife taking my kids to school. . . . Have you ever seen those little commercials they have on TV where somebody new comes to the neighborhood, and these people come over with these trays of food. I'm still waiting for my tray. I thought that would happen, and it didn't. It never dawned on me that in all those commercials there was only one Black family in the group. They seemed to be very content, and they were well liked by everybody. But it isn't that way out here. So I was out here on a dream.

Racial Prejudice and Exclusion of Children

While the exclusion that mothers felt was unpleasant, their most painful experiences were seeing their children encounter racial prejudice and exclusion. Many of their children's experiences were caused by adults. Geneva Rivers found that many neighborhood parents didn't allow their kids to play with her daughter: "[My daughter] is a very nice little girl. She's not bad. One mother told me her daughter could no longer play with mine because my daughter didn't pronounce her words properly, and that her daughter would pick up from it."

Often the Gautreaux children were accepted by other children, but some parents interfered. As children became closer, visiting and interacting outside of school and in each other's homes, some white parents created barriers. Eva Bethel's son could sleep over at some white children's homes, but he faced problems from some other parents: "As soon as he tries to act normally within their lives from day-to-day as the other children do, he runs into a little trouble. Parents responded when the Black children attempted to enter their worlds." Some white parents prohibited Black children from playing in their homes and their own children from playing in their Black friends' homes. Claire Monroe described their rules: "Even my daughter has attempted to mingle with them. They are not allowed to go into their homes. They are kept like arm's distance away."

Children were confused and upset by the mixed message. Often white children wanted to play with Black children, but parents prevented them from doing so, and penalized their own children in the process. Angelique Dillon described her daughter's experience:

> The worst thing about living here has been some of this racist stuff. She didn't understand why—it kind of hurt her feelings. They didn't want to play with her or talk to her or anything. I never taught her to fight back, but I taught her to speak up and don't just go off in a corner and cry. Sometimes she would have a friend, and then find out that her parents don't want her to play with her. She's been a little lonely, for quite a while. Right next door the man said he doesn't want his kids playing with Black kids. But they were having a ball. It was so stupid. Now his kids are over there looking here, wanting to play. He's penalizing his family because he's a racist.

Evelyn Maxwell's daughter Alexis was barred time and again from entering several friends' homes, even when other children were welcomed. Most of her friends were also prohibited by their parents from entering her home. Children had difficulty understanding these behaviors:

The hardest thing for her is understanding the racial problem. She sees things she wouldn't see otherwise. She recognizes a difference with her friends because of her race. She tells me things that people say about Blacks at school. She can't visit her friends in their homes. The other parents will let her play with the other children outside, but she only has a couple girlfriends whose house she can go inside. And most of them can't come in here. They'll come to the door and ask if she can come outside, and I say, come in, but they say, "No, my mama says I can't come in." Alexis had questions about it at first, but now she understands that some people are just like that. She accepts it, and doesn't get upset about it now. . . . Another classmate invited her over to her house after school to do homework together, but she just couldn't get in. It was nothing but prejudice, because she had another girl there. The girl didn't think anything—*kids just don't think of prejudice*—but her mother sent her away. It worries me a lot, because she doesn't have anybody's house she can go into to relieve me sometimes.

Alexis Maxwell was also excluded by parents who refused to drive her to school with the other children or even take her to the ice-skating rink with the other children:

One real cold day the [school] bus didn't come or was late, and this mother came by on her way to work, and she told all the kids to get in the car and she would take them to school, but she told Alexis to go home, that she couldn't take her. This other lady standing there heard it, and she told me. She said it's a shame the prejudice some people can have. She said, "I bet that hurt but I guess you have to deal with stuff like that." I said, "Yeah, I'm used to it." Alexis looked down and started crying because she couldn't go to school. My car wasn't running so I couldn't take her.

The mother [who refused to take Alexis] has a boy Alexis's age, in fact they were in the same room last year. She lets him play with Alexis, go swimming, and play with him outside. But she doesn't want her in her home, or in her car. Alexis understands. Her friends' parents take them skating, but she can't go with them. I have to take her if she wants to go. She asked me if she could go with them, and I said, "Yes, if their mothers will let you." She asks the kids, but they never call back to say she can go. Especially when my car wasn't running, there were things she would have liked to do that she couldn't. The kids would say, "My mommy will take you." But then the mother never calls.

Ms. Maxwell also tried unsuccessfully to enroll Alexis in the local Brownie troop:

> She knows that she does get left out of activities because of her color. The Brownies wouldn't take her in. She's been trying to get into Brownies for two years. I tried to sign her up last year, and they said she was too late, so I said, "OK, put her on the list for next year." So this year I called up the first week of school, and they said they had already filled up their list. The next day Alexis said another mother called up and got her child in.

CHILDREN'S POSITIVE INTERACTION

As was the case with their mothers, children's negative experiences were often accompanied by positive interactions. Averaging over all children, suburban movers were as socially accepted as city movers. Suburban mothers reported that their children had the same number of friends in the suburbs as they had in the city (6.2 and 6.3), and this was not significantly different from the number of friends city mothers reported their children had (6.0). In both retrospective and suburban/city analyses, mothers reported that suburban children spent the same amount of time playing alone as city children.

Many suburban children seemed to have no trouble making friends, as reflected in the accounts of Lenore Sowell and Dee Scott:

> She never really has been alone. Some of the children from down the block came over and said they wanted to make friends, so they asked if they could come in and meet her, and they started playing with her, and then they asked if she could come over. She makes friends easily.
>
> The friendliness everybody shows. Everybody seems to be really nice. She [my daughter] hasn't had any problems. I haven't heard her say anything about the kids being prejudiced or anything like that. The Friday before last, for instance, the eighth graders always go into Springfield for a historical trip. . . . It ended up that she was the only Black on her bus. The kids didn't discriminate or anything like that. In fact, she said everybody was fussing over her to see . . . to say, "Well, I'm sitting by Ruth," or something like that. Everybody's just real friendly to her. She's never had a problem with someone calling her a name or acting prejudiced toward her. And I like that.

Mothers were also asked how often their children played outside when the weather was good, as an indicator of children's comfort in the neighborhood. Contrary to the concern that suburban children's experiences of prejudice might keep them from venturing outside, the city and suburban children spent the same amount of time playing outside. Indeed, the retrospective analysis showed that children played outside significantly *more* often in the suburbs than they had in the city, perhaps because they felt it was safer to do so. Carol Reddon said,

> [In the city] I didn't trust the kids and plus I didn't trust them outside so long, because of the neighborhood I was living in. Yes [I think he would have preferred playing outside more often in the city] . . . [In the suburbs] they have good behavior. They don't fight, and they don't talk bad. When they go outside, their mothers know exactly where they are. And before nightfall all kids are in the house.

A number of mothers, like Hazel Tucker, expressed positive reactions to the friendships with whites: "She knows about all the kids in the neighborhood [mother lists the different buildings where she has friends]. You go outside, everybody knows Jolene. A good forty friends. They are mixed races. White, Black, a little Mexican friend, one Chinese from school. The majority of them are white."

MIXED REACTIONS AND CHANGES OVER TIME

Most (74 percent) families experienced friendly neighbors, and some experienced negative incidents, but these were often overlapping groups. Most of the suburban movers who experienced negative incidents also reported that their neighbors were generally friendly. Several women, in fact, described *mixed experiences* in their communities, ranging from hostility to neighborliness. Some of Marie Austin's neighbors circulated a petition to have her family evicted but failed to get many signatures. Indeed, even as a few neighbors were trying to get her evicted, she also had developed a good friendship with a neighbor in a nearby building.

Women's experiences were neither uniform at any point nor consistent over time. They may have reflected dissimilar relationships with different community members or even the ambivalence of their neighbors. Janice Vaughan perceived such mixed reactions among the same neighbors, describing them as "friendly," yet "afraid of Blacks." Eva Bethel described four different kinds of reactions that her son Jarvis encountered from whites:

> There are people who are definitely *always prejudiced*. They don't make any bones about how they feel. And then there are the people who re-

ally *don't know if they're prejudiced* or not. And then there are the people who are kind of *two-faced.* . . . [Finally, there are *families that fully accept him,*] families that he can visit. He slept over. They go to little affairs together, and there's no problem.

It was often difficult for participants to ascertain the extent to which relationships reflected neighbors' racial prejudices—as opposed to community norms of social distance. When her neighbors said little to her, Priscilla Wilks did not necessarily attribute her neighbors' unfriendliness to racial intolerance.

> I don't really know their names because I don't walk into their homes and say, "Welcome to the neighborhood," because they would look at you kind of funny and think you must want something. They don't come over and say hello to me and I don't say hello to them. If I meet them outside, I may say something, but if they don't speak to me, I don't speak to them. I have said hello to some, and they didn't respond or speak. Most of these people don't socialize too much, it seems. They don't have time.

Besides the mixed and ambiguous reactions at any point in time, reactions seemed to change over time. In response to the question asking about "incidents where people treated you or a member of your family badly," suburban movers said they experienced progressively fewer negative incidents in their first six months after moving than at the time of the 1982 interview (36 percent versus 18 percent), and negative incidents declined even further by the time of the 1989 survey.

Mothers described the ways that social acceptance increased over time. Nia McFar recounted her son's experience: "I think it was harder to make friends here than if he was in school with more Blacks [as he was in the city. But] . . . after the kids [in the suburbs] began to show him around, he found out that they are nice kids, too . . . he has no problems in school now." Camille Johnston described her daughter Darlene's adjustment:

> The worst was getting adjusted to the schools. She had a problem getting along with kids and they with her. . . . For awhile she couldn't cope . . . with the name-calling. She wasn't prepared for that. Because more or less they were like pioneers—the first ones here—the white kids couldn't understand about these Blacks invading their privacy. Eventually she got around to them understanding her and she understanding them.

Michelle Holman's son Rodney experienced some resistance initially because of his race, but was well accepted by friends who shared similar interests:

> At first, they wouldn't let him on the basketball team. I think because he is Black. At least the reasons they gave didn't make sense. But now that we've been here about a year, they have accepted him. He gets calls from them all the time, wanting him to spend the night in their homes. He likes the suburbs now, not the city. His friends are better here than in the city. They're not really bad kids, so they won't get him in trouble. He's around kids who like to do things in school, or to movies, not gang-banging type kids.

Part of the change may have happened because families learned to ignore racist behavior. Florence Baker and her daughter ignored the frequent name-calling and appeared to minimize it, and sometimes it declined: "People call me nigger sometimes, also. Walking up to the 7–11 they holler "Hey nigger" out of their cars. It happens to my daughter too. She just ignores it. Big deal." As Hazel Tucker noted, "Sometimes I would ignore it. . . . It doesn't happen now. They are probably used to us being out here now. It did happen more in the beginning."

Sometimes white neighbors' awareness of prejudice actually led to its decline. The petition to evict a family from the building was clearly offensive to some neighbors. They not only refused to sign, but they were friendlier to their new neighbors as well. The reports of social exclusion provided a catalyst for change. Marguerite Jones's son Kenny and his white friend were ostracized by a few students until a newspaper story prompted people to act differently: "When Kenny first came here he had that problem . . . kids . . . would always say, "Why aren't you with your own kind?" One of the kids kind of ridiculed his friend for being with Kenny. But now, since . . . the newspaper article [that reported Kenny's experiences], they've changed." The article highlighted the racial tensions that surfaced in a predominantly white suburb when a Black and white teenager became friends and other white teenagers objected to their relationship. Then neighbors, apparently embarrassed, rallied to reach out to this family and accepted Kenny. Since the article,

> some of the grown people said they didn't know that Kenny felt the prejudice. I think the [newspaper] article coming out really helped a lot of them. They showed them. When he first came, some kid wrote

"nigger" on his desk. It surprised me, you know, that it got into the paper. . . . [Now Kenny goes] to everything that's going on at school. There was a party at school on Saturday, . . . Kenny was going on his own. There was a time when [he] would be scared to do that. He is doing well, he's not afraid. The article coming out shook a lot of them up.

Low-income Black families moving to mostly white suburbs had good reason to fear that they would not be socially accepted. As they anticipated their move to the suburbs, many feared that they would face racial prejudice and exclusion. However, their experiences were more complex than anticipated. Most of those who were harassed by a few neighbors were accepted by most of their other neighbors. Families who were antagonized by some neighbors found friendships with others. Children who were excluded by some friends were invited to the homes of others.

Indeed, negative incidents sometimes precipitated a backlash, leading to increases in neighborhood acceptance. This may also explain why the negative incidents declined over time. While it is not clear why harassment declined, it is possible to speculate. When prejudiced individuals saw that their hostile actions did not win general approval, they had to realize that their neighbors were not going to support them. When some of these hostile actions led to increased public support for these families, the bigots may have decided that they, not their targets, were the unwelcome ones. Their views were rebuffed, and, contrary to their aims, their actions led to greater sympathy and support for their targets. While the harassment made the newspaper headlines, the real story was the quiet general acceptance by the larger community.

SOCIAL EXPERIENCES OF A LARGER SAMPLE

The following sections examine whether the social experience of the original small sample was evident in a larger sample at a later period of time. A random sample of Gautreaux participants was surveyed in the fall of 1988. The response rate for the survey was 67 percent, yielding a final sample of 230 suburban movers and 112 city movers. This sample matches the distribution of participants in the Gautreaux program. (See table 5.1 for sample characteristics.) To understand respondents' experiences, in-depth interviews were conducted with 95 participants in their homes (52 suburban movers and 43 city movers).

Table 7.1 Comparison of City and Suburban Respondents on Post-Move Social Integration

	City $N = 112$	Suburb $N = 230$	t	Significance
Individual Scale Items[a]				
Lend things to a neighbor	1.96	1.84	1.22	n.s.
Let neighbor use my phone	1.81	1.83	0.30	n.s.
Watch neighbor's kids	1.81	1.98	−1.54	n.s.
Eat lunch or dinner with neighbor	1.65	1.75	−1.05	n.s.
Greet neighbor in street/hallway	3.36	3.32	0.46	n.s.
Talk to neighbor for ten minutes	2.79	2.80	−0.14	n.s.
Interaction scale[b]	2.23	2.26	−0.36	n.s.
Neighbor friendliness rating[c]	3.86	3.81	0.43	n.s.
Neighbor help	24.8%	25.0%		
Harassment[d]				
Number of times treated badly first year	0.79	2.60	−2.23	*
Number of times treated badly now	0.84	1.29	0.62	n.s.

[a]Scales range from 1, never to 4, often.
[b]Scale ranges from 1, no interaction to 4, frequent interaction.
[c]Scale ranges from 1, very unfriendly, to 5, very friendly.
[d]Based on interview data: suburban $N = 52$, City $N = 43$.
*$p < .05$.

Racial Harassment

As noted, in 1982, suburban movers reported significantly more incidents of harassment than city movers (2.60 versus 0.79; see table 7.1) in their first year after moving, and about twice the proportion of suburban movers experienced harassment as city movers (52 percent versus 23 percent). However, in the larger sample in 1988, suburban movers reported levels of harassment not significantly different than the level in the city (1.29 versus 0.84; see table 7.1). While 52 percent of suburban movers reported harassment in the first year after they moved, by 1988, 25 percent said they had such problems in the previous year. Most incidents involved children using racial epithets and insults like "niggers" and "Blacks go home." Some neighbors complained about them to management, but often found managers unresponsive: "The manager of the apartment complex wouldn't speak to Blacks. She would just stare right through you. If you came to her office, she would just ignore you. She was the only problem here."

Some suburban movers reported more severe problems, such as

Table 7.2 Comparison of City and Suburban Respondents on Post-Move Numbers of Friends and Interracial Friendships

	City N = 112	Suburb N = 230	t	Significance
No friends in neighborhood	33.0%	25.7%	1.79	n.s.
Number of black friends	3.33	2.64	1.96	*
Number of white friends	1.25	3.02	3.96	***
Total number of friends	5.36	6.69	1.59	n.s.

$*p < .05; ***p < .001.$

fighting, stone throwing, and police harassment. Of the twenty-seven suburban movers reporting harassment, eight reported physical violence or police harassment. Most of those reporting such incidents believed they were racially motivated: "A white woman told her son to throw a rock at my kids." Another said: "Someone broke my tail-lights at work. My tires have been slashed."

In sum, suburban movers experienced more harassment than their city counterparts. However, most incidents involved racial epithets rather than physical threats. Moreover, suburban movers reported that these incidents generally abated over time, which suggests that their neighbors gradually became accustomed to their presence in the community.

Interaction with Neighbors

No significant differences emerged between city and suburban movers on the six interaction measures or on the combined interaction scale (table 7.1). With respect to everyday interaction with neighbors, both city and suburban movers reported that they frequently talked with their neighbors for more than ten minutes and greeted them in the street or hallway. They engaged less frequently in other activities: lending them things, letting neighbors use their phone, watching a neighbor's children, or eating lunch or dinner with a neighbor. Indeed, on all of these measures, suburban movers interacted with neighbors as much as city movers did.

Interracial Friendships

On the subject of friendships, some participants in each group had no friends in their new communities (table 7.2). However, suburban movers were slightly less likely to say that they had no friends than city movers (26 percent versus 33 percent).

Further, suburban movers did not restrict their friendships to Blacks. Although suburban movers had slightly fewer Black friends than city movers (2.64 versus 3.33), they had significantly more white friends (3.02 versus 1.25). Suburban movers reported having slightly more friends than city movers (6.69 versus 5.36), but this difference is not statistically significant.

It is noteworthy that many of those with "no friends" felt their neighbors were friendly. On that question, 69 percent of city movers with no friends said their neighbors were friendly, and 57 percent of suburban movers with no friends said this (not a statistically significant difference). This high neighbor friendliness suggests that having "no friends" did not indicate neighbor rejection; rather, it may indicate a higher standard for what it took to be a "friend," as opposed to a "friendly acquaintance."

Multivariate Analyses

Since the equal-status hypothesis implies that individuals with more middle-class attributes will be more socially integrated, the best test of the suburbs' effects required controlling for individual attributes that indicate middle-class status. Using linear, multivariate regression, the analysis examined whether adult suburban movers had fewer friends and less social interaction than adult city movers, controlling for many attributes of the adult: years of education, whether family gets AFDC, second-generation AFDC (whether an adult's parents got AFDC when she was in high school), number of children, and sense of control over her life.[9] In addition, age and age of youngest child were controlled, because younger women and those with younger children may have had more opportunity for interaction. Years in the program were also controlled, because social integration may have increased with experience in the program. Possibly after controlling for these individual attributes, the suburban movers would be less socially integrated than city movers, contrary to the preceding univariate analyses.

However, this lack of difference in social integration between city and suburban movers persisted even after controlling for individual attributes (see table 7.3). Suburban movers did not have fewer friends or less social interaction than city movers. Individual attributes also had little influence on participants' friendships or social interaction. Only those who were not AFDC recipients made more friends. No other individual attributes had significant effects. In sum, these analyses confirm the

Table 7.3 Multiple Regression Analyses Predicting Numbers of Friends of By Race of Friends

Variable	Total Friends		Social Interaction Scale	
Suburb[a]	1.445	(.917)	.099	(.079)
Number of years on program	0.244	(.151)	−.015	(.013)
Education	0.354	(.261)	.012	(.023)
Fate control	0.642	(.584)	.068	(.051)
Age	−0.054	(.074)	−.006	(.006)
Number of children (log)	.308	(.310)	−.033	(.027)
Age of youngest	0.109	(.082)	−.008	(.074)
Getting AFDC	−1.744	(.862)*	.043	(.071)
Second generation AFDC	1.469	(.825)	.769	(.441)
constant	−2.227	(4.619)	2.066**	(.399)
R	6.3%		3.9%	
R (adj.)	3.5%		1.1%	
N	325	325		

Note: Numbers in parentheses are standard errors.
[a]Dummy variable with 1 indicating suburb, 0 indicating city.
*$p < .05$; **$p < .01$.

previous finding: Participants who moved to suburbs were no less socially integrated than those moving within the city.

CONCLUSION

Although suburban movers encountered more racial discrimination and harassment than city movers, these incidents decreased over time, and by the time of the 1988 study, there was little difference between city and suburban movers in whether they had friends, their number of friends, their interaction with neighbors, or their rating neighbors as "friendly."

Thus, there is little difference in overall social integration between city and suburban movers. Race and class differences between suburban movers and their new neighbors might have reduced social integration; however, the results do not support this expectation. City and suburban movers reported similar frequencies of interaction with their neighbors on six different activities, and both groups rated their neighbors as being "friendly." Over two-thirds of both groups reported making friends in their new communities, and there was no difference in the overall number of friends that city and suburban movers reported. However, not surprisingly, suburban movers were more likely than city movers to form interracial friendships.

Suburban movers experienced more harassment than city movers in the first year after moving, but there was little difference between the city and suburban movers in later harassment or in overall social integration. The number of friends and the level of interaction with neighbors were about the same for both. These findings are striking and unexpected.

Both Gautreaux participants and their new neighbors were able to interact normally and form friendships. This is not to say that all suburban neighbors were equally friendly, but, of course, that was not true in the city either. Rather, most suburban movers received enough acceptance from their new communities to feel socially integrated.

Participants who moved to white suburbs had more white friends than the city movers, and those who moved to Black city neighborhoods had more Black friends than the suburban movers. This did not have to be true. Indeed, some suburban movers had more Black than white friends. Yet this program accomplished a considerable amount of racial integration, including a substantial number of individual friendships.

EIGHT

Schooling

The Gautreaux program was a housing program; not an education program. For the most part, participants viewed it as a way to improve their housing situation. In the survey of 330 female heads of households, respondents reported that their most important reasons for applying were better housing (28 percent), help with rent (25 percent), and a safer place to live (12 percent). Other considerations were rarely the first priority—no one said moving near jobs was a concern, a few said getting their own apartment was a concern (just under 6 percent), and a similar small number said they moved to get better schools for their children (slightly over 6 percent).

Adding their first and second most important reasons, better housing is still the most common response, and schooling remained a relatively low priority. Half named better housing, and 37 percent named help with rent as one of their top two reasons. Only about 25 percent of respondents listed safety or schools as one of the top two reasons (a safer place to live, 27 percent; better schools, 26 percent). Thus, families entered this program seeking better housing; schools were a less common concern for most families.

The nature of schooling in the United States made this housing program into a schooling program. Unlike many other nations that have national curricula and national funding and control of schools, schools are locally controlled in the United States, and their quality varies greatly in different localities. As a result, suburban moves had the potential of making dramatic changes in children's education. While 75 percent did not consider schooling as a top priority when they contemplated the move, by the time they were interviewed, the suburban movers had noticed some striking changes in their children's schooling.

The suburban schools represented the children's main entry into public life and reflected the complex interaction between social and educational processes. Gautreaux children benefited from the greater resources of middle-class schools, and they encountered a variety of new experiences in the mostly white school environment.

This chapter examines the school environment. It focuses on the educational resources, curricular and extracurricular programs, class size, discipline and safety, and educational standards. It looks at suburban and city schools through the eyes of parents whose children went to both. While statistical studies can compare city and suburban schools through objective indicators, they do not necessarily reveal what is salient to parents.

Mothers' reports are a good way to learn about some aspects of schools. While objective indicators are better ways of describing schools' achievement outcomes, and systematic observational methods are better for describing teaching techniques, mothers can describe many aspects of suburban schools that are otherwise hard to discern. In particular, mothers whose children were formerly in inner-city schools may be especially perceptive about whether urban and suburban schools treat the same children differently. Mothers could see how their children fit into these new schools compared to the old, the ways teachers treated their children, and the ways the teachers communicated with parents. They could also note if their children were in special programs in one school but not the other.

Of course, these are low-income Black children, moving to schools where nearly all students were middle-income and white. Among the questions to be addressed are whether they would be neglected and ignored, or separated, perhaps in lower tracks or special education. Although these were better schools, that does not necessarily mean that they offered better education to these children. The answers to these questions are complex. They simultaneously had both positive and negative elements and also changed over time, as the suburban communities seemed to adapt to the children and the children adapted to the suburban communities.

Our society generally believes that suburban schools are better than inner-city schools. What is striking in the suburban movers' accounts is the wide variety of dimensions on which they reported differences. This chapter first describes the suburban movers' perceptions of the schools' physical resources, programs, and class sizes. Then it describes their perceptions of safety and discipline, and of the educational standards.

Educational standards turn out to be more complex than sometimes assumed. High educational standards led to better education, but they also accentuated the glaring inadequacies of these children's past education. The suburban mothers reported great enthusiasm about the schools' commitment to small classes and the schools' high standards. Yet, high standards also demanded a reassessment of their children's skills and performance that was often disturbing. This reassessment was particularly painful for the mothers of children moved into special education.

This chapter ends on a tentative note. While the suburbs offered much safer schools, smaller class sizes, and much higher educational standards, the higher educational standards were both a benefit and a problem. Many mothers reported that the higher standards helped their children improve their achievement far beyond the levels that city schools even aspired to attain, but many children initially had to face the realization that their achievement was substantially below the suburban schools' norms, and their capacity to meet those norms remained in doubt. Some mothers were understandably upset by this circumstance. While some blamed the city schools, others blamed the suburban schools for posing inappropriate criteria or even acting in racially biased ways.

SCHOOL SATISFACTION

Satisfaction is almost always relative. While surveys usually ask questions about satisfaction as if it were an absolute, people can only answer relative to what they know or expect. Most city mothers reported that they were satisfied with what their schools taught (83 percent). However, when suburban movers were asked the same question, even more of these mothers—96 percent—were satisfied with what their schools taught. Moreover, while suburban movers left city schools very similar to those the city movers were still attending, when the suburban mothers looked back on their city experience, they were significantly less satisfied with the city schools their children had been in a few years before. In contrast with their 96 percent satisfaction in the suburbs, only 55 percent were satisfied with the city schools.

New experiences showed parents that schools could be different than they had previously imagined. Many suburban movers reported that they were quite satisfied with the city schools when their children were still in those schools, because they did not know any better. Only after they moved to the suburbs did they have a point of comparison, and then their evaluations of the city schools drastically declined. This chapter examines what they saw in the suburbs that caused this reevaluation of the city schools and how this new vantage point revealed aspects of the city schools that other parents may overlook.

Many of the mothers were happy that their children were attending schools that offered more resources and safer environments. They were also pleased by the higher standards at their suburban schools. However, for low-income Blacks moving to middle-income, white, suburban schools, the experience was always complex, and even some of the positive features were associated with disadvantages and problems. Almost every aspect of these moves was ambivalent—full of potential advantages and disadvantages. Even suburban schools' discipline and achievement standards, which mothers mostly praised, sometimes had disadvantages and raised problems that some individuals reported as racism.

Resources and Programs

Like the suburban neighborhoods, the suburban schools offered a physical environment that was vastly superior to what these families had seen in the city. While city schools were often old and run down, the suburban schools were usually newer and well-maintained. There were no broken windows or leaky roofs; the outside walls did not have graffiti, the inside walls did not have peeling paint or water stains. While the city playgrounds were small, asphalt-covered, and often littered with broken glass, suburban playgrounds were large and covered with grass and trees. While textbooks were old, worn, and in short supply in city schools, suburban schools offered plentiful new textbooks and other resources.

In the classrooms, other resources were evident. Katrina Anderson described the differences she observed between the suburban and city curricula: "The [suburban] schools have more programs. [My daughter] was in a college prep class where they were using computers, which I don't think they have too many of in the city. She liked that."

Many mothers praised the extracurricular programs, which were more extensive and of higher quality in suburban schools than in city schools. The range of athletic activities and the associated facilities were particularly salient in the suburbs. As Carolyn White said,

> The beautiful school [offers] the first real football field [they had] ever
> seen. [It also offers] golfing, track, tennis, swimming team, track team,

football, soccer, hockey, wrestling, volleyball, girl's basketball and softball, boy's softball. . . . They didn't have as much concentrated [sports
activities] in the city as in the suburbs. Here there seems to be more emphasis and more activity. [These] sports sometimes may be in some of
the city schools, but [not in all city schools, so] he wouldn't have had a
chance to have access to them.

Jenny Moseley, Claire Monroe, and Gwen Larson commented on the
opportunities offered by other activities:

He's playing a cello now; he wants to go into the horn next year. It has
given them a greater opportunity to spread themselves, to build.

There is a music program that is excellent. She's learning a lot from it
and has really excelled in it. She has access to a lot of activities that are
not very expensive to cover. She's contented, and she finds it challenging, not in a negative way.

I like the fact that the school has a variety of activities that the children
can participate in. They have lots of sports, they have a Black student
union that offers drama, fashion, etc.

Thus, the women were more satisfied with curricular and extracurricular
offerings in the suburbs than in the city.

Class Size

Smaller class size was one of the most obvious results of superior resources in the suburbs. The suburban movers reported class sizes were
significantly smaller in the suburbs than they had been in the city, shrinking from 29.6 in Chicago to 21.9 in the suburbs. Even after removing
special education classes (which tend to be smaller), the difference remained significant and nearly as large: 28.5 in the city and 22.3 in the
suburbs. Even though the children were older in the suburbs, and class
sizes increase with age, the class sizes were much smaller in the suburbs.

Moreover, mothers believed class size affected the quality of education their children received. Some mothers thought that class size influenced the school's ability to assess and respond to their children's needs.
Carol Reddon found that her son Denard "wasn't improving any" in the
city, "The school was too crowded and they didn't have enough staff to
detect Denard's needs. His learning ability or anything. . . . So he was
just going on and on and getting farther and farther behind."

Some mothers felt that class size affected the amount of attention and assistance their children received. Carole Phillips contrasted the conditions in her daughter's city and suburban schools:

> I did not like anything at those [Chicago] schools. The teachers complained that there wasn't enough room in the classroom. It was so crowded. . . . In the city, they don't really care. The schools are overcrowded. They don't have the time to put towards the effort to help this one individual who needs this help. . . . [In contrast, the suburban schools are] not overcrowded. They had time to give them the help they needed.

Reduced class size in the suburban schools is particularly important, for it may have implications for other aspects of the changed environment, including the amount of assistance teachers gave to individual students and the communication between the teachers and parents.

School Environment, Discipline, and Safety

Mothers generally favored the school environment in the suburban schools. While 56 percent of the city movers said that the schools provided the right kind of environment for their children, 92 percent of the suburban movers did. Moreover, when these suburban movers looked back at their children's previous city schools, fewer than one-third (33 percent) reported that the city schools provided the right kind of environment for their children.

Safety was an important factor in mothers' assessments of their children's school environments. Mothers regarded city schools as significantly more dangerous than suburban ones. Suburban mothers were much less likely than city mothers to feel that the schools were dangerous during school hours (6 percent versus 33 percent), and the same was true after school hours (24 percent versus 71 percent).

Moreover, the difference was even greater when suburban mothers reflected on their children's previous city school in light of what they had seen in the suburbs. During the day, few suburban mothers (6 percent) felt that the suburban schools were dangerous, but most (71 percent) felt that their children's previous city schools were. After regular school hours, 24 percent felt that the suburban schools were dangerous, while 89 percent felt that the previous city schools were dangerous.

City classes were also generally more unruly. Mothers primarily blamed the disorder on city children's behaviors and secondarily on the teachers' inability to maintain discipline effectively. Doretta Sparks underscored the dramatic differences: "The kids [in Chicago schools], they fight and they go on something terrible. And they are not manageable. But I mean, you know, the teachers were doing the best they could with what they had. . . . The kids are more under control [in suburban schools] . . . there's just more discipline."

The potential danger in the city sometimes extended beyond the classrooms and the school buildings themselves. School playgrounds, field trips, and even the routes to and from school posed safety risks, as well. Mothers feared for their children's safety because of the fighting in and around city schools. Annie Winters walked her daughter to school and even called the police when a girl drew a knife on her older daughter in the city. Denise Brown emphasized her frustrations:

> There was fighting [in the city schools], and no one did anything. When I would go with them, like on a field trip, and they would be outside, they would be fighting and kicking, fighting and kicking, and no one would do anything about it. If I would say something to them, like don't do that, they would say something smart to me.

By contrast, suburban schools experienced *few discipline problems.* Mothers regarded suburban children as better behaved, and also emphasized the *greater control teachers and administrators exercised.* Patrice Marsh presented an image of her son Leo's suburban school that contrasted sharply with the urban dangers: "When they are let out of school . . . the kids are playing, talking, they seem to get along. It's a pleasure taking him to school." Claire Monroe stated that the "freedom from fights" was the best thing about her daughter's move to the suburbs:

> Where we used to live, there were fights all the time. She would come home from school nervous. She wouldn't fight back. She would always get beat up. Here, the fights are not physical. They are exchanges of words. The words they say to each other are really not anything. So there is no real damage, no real hurting involved there.

Gloria Reno emphasized that suburban school officials took greater control and maintained a safer school environment:

> They have so many different kinds of children [in city schools]. It was less controlled. More strangers can just be . . . around the [city] school and nobody would be suspicious. But here [in the suburbs], anybody looks funny, they're going to check it out and have the police there. . . . It's more controlled [in suburban school]. In terms of inside

and outside protection. Nothing like wondering if your child is going to come in beat up or come in at all.

While suburban movers generally praised the greater discipline and safety in the suburban schools, some noted that it posed some risks for their children. Some mothers reported that because their children came from the less-controlled city schools, they initially had difficulty getting used to the new expectations in the suburban schools. The mothers were not always sure whether the accusations were fair or biased. Nor were they sure whether teachers' complaints were branding their children with a lasting stigma of being trouble-makers that would affect their later school careers.

Educational Standards

It is hard to measure standards directly, especially for this study, which spans many schools. However, when their children moved from city to suburban schools, mothers had a chance to see how the same children were treated differently by their new schools.

Many mothers made explicit comparisons between city and suburban academic standards. They emphasized that the academic standards were much higher—sometimes dramatically so—in the suburban schools. While the mothers' accounts lack the precision of documenting the differences in terms of test scores, they are richer in detail, describing kinds of achievement and the ways it was visible.

Mothers often measured these differences in years and grade levels. Hazel Tucker concluded that her daughter Marcella's suburban school was a whole grade level ahead of the city schools: "The move affected my child's education for the better. *I even tested it out.* . . . I let her go to summer school by my mother's house [in Chicago] for about a month; . . . she was in fourth grade at that time. . . . Over in the city they were doing third-grade work. What they were supposed to be doing was fourth grade." This disparity was evident in a number of ways. Many mothers described a much more demanding level of work in their children's suburban schools than in city schools. Dee Scott emphasized that "the level of everything is so much higher than it was in the city. . . . Everything is just more advanced."

Mothers also said that there was more schoolwork. April Jackson described the combination of differences that her daughter Romana encountered with the move: "The work is different. I think it's harder than what they are taught in the public schools [in Chicago]. They have more homework. There's always an assignment. They have certain novels they have to read which is a part of their schoolwork."

Moreover, some mothers reported that suburban teachers had higher expectations of their students than the city teachers did. Suburban teachers demanded responsibility and performance. Sally Fletcher's mother was pleasantly surprised when Sally was expected to complete her assignments when she stayed home with a broken finger. Her mother explained, "They don't accept any excuses like they do in the city. . . . It made Sally feel her teachers really cared, that they're not just there for money."

Several mothers were struck by the marked differences in skill and knowledge between city and suburban students. They attributed the superior position of the suburban children to their having had access to better schools from the beginning of their formal education.

Unfortunately, the higher standards in the suburbs also had another side. Students who had done well in the city schools found that they were not that good in the suburbs. April Jackson recounted the challenge her daughter Romana encountered:

And she's competing now with kids that are at a different level. Whereas she was the smartest in the public schools, here there are kids who are geniuses almost. I think that's the difference there. These kids started out maybe in the better schools from the beginning, from day one. So they are used to all of these things.

The differences in academic standards were reflected in the city and suburban schools' evaluation of student performance. While city teachers told mothers that their children were achieving at a satisfactory or better level, the suburban teachers' assessments were markedly different. Passing grades in the city did not mean achievement at grade level in the suburbs, and even honor-roll students in the city were sometimes years behind grade level in the suburbs.

Michelle Holman's son went from being an honor-roll student in his city school to a grade level or more behind in his suburban school: "The school work is much harder here than it was in the city. He's just learning what they have had already. Now that he's picking it up, he's doing OK. . . . He was an honor-roll student in Chicago. But when he came here, he realized that the honor roll [in Chicago] wasn't the honor roll [in the suburbs]."

Mothers often had strong reactions to the suburban schools' higher standards and reassessments of their children's performance. Dee Scott acknowledged the benefits, but found this realization painful:

> When Caleah was in the city, she was considered a rather bright child. She was really good in reading and stuff. In fact, she was getting merits and stuff like that. When I moved out here, it was different. She was considered an idiot as far as they're concerned. I didn't like that. It was good in a sense that they were concerned and were taking a lot of time with the children. The levels of everything in the city are much lower than they are out here.

The increase in standards was even more difficult for slower students. Marie Austin acknowledged that her son Marcus "was kind of slow," but city teachers gave him "passing grades and he didn't even deserve it. . . . Here, it's hard for him to get passing grades because he has to study in order to get his passing grades."

Suburban schools often viewed the Gautreaux children's performance as below par, sometimes dramatically below their standards. Margaret Harper reevaluated the city school's standards in light of her daughter's progress in her suburban school: "I was concerned in Chicago; but the teachers were saying she was doing OK. When I moved out here, we had a different reply from this school; so evidently she wasn't doing that great in school in the city."

Erica Bennett recounted an even more dramatic disparity. Suburban educators determined that her son was performing years below grade level: "[The suburban school] said it was like he didn't even go to school in Chicago for three years. That's how far behind he was. And he was going every day and he was getting report cards telling me he was doing fine." While many mothers hoped that suburbs would offer their children improved educational opportunities, many were surprised at the magnitude of the disparities.

The high educational standards in the suburbs were a mixed blessing: they offered better education, but also revealed the glaring inadequacies of their children's past education. As the above accounts indicate, in the early years after moving, the reassessments of their children's skills and performance were often disturbing. Mothers came to realize that their children's past achievement was lower than they had thought in the city, sometimes by several grade levels, even for children who were on the honor roll in the city. This is particularly true for those children who moved into special education.

SPECIAL EDUCATION AND OTHER PLACEMENTS

Special education was also an area where some mothers received a disappointing assessment. The suburban mothers reported that schools placed their children in special education programs—learning disabled (LD) and educable mentally handicapped (EMH)—at a significantly higher rate than they had in the city (19 percent versus 7 percent), and at a significantly higher rate than the city control group (5 percent).

Having a child placed in special education for the first time is a shock to any parent, but for these mothers, it was especially difficult. On the one hand, they had great respect for the superior professionalism of the suburban schools, their dedication to small classes, good instruction, and communication with parents. On the other hand, being a small minority in these white middle-income schools, they were concerned that these assessments may have been racially biased. Thus they had a variety of reactions.

Some mothers were satisfied that the suburban schools had made a sound decision and that the placement was appropriate for their child. Eliza Fitzpatrick came to believe that special education was the appropriate placement for her daughter Joselyn, because of the disparity between the level of her work and that of her peers:

> When we left Chicago, she was in first grade. When she got out here, she couldn't read. She couldn't keep up with the second grade out here, so she got retained. But she still didn't know how to pick up, in the regular second grade. She wasn't doing the work, and the other class was, so I think they should have put her back in first grade. But they did a lot of tests on her. They were really nice about it. They ran tests on her to try to get her in the right grade, but she just couldn't read. So they got her into the special education out here, and she's been doing really good. I didn't know Chicago was really that far behind compared to the suburban schools. They are more advanced than the Chicago schools. That's why she was retained, because she was in the Chicago school, an average student, but out here she was way below the other students.

Marie Austin approved of her son Marcus's special education placement because she recognized that he needed the extra attention he received there: "By him being in special ed, that shows you right there that they're giving him more attention because there's only about five or six kids in one class. They have to be giving him on the one-to-one basis with attention and dealing with him. I've been very satisfied with that." Margaret

Hopper also appreciated the efforts of suburban school personnel to diagnose her daughter Lorenza's problem and "work with it":

> I've been out here four years, and they have been tested three times. When they found out that the child has a learning disability or something, they really try and work with it. The school nurse did a home visit. We sat down and talked about their earlier childhood. To me, that was really good. You never find that in the city.

Some mothers were initially suspicious about racial motives for these placements or the potential stigma that could result. However, the classes were much smaller and offered more individualized attention than the regular classes. Consequently, some who had opposed the special education placements changed their views over time. Kama West spoke of her gradual acceptance of her son's abilities and needs, and the reality of his mental retardation:

> [A psychiatrist] told me that Roberto had motor skill problems and he should go into in-depth testing, and I couldn't afford it, and I didn't believe him anyway. Because no one else had it in my family. I was like the first one, so I didn't believe him. When I moved here I put him in school, in kindergarten, and they told me that he had problems, and I didn't believe them. So they sent him through all these training with the help for EMH children, and there was real documentation that there really was a problem. So I believed them. It took me almost a year to really accept it. It's kind of hard to accept the fact that your child is mentally retarded. It is not easy to accept that you have less than a perfect specimen. That may sound cold but it is true. . . . Now I can handle it; otherwise I couldn't have told the truth right now. . . . I hid it for a long time from my family. They now know.

Some mothers retained an intense ambivalence about their children's placement. They were not sure what was appropriate, and they worried about what outcomes it would lead to. Dee Scott expressed such ambivalence, both a respect for the suburban standards, and a strong mistrust of what it meant about her daughter's capabilities:

> The levels of everything in the city are much lower than they are out here. Everything is much higher out here. . . . When she moved out here, everything just changed. They wanted to hold her back. . . . They were putting a label on my child. She was in learning disability classes, and I didn't like that. I guess it was good . . . well, I really don't know if

it was good or bad. *I guess she's smart as long as she's in the city* going to the schools there. But then out here, trying to live up to the standards of their teaching, she's just an average and below average child in some things.

Thus, Ms. Scott felt she had a choice of which standards to use in judging her daughter. Despite her respect for the suburban standards, she had trouble accepting their assessment of her daughter. Indeed, she indicated considerable mistrust of the school's procedures and what it might have done to her child:

> They send me all these different papers and stuff, wanting me to sign so they could do all these different surveys. My child isn't a guinea pig. . . . She doesn't have a problem. She's just not up to the standards of these white folks out here like they want her to be, which I didn't appreciate at all. . . . I think it's really silly, I can't understand all this prying. Trying to find out if she has a legitimate reason for being a dummy! I really don't know what they're trying to do.

Some mothers blamed the city schools for their children's need to be placed in special education. For instance, Erica Bennett blamed the Chicago schools for failing to assess her son Keanu's learning problems, which the suburban school was assessing and approaching appropriately:

> Mostly the kids that came from the city were kind of behind the regular kids. So they started testing them. Every child here, practically, had to have some kind of special help. So Keanu was . . . too far gone. The only place that they could find for him in school was to put him in the EMH program. . . . emotionally mentally handicapped, that's the title. They had other programs, but they said that was the best for him, because he really needed one-to-one. They said it was like he didn't even go to school in Chicago for three years. . . . To know that a big city like that would allow your child to be abused and misused to make him emotionally mentally handicapped. . . . He would have been EMH all right, a cripple all his life. . . . If a teacher saw that he was slow, he should have brought it to my attention. Nobody ever did. . . . I don't think they ever even tested him. If they did, I didn't even know his scores or anything. I just assumed there was no problem because nobody brought it to me. And I think it was just pure negligence.

Other mothers blamed the suburban schools. They mistrusted suburban school officials and suspected that the diagnosis was arbitrary or racially biased. Some also feared that the special education placement would label or stigmatize their child. As Ms. Scott stated, it sent the message that "this is as far as you can go."

Some of the mothers believed that racism tainted school officials' special education placements without adequate assessments. Jacy Arnold suspected that suburban schools used a systemically biased approach in placing city children:

> The first thing they do to 90 percent of our children . . . is to say they are retarded or mentally handicapped or have emotional problems when they come from Chicago. . . . They don't have a chance to really prove themselves before they drop them down and stick them in a lower class. And I think that's part of society's really holding them down so they won't advance as fast as the white kids.

Some mothers opposed the suburban schools' placements. Dolores Gale believed her daughter was misclassified on the basis of cultural differences and strongly objected:

> The principal called and said that she had a learning disability. But that was false . . . they didn't understand that she had just got out here, and she doesn't know the culture. . . . After they got to know her and me as a different culture, they found out it wasn't a learning disability. . . . They say all Blacks have learning disabilities. I was raised around Caucasians, because my mother is white.

Occasionally, they were successful in battling these placements. Karen Stamps persuaded school officials to reevaluate her daughter's placement:

> They decided to put her in a class for slow learners. I didn't let them do it because I knew my daughter was really capable of doing what she was told to do, so far as her homework is concerned. Then they brought in their psychologist from the school and she came up with the conclusion that she didn't need to be placed in the special class. The psychologist said she needed more time to adjust. . . . And believe it or not, her grades have been improving . . . in regular classes.

Once students' special needs became apparent, special education may have been an appropriate response. Alternatives to special education are possible, but they too have disadvantages. Some schools responded by placing children back a grade, but placing older children with younger children can create problems of social interaction. Moreover, mothers were similarly divided on the practice of holding children back a grade. Some saw it as appropriate response to students' achievement needs, while others feared that it reflected racial biases.

Being in predominantly white suburbs, some mothers suspected that racial biases affected school officials' decisions. While misclassification based on implicit racial stereotypes and class biases was suggested by persistent claims and some research findings, it was difficult for the women to determine the extent of bias, especially since their children experienced poor schooling for several years in the city and then faced higher standards in their new schools.[1] In addition, special education introduces the risk of social stigma and of permanent classifications that may be hard to escape in the future. But the issue is complex, because special education classes offer certain advantages. Special education provides very small class sizes, so teachers can devote more time and attention to individual students. It also provides teachers who have special training. Some special education programs are successful at returning children to regular classes. Mothers were uncertain and divided on whether the increased incidence of special education was appropriate and helpful for their children.

Without doing extensive testing of students, it was not possible to determine the validity of the schools' assessments or the appropriateness of their placements. It is not clear whether suburbs were "overdiagnosing" or city schools were "underdiagnosing" special needs, or whether both were correct for their own level of standards.

A number of features of suburban schools were conducive to increasing special education placements. First, the higher standards in the suburbs may explain the increased placements. Children who performed within the normal range in the city were below the common norms in the suburban schools. While racial biases may have had some influence, some of the performances identified by the schools were highly specific—whether children could read or write at grade-level standards. Moreover, city schools were ill-suited to identify special needs if, as some mothers asserted, they had large, disorderly classes, and if they lacked the funds to evaluate students and to provide special education to all students needing it. Special education classes tend to be several times more expensive than regular classes, and city schools may have more children who need these services. In the suburbs, the small class sizes and increased teacher attentiveness are consistent with the interpretation that suburban schools could more readily detect children's learning problems, and they had more funds for evaluating students and for operating special education programs. Accounts of racial prejudice in the suburban schools were also consistent with the possibility of bias tainting some of these placements. Thus, for a variety of reasons, the suburban move made special education placements more likely.

It is difficult to know whether the suburban schools overprovided special programs, whether the city schools underprovided these services, or whether the different settings required different levels of services. Moreover, it is not clear whether being assigned to these programs was good or bad for these children in the long run. What is clear is that at the time of this study, mothers were often quite disturbed by the assessments of their children and by these special placements, and their concerns about these disturbing events seemed related to a combination of factors, including racism and the higher educational standards in the suburbs, compared with the preparation these children had gotten in the city.

TEACHERS' TREATMENT OF CHILDREN

The most important factor in education is the teacher. This section examines how mothers viewed teachers' commitment to instructing their children, teachers' efforts to keep them informed about their children's progress, teachers' efforts to show parents how they could help their children learn, and teachers' discrimination against Gautreaux children.

The mothers generally credited suburban teachers with giving their children more assistance and treating them better than the inner-city teachers. While most suburban movers (92 percent) approved of the ways teachers treated their children, fewer city movers did (83 percent). Moreover, this difference may underestimate the differences in actual behaviors. After seeing how suburban teachers treated their children, many fewer suburban movers (67 percent) approved of the way the city teachers had treated their children (both of these differences are statistically significant). Mothers' opinions of city schooling may have changed after they saw what schools were capable of doing in the suburbs.

A 92 percent approval rating might not seem at all worrisome, but the small numbers who did not approve sometimes raised very serious concerns about discrimination against their children. Indeed, some mothers who generally approved of most teachers also reported that one or more teachers showed racial bias against their children. Thus, an apparently simple statistic conceals a more complex picture. Suburban mothers reported general approval of instruction, treatment of their children, and school-parent communication, yet a number of parents reported incidents of teachers' racial discrimination.

Instruction and Assistance

When families moved to the suburbs, children were enrolled in the local schools. Just as neighbors were not aware of the Gautreaux program, the local schools were not notified of the program either. No one told the schools that some low-income Black children would be enrolling. This had some advantages; it reduced visibility and the potential for political backlash and demonstrations that sometimes accompanied busing programs. However, unlike the teachers involved in school busing programs, these children's teachers were not given any special notification, preparation, or sensitivity training for how to deal with these children or with their classmates' reactions.

Teachers in middle-income, mostly white schools probably lacked experience with low-income Black children. However, compared with the city movers, the suburban movers reported that teachers were significantly more helpful to the children, more responsive to their educational needs, treated them better, went out of their way to help them more, and helped them much more often. When asked whether suburban teachers went out of their way to help their children more, less, or the same as city teachers, 45 percent of the women said more, and 21 percent said less. Similarly, when asked whether teachers had gone out of their way to help their children during the past three months, suburban movers were twice as likely to report such extra help as city movers (59 versus 30 percent). This difference occurred on questions about the amount and recency of teacher help, and it remained strong even when analyses excluded students in special education (who receive much greater teacher help).[2]

Many mothers were impressed with suburban teachers' efforts and commitment to their students compared with what they had come to expect from city teachers. Others, such as Debra Scott, emphasized the city teachers' shortcomings:

> They [Chicago teachers] don't really care. They're just getting a salary. They should be able to tell if a child is not on a fourth-grade level, but they just keep on passing them. They don't pass them out here if they're not on the right level. . . . They [city teachers] just did what they were supposed to, nothing out of their way. They drank a lot of coffee, hung around in the hallways and over at the currency exchange gossiping about the kids.

Mothers often regarded the amount of time teachers invested in the job as evidence of their commitment and critical to their child's failure or success. Veronica Bolden blamed city teachers for her son's academic problems because they "did not spend enough time with the children in teaching them the things they needed to know for the grade level." Cherie Lord emphasized the willingness of suburban teachers to give extra time to their students: "[In Chicago] after their [the teachers'] eight hours are over, they're over. That's the way it was—the attitude was. He has teachers [in the suburbs] that would work overtime to get things right if it looks like it's [his work] is messed up."

Other mothers emphasized the support and encouragement suburban teachers gave their students. They also viewed teachers' unwillingness to simply pass their children without merit as a sign of care and concern. Claire Monroe emphasized the extent of these efforts: "The teacher is concerned about the student. Most of the teachers are fair in their assessment of the child's progress. And they will work individually with the child. They'll stay after school until 6:00, if necessary, with that child. They will walk that extra mile."

Several mothers described unusual efforts that teachers made on their children's behalf. Claire Monroe recounted that when she was unable to drive her daughter to a band concert, her band instructor picked her up at home and brought her to the concert. When Robert Shannon's mother could not afford to pay for a three-day class trip to a ranch, Robert's teacher paid for his expenses so he could take the trip with the class.

Some schools built extra assistance into the normal structure. Mabel Porter described the study room at her son's school where extra help was made available to students: "When a student is having trouble in math or science, they can go there during their study period and get extra help in almost any area. In almost any area that they want to study or do extra work in, it's there for them. There's a teacher for that particular subject in that area when they go in."

Mothers' comments confirmed that this assistance extended beyond the classroom teachers. Alesa Butler praised the entire staff at her son's suburban school:

> Every week someone is trying to help. Not necessarily his teacher. It could be someone else. They would give him talks over the telephone, telling him they understand he may not like to read, but to keep on trying. They would give him things to work on, and they would make themselves available. In case his teacher was unable to help, he was welcome to come to their class and speak with them. There were some teachers who were very motivated, who would talk to me after hours.

Some mothers also acknowledged the emotional support that suburban teachers gave their children. Claire Monroe described how Onika's teachers motivated students to learn:

> The instructors are excellent. They are warm toward the students. They are encouraging. They don't browbeat them. . . . Whenever the school have activities, the teachers are involved in them. They don't just send the children up to perform. They get in with it. They will dress up in clown costumes, act like hippies. They are not too good to be on the kids' level and have fun with the children. They can do that and still maintain a respect between them and the kids. It's like a big, close-knit family.

Florence Peterson described her daughter Lizzie's teacher as particularly caring. She refused to review Lizzie's file when Lizzie entered her class, which was said to show Lizzie's "bad habits," choosing instead to get to know the child herself and form her own opinion:

> After she got to know what kind of child Lizzie is, then she read the folder and said everything in it was wrong. She doesn't know if Lizzie changed over the summer, or what. She said she was so glad she did it that way. . . . She makes me feel that she really cares about my child. There have been teachers in the past who have said, "It's my job, I'm going to get paid anyway." Her caring makes me feel comfortable; if you are nice to my child, you're for her best interest.

Principals play a central role in many facets of the school's operations, including setting a tone for how the school treats its students. A few mothers commented favorably on the support principals and other administrators gave students. Claire Clinton observed that the principal and the assistant principal at her son's suburban school "seem genuinely concerned about the students and about them being at school every day. And about them being happy here."

School-Parent Communication: Helping Parents Participate

Parental involvement in schools can have an important influence on students' experiences and performance. Parents may volunteer in the classroom on a one-time or ongoing basis. On a more individual level, teacher-parent communication can inform parents about and involve them in their children's education in many ways.

Parents identified school-parent communication as another area that improved with the move to the suburbs. They believed that the suburban schools provided them with more information about their children's progress and school programs than city schools. More mothers liked the school-parent relationships than any other aspect of the suburban schooling process. The amount and quality of communication between parents and school officials was a key component.

Interaction between schools and parents served various functions and represented another way that teachers gave attention to students. It kept parents informed of their children's progress or problems on an individualized basis. It was also a problem-solving strategy, allowing teachers and parents to address children's problems together. School-parent contact facilitated the exchange of information in both directions and could be initiated by either party. Teachers advised parents on how to help their children with homework. Parents advised teachers on how to work most effectively with their children.

The pattern of communication varied. Sometimes it was routine, and sometimes it occurred only as a need arose. It took place during school hours, evenings, or weekends. Mostly it happened at school, but sometimes it happened at the parent's home, and occasionally even at the teacher's home. It occurred in person, by telephone, or in writing.

Some suburban schools and teachers made a practice of contacting parents on a regular basis, involving them in their children's ongoing educational process. Suzie Taylor described the system that her son's teacher designed to keep parents informed about their children's progress:

> [The teacher puts all the child's work for the past week] in a folder, and the child will bring it home and the parent has to sign it. If there was work in there that was incomplete, they had to finish it and bring it back. They'll let you know how your child is doing in school. That was really good. . . . When your child sees that you are interested in the school, he will do more.

Carole Phillips also regarded the regular phone calls and notes to parents as indicative of the teacher's concern. "It makes me happy because she really doesn't have to call me and let me know these things. But she does."

Frequently, mothers said that teachers contacted them when their children were experiencing problems in school. While this approach was not as positive or extensive as the regular contacts, mothers often said that this was better than in the city, where they sometimes did not learn about their children's problems until it was too late to do anything about them. Gwen Larson observed that the suburban school required parents to stay involved through meetings and "special sessions. . . . It's mandatory that you participate, or at least know what your children are doing."

Katie Hopson also favored the aggressive approach that her daughter's suburban school used to involve parents:

> The school system *makes you participate.* They sort of bring you in. It's the truth. And they'll call you in and say, "I want a conference, because so-and-so is not doing well. Is there a problem at home, something we can help?" They really bring you into your child's education, whereas you notice in the city there's so much apathy. I'm sending him to school, if you can't do it that's your problem, not mine. None of that here, none of it. They will work with the child, and with you as a parent. . . . I like that a lot. I like being involved in my children's education. And I like the way that they do it. . . . You know everything that they're doing in the school.

Suburban schools' prompt reporting of tardiness or absences was a common example. None of the mothers mentioned such an arrangement at their child's city school. Suburban school officials frequently contacted parents by phone or through notes about their child's lateness or absence to seek their cooperation in remedying the situation. Marie Austin described such an arrangement at her son's suburban school:

> If a child is tardy or doesn't come to school they'll give you a call. They'll call you here at home and let you know that they aren't there. If a child misses three or four days, they call you to ask you what happened. They show more concern about their presence in school [than in the city schools]. . . . If the child is not attending his classes, we'll know that right away. The teacher wrote me a note. I called the school. We had a meeting previous to that. Usually they write you a note and you come to see the teacher for a conference. . . . Teachers are easy to talk to. They really show real good concern for Marcus. They let me know that he's trying hard, and they're working with him to the best of their ability.

Anita Higgins also emphasized the school's efforts to keep her apprised when her son skipped classes or homework assignments. That permitted her to take measures to get him back on track:

They [teachers] keep up with it. They don't let him get into any trouble. They just keep in touch. . . . They call. Anything that happens, they will call you. That's what I like about the school. They really are concerned about what's happening. They want you to know what's happening with the child.

Some teachers and administrators actively sought parents' advice in addressing their children's problems. Claire Monroe liked the teachers' "warmth and kindness":

They are concerned. If you feel as though there is a problem, they will call you; they will call you to ask if you have any suggestions on what they can do to help to improve the situation with the child. They want you to call any time, call their homes anytime if you feel that you have a problem or if you need some questions answered.

Marlene Savage praised the ways school officials explained her son's problems to her and involved her in the difficult decisions about how to resolve them. She appreciated "the way they treat you": "Before they failed Douglas, they asked me if it was alright if they could. If I didn't go along with them, they wouldn't. They talk to you if they are going to do anything, explain everything."

In some instances, teachers urged parents to be more supportive of their children. Gwen Larson also described the consultative process between herself and the suburban teachers, who offered her practical assistance with her son's schooling:

I wanted to get much stricter on him, but they [suburban teachers] encouraged me to not be quite as hard, and to give him rewards along with punishment. They offered suggestions, things that they might know in educating children. They said whenever I had a problem to be sure to get in touch with them. They stress that they are there and encourage us to talk to them if there are any problems. They seem to respond toward your child better if they know you are concerned.

Some schools went further to involve parents. Carol Phillips noted that teachers sent directions home "so the parents can help" children with schoolwork. Nia McFar said teachers "are really friendly with the students and parents. . . . I like the way the teachers interact with the parents. They give programs for the parents, and try to get the parents to come and volunteer."

Some mothers also commented favorably on the way suburban

schools responded to parents who initiated the contact. Florence Baker emphasized the staff's responsiveness at her daughter Merlissa's school:

> I like the concern that the schools have for the parents and the child. If you show them that you are concerned—I try to make a visit at least once per marking period to talk with the teacher and establish an open relationship from the beginning. They seem to be real good about keeping you informed about how they're doing. . . . It's easy to talk with her [suburban] teacher. We've built a good relationship with each other. The school helps too. If you call there, they will take your number and ask the teacher to call you. Otherwise I usually send a note with Merlissa and ask her to call me or write me back. We cooperate.

Interaction between parents and schools helped to establish a three-way relationship among parents, children, and school officials—including teachers, administrators, and counselors—that assisted and supported the children in school. School officials' initiative and accessibility also played a symbolic role in demonstrating care and concern for the children. Phone calls, notes, and meetings were evidence of that commitment.

Teacher Discrimination

Despite a 92 percent approval rating, some mothers perceived the suburban teachers as mistreating their children, usually because of their race.[3] Although there was no specific question about why the mothers thought the teachers treated children as they did, mothers' reports often pointed to discrimination. Moreover, some mothers described incidents that indicated racial bias; some of these were reminiscent of events reported in the South decades earlier.

Mothers catalogued a number of ways in which teachers manifested their prejudice. Some involved verbal disrespect, such as name-calling, harassment, and humiliation in front of the class. These hostile behaviors overlapped with what mothers interpreted as favoritism toward white children, including providing assistance, giving time and attention, tolerating troublesome behavior, permitting work to be made up, and even leniency in grading students' work. Moreover, the teachers set the tone for the class. When teachers permitted racial bias, they created an atmosphere where such language and behavior were permitted and encouraged other children to follow suit.

Mothers suggested that children were exposed to a constellation of racist actions. Gwen Larson stressed the differences in the way teachers treated Black and white children:

> Some of the teachers are prejudiced. . . . If my child approaches the teacher about making up work from when he was sick, they would say no. . . . They give white children more opportunities to make up work. . . . If a Black kid said something like "You didn't tell us that the test was today," they would make them feel really bad in front of the class, or they would ignore them totally. So the Black kids sit there watching the white kids be able to have a better relationship with the teacher.

Katrina Anderson emphasized the devastating impact that the day-to-day racial harassment by teachers and other students had on her daughter:

> The tension in the school—problems with both teachers and students—affects her. She tries to overlook it, but you can't overlook something that's there every day, over and over and over and over. Sometimes she will be so despondent she just stays in her room. . . . I dislike the favoritism, from Black to white, the aggravation, the way some kids treat kids of other colors, and the grades they give, the way they grade between Black and white students. . . . The teachers call the kids names. They ask them questions to make them feel dumb. My daughter had a job at the school Tuesdays and Thursdays but she quit because of how the teacher treated her. If she used one word, the teacher would use another that meant the same thing, to try to make her feel she was wrong. She would come home all upset, so she finally quit.

Mothers also reported discriminatory treatment by other school staff. One school bus driver made Black children go to the back of the school bus until a mother complained. Viola Hodges criticized the way school staff isolated the small group of Black children at her son's suburban high school:

> The [Black] enrollment . . . [is] about ninety. They have one little space in the corner where they can sit for lunch. They can't even venture out. The monitors, the guards in the hall, they put them in the corner for their lunch. All the Black kids. It's like down South on the plantations. . . . The suburbs are pretty good and all, but it's still the plantation.

Some mothers expressed greater discomfort talking with suburban teachers because they were nearly all white. Annamarie Palmer described a better relationship with her son's Black city teacher than the white one in the suburbs, "The [city] teachers were more open with me and him, because there were more Blacks there." Ivory Stewart was not sure how much racial tension came from the suburban teachers and how much was based on her own expectations:

I was raised mostly around our people and sometimes if I talk to the [white suburban] teacher. . . . I feel sort of uncomfortable. It's getting better; had a big problem with that in the beginning. . . . As far as school goes, I guess you feel lower than you should feel. Maybe they don't feel that way about you. I feel it because I've heard so many things [about race problems]. Then when I go to school I think, everybody is looking at me, as if I'm singled out. The school welcomes you, but I still feel I have to get that out of myself.

Several mothers advocated hiring Black teachers and other adults in the suburban schools because Black children needed teachers who understood them, could act as role models, and could respond to racial harassment incidents. Priscilla Wilks regarded the absence of Black teachers as a major factor in perpetuating racial discrimination against Black children in school. Mabel Porter emphasized the need for Black staff:

The Black kids really need a Black adult that they can relate to when they are having problems. There's a lot of name calling. . . . The (Black) kids are really outnumbered. It's only maybe 75–80 enrollment, in almost 3,000 kids. The kids just don't have anyone, an adult, that they can relate to.

While some of the incidents of teacher bias in these Chicago suburbs in the 1980s were similar to reports about southern teachers in the 1940s and 1950s, there were two important differences. First, the teaching staffs were rarely universally biased. Second, teachers who exhibited racial bias were often the same individuals who offered extra assistance to students.

Few of these suburban schools in the 1980s presented a united front of discrimination. In the first years of desegregation in southern schools, teachers often presented a united front of resentful compliance, which rejected and belittled the Black children that the courts had imposed on them. In contrast, very few mothers felt that all teachers were prejudiced.

Alberta Geoffrey was one of those few. She believed that the entire faculty at her son's school was racist: "The school was prejudiced from the beginning. The teachers—all white—did not want the Blacks to come to their school. They let it be known. They'd say, 'We didn't ask your kids to come to this school.'"

Some, like Katrina Anderson, felt the problem was extensive, but not total: "You have a lot of prejudiced teachers out here." However, most mothers felt that the problem was generally limited to a few teachers. Veronica Bolden reported that some of the teachers "have definitely displayed real signs of being prejudiced." Very few mothers reported that the entire school faculty presented a united front against the presence of Black children or that all teachers exhibited prejudice against their children.

While some prejudiced teachers were totally unhelpful, some of the teachers who showed biases were good teachers to these children. Not only did many mothers report mixed experiences with different teachers, but some mothers reported mixed experiences with the *same* teachers. Carole Phillips emphasized that the suburban "teachers are excellent. *They are very prejudiced, but . . . they are right there to help you. . . .* In the city they don't really care . . . They don't have the time . . . to help . . . My son . . . now his grades have really come up [since leaving the city]."

Similarly, Gwen Larson, who complained that teachers were prejudiced, also described having a healthy relationship with the teachers. She is the mother who reported that suburban teachers encouraged her to reward her son and not be so hard on him.

In sum, while the mothers had abundant reason for offering a 92 percent approval rating of the suburban teachers, the small numbers who did not approve raised very serious concerns about teacher discrimination against their children. Some mothers who expressed a general approval of most teachers also reported that one or more teachers showed racial bias against their children. Thus, this apparently simple statistic conceals a more complex picture.

EARLY OUTCOMES

This section focuses on the effects of the suburban move on students' achievement and behavior. It is obvious by now that *nothing is as simple for these families as it seems at the outset.* Newspaper accounts assume that higher achievement results from well-maintained buildings, new textbooks, plentiful supplies, and high teacher salaries. But most children in suburban schools have many advantages in their homes, which these low-income children may have lacked. Therefore, it is not certain how much the high test scores in suburban schools result from family advantages rather than from resources (a matter of dispute among social scientists). Nor is it certain how much low-income children gain from suburban school resources. This section compares a variety of educational outcomes in the city and the suburbs.

The mothers' reports permit comparisons between the city and suburban movers on their children's attitudes, attendance, behavior, and achievements at school. The picture of attitudes, attendance, and behavior comes from the children and their mothers, while the achievement analysis is based on mothers's reports about their children's performance.

The formidable challenges that these children faced in entering suburban schools might have caused a great amount of problem behavior, and in the first days and months after the move, mothers reported that children actually did experience great problems. One girl who had seen very few whites in her life entered the school building, saw a sea of white faces, and immediately ran home. Many other children faced enormous difficulties in catching up to the suburban school standards, both in terms of academic achievement and classroom discipline. Most children face difficulties when they move to a new school, and these children had to deal with drastic changes; nearly every child faced initial difficulties in the first year after moving. Recognizing that all moves are traumatic and entail short-term dislocations, this research focused on children's situations after they had been in their new schools for several years.

Attitudes Toward School and Attendance

The debate about raising educational standards often arouses concern that increased standards would reduce the attendance of low-achieving students. If this is a potential problem in urban schools where many students have low achievement, it might even be more likely when a few children arrive in schools where most students already have higher achievement. These new arrivals might find the challenges too formidable. In general, however, the Gautreaux children said that they felt much more positive toward their suburban schools than their city schools. When asked how they felt about their schools on a five-point scale, their average response corresponded to "like school a lot," while their response about their previous city school corresponded to "like school a little"— a significant difference. Their responses indicated that they liked their schools more than the city group, but this difference was not large enough to be statistically significant.[4]

To examine how their attitudes might affect their attendance, children were asked how often they *wanted* to stay away from school when they were not sick. The suburban movers' responses indicated no difference between their pre-move and post-move reports. Children were also asked how often they *actually* stayed home when they were not sick, and this question revealed no differences between pre- and post-move attendance.[5] Thus, while there were reports of initial problems of attendance when children arrived at the suburban schools, these attendance difficulties did not continue to the time of the study.

Fear seemed to be a likely explanation for children's desire to stay home from school and for actual absences, both in the city and the suburbs. Their mothers seemed to think that fear influenced their attendance. Children had different fears in the city and suburbs. In the city, they feared the violence; in the suburbs, they feared the biases, exclusion, and achievement difficulties. But these fears did not affect school attendance equally in the city and suburbs. Suburban movers reported that their children experienced fewer fear-motivated attendance problems in the suburbs than they had in the city (11 percent versus 21 percent), and they also reported lower rates of fear-motivated attendance problems than city movers (11 percent versus 17 percent).

Another way to test whether fear influenced attendance is to examine whether children's fears correlated with their attendance. Children were asked about how safe they felt being out alone in their neighborhood, and these reports were correlated with their attendance. For the city group, there was a very high correlation, indicating that fear could explain almost one-third of the variation in school attendance. In contrast, the suburban correlation, though significant, indicated that only 6 percent of the variance in attendance could be explained by fear. While fear for one's safety may have been a major contributor to children's absence from school in the city, it was not a large influence in the suburbs.

This is consistent with mothers' reports, which suggested that gangs and other safety problems were deterrents to children attending school in Chicago. As Marie Austin stated, "The boys would threaten him to bring money to school. If he didn't give them money, they'd threaten him and they'd fight him. There were always a lot of problems all the time with the kids."

In contrast, in the suburbs, some mothers cited racial incidents and discriminatory treatment as factors that kept their children home from school. These problems were mostly temporary, however, and children overcame them. Gloria Reno recounted her son's successful adjustment:

"He didn't want to live out here. . . . He just rebelled at first. He didn't want to go to school. . . . He didn't want to become involved. . . . But now he's altogether different. I can't keep him from becoming involved. It took him really almost a semester of school to get adjusted."

Behavior

Attendance may only indicate minimal and grudging compliance with legal imperatives, since nearly all of these children were under age sixteen, the age of compulsory attendance. A further indicator is the question of children's behavior in school. Gautreaux children might have been more likely to get in trouble in suburban schools than in city schools, because the suburban school norms for behavior were stricter, the teachers were more likely to be critical of Black children's behavior, or the children were rebelling against the greater academic and social difficulties they faced.

The results do not support these expectations. When suburban mothers were asked if their children got in trouble with teachers more, less, or the same in the suburbs than they had in the city, the average response was the same. Slightly fewer suburban mothers reported school trouble than city mothers (25 percent versus 29 percent). This is not a significant difference, but it is the opposite of expectations based on the suburban standards. It suggests that the suburban movers were able to adapt to the higher standards in the suburbs. Ruby Nelson said that her son's "constant talking" became less of a problem in the suburbs because the teachers would not permit it. Roseanne Johnson also noted the improvement in her son's behavior with the move:

> I've been up there [at the suburban school], and I could see the improvement [in his behavior]. I can see him trying. I think that's the best part of it. He's trying harder. He was around a lot of aggressive children in the city. Fighting, talking back to the teacher. . . . Speaking when not spoken to. He just shies away from things like that now.

Jackie Bryant indicated that her son responded to the stricter behavior standards in the suburbs:

> [In Chicago] He just didn't concentrate or something. . . . He was always just watching the other students. A few times I used to go back and check on him in the school room, and he'd be playing around in his desk. Out here . . . in the schools here, they don't have time to be

playing around. They're real strict on them. The change is because of the move. . . . It's so different out here.

Thus, while children moving to suburban schools often experienced initial problems, they generally adjusted to the new behavioral standards. Even though they faced higher standards, they met them as well as city movers met their school behavior standards.

Academic Achievement

While this study tried to obtain achievement test scores as outcome measures, that was not feasible.[6] In the retrospective analysis, mothers' reports indicated that their children's grades declined slightly with the move, but the difference was not statistically significant. Similarly, there was no difference in the grades of the suburban and city movers. These findings were the same when the analyses were restricted to children in regular classes—excluding those in special education programs. The analysis of the limited number of school transcripts using overall grades for each child for Chicago and the suburbs also indicated no statistically significant differences from pre- to post-move schools, and no differences were more than one-half grade (on a five-point scale). The results indicated that the new suburban students did not have lower standing in their teachers' eyes.

A second measure of academic achievement was the children's performance on schoolwork relative to that of their classmates. Neither the mothers nor their children perceived a change in relative performance with the move to the suburbs. Both the retrospective analysis and the comparison with city movers supported this finding. Several factors could account for this lack of change in children's grades and academic performance in the face of suburban schools' greater demands and higher standards. First, this may reflect previously untapped abilities coming to the fore. The children had to adjust to very different curricula and expectations. Some accounts suggested that the children and their mothers responded to the challenges of the suburban schools by investing more in academic work.

Michelle Holman credited the quality of the white schools for her son Rodney's extra effort: "All white [schools] are better than Black. . . . Plus it . . . brings the best qualities out of [my son]." This assessment reflected the recognition that white schools generally had more resources, better trained and more experienced teachers, and higher academic standards. Moreover, this mother's statement indicated confidence in her son's ability to rise to the occasion and meet these higher standards.

Many aspects of the suburban school environment may have contributed to children's performance, such as more assistance from teachers, increased school-parent communication, and greater physical safety. At the same time, students may have worked harder in the suburban schools, as Ivory Stewart found: "James has the same grades as in Chicago, but he has to work harder to get them because the standards are higher (in the suburban schools)." Aretha Smith expressed her surprise at her son's ability to maintain his academic standing in the face of the higher suburban standards: "I was amazed when we came out here that he was able to stay in the same grade, because you knew the city schools are behind. And he was going to an inner-city school. I was amazed that he was able to come out here and compete on the same level."

Some mothers credited the suburban teachers with improving their children's grades. Tanya Farris described the successful efforts of her daughter Lenise with her teacher's assistance:

> In the last marking period . . . to help her bring her grade up so she
> could pass, [the teacher] had her come early in the morning, and she
> helped Lenise with her studies. She went over a particular test with her
> that she didn't understand and let her take the test over after she had
> gone over it with her.

While there was little change in average grades with the suburban move, a few mothers said that their children's grades did decline after the move to the suburban schools because of higher academic standards, teachers' bias, or the children's difficult adjustment to the new school. Marlene Savage explained why her son Douglas's grades went down with the move:

> [His] grades were better in Chicago. . . . The standards here in the sub-
> urbs are higher. That brought them down when we moved out here.
> He didn't catch up fast. The work is harder. He's failed since he's been
> out here. First year, fifth grade, he failed. He couldn't keep up with the
> class. Their work was more advanced than what he had. He was sup-
> posed to have used cursive in Chicago but hadn't. They didn't write in
> cursive in his school there [in the city]. When he came here, all his
> schoolmates were doing so. It was hard for him to catch up to their
> level. The schools are good here. . . . They take up so much time with
> them here; they really work with them. . . . He's doing much better

now. I think he is more at ease now in this area than he was when we first moved out here. Because he is shy, it takes him longer to get along.

Katrina Anderson attributed her daughter Charmaine's initial academic problems to the prejudice in her suburban school. Once Charmaine felt that her efforts did not pay off, she did less work:

> With the teachers, she was getting low marks, no matter how hard she tried or how many books she brought home at night. So she got kind of despondent. So I would keep going to the school but they always made an excuse for the teacher. They still do. She would spend a couple hours a night on homework, as well as during study period, during the first quarter. But when she got her report card, and saw something that she worked really hard for didn't materialize, she [began to do just] enough to get by. Why should she do a lot of work and go out of her way when all she's going to get is a low mark anyway? She'd compare with other students who didn't do much work and got A's and B's. Three weeks never pass without something happening, either with the students or with the teachers. I'm always at the school for one reason or another. The last [suburban] school was just like living with the KKK, going to school with them. It was a horrible school.

While some students' grades declined with the move to the suburbs, others improved. Edward Phillips, a fifteen-year-old, had a mediocre record in the Chicago public schools and had been identified as having modest ability and a tendency to cause trouble. In his initial experience in the suburban schools, he showed the same patterns of poor motivation and mediocre performance in class. However, one of his teachers believed that he had more ability than he was demonstrating and recommended transferring him to a higher-ability group. Edward responded to the greater demands and became a good student. The reassignment served as motivation, which brought out previously undiscovered talents.

Athletics and Academic Achievement

The children who moved to the suburbs did significantly better in sports than the children who moved within the city. Both the retrospective and the city movers' comparison showed a significant improvement in the children's relative performance in sports in the suburbs. It is not clear how much this was attributable to the children's improved performance and how much can be explained by lower athletic standards in the suburban communities.

Regardless of the reason, their athletic achievement had a positive impact on children's academic performance. Mothers noted that unlike the city schools, suburban schools had strict academic standards for participation in athletics, and these requirements motivated some children to strive to maintain their grades. Moreover, some of the mothers noted that their children's athletic prowess led suburban teachers and administrators to encourage their children and assist them with their class work so they would qualify for the teams. Thus, children's sports performance was significantly positively correlated with their academic grades in the suburbs, but not in the city.

In contrast, city schools permitted some of the children to participate in sports and other activities even with low grades. Yasmin Coleman attributed her son Jermaine's improved grades and interest in his suburban school to his participation in sports and the benefits it offered:

> His grades are better now than they were in Chicago because he studies
> better now. He's more interested now. . . . Maybe in the city he didn't
> understand the necessity of good grades. . . . I think it has something to
> do with the participation in sports. He has to have good grades to be in
> the sports [in the suburbs]. I like the attention that they give him in
> sports. They have teachers and coaches who are concerned and who
> take time and patience with the kids. They want them to do well.

Margie Shannon credited her son Martin's athletic coaches with encouraging his academic efforts: "If the coaches can help you in any manner, they have. In the past, if Martin's grades had fallen, . . . the coach got on him a little bit, you know, gave him that extra push. 'C'mon, you gotta keep them grades up.'"

Similarly, Carolyn White reported that athletics became a source of motivation and accomplishment for her son Michael:

> Michael had excelled in athletics and had been allowed to stay on the
> football team at his Chicago school even though he was getting very
> poor grades in his classes. When he moved to the suburbs, the coaches
> were also enthusiastic about his being on the football team, but they in-
> sisted that he get satisfactory [passing] grades in order to continue play-
> ing on the team. They arranged for him to receive extra help in the
> classes that were giving him trouble, and the teachers went out of their
> way to help him. The coaches and other school officials helped him aca-
> demically, as well as with his athletics, and showed a great deal of con-
> cern for him. There were times when he didn't have a way to get to the

practices, and the folks in the community, the white people, just took him. There were times when they would win at the wrestling tournament, and I didn't have money for him to buy pizza or whatever, but the community would pitch right in and buy him whatever he needed or bring him home if he needed a ride. . . . Michael went on to wrestle, play football, and to do good [academically] — to keep a C average. With all of his activities, he still managed to keep a C average. . . . In 1978, he was supposed to go to training camp and I didn't have money for him to go. The mayor of this town and the Rotary Club sent him to California for Olympic training and paid all of his expenses. . . . He gained from that a scholarship offer from two universities.

Mabel Porter reported that football led her son Christopher to real accomplishment in the suburbs:

It may sound stupid, but I'd say football is the best thing for my son about living in the suburbs, because it seems like everything is built around his football. The football motivated him to study. He doesn't get the best grades in the world, but it still motivated him. He had a goal. . . . He wanted to be all-conference in his senior year. And he knew that was something he had to do to make it. He really stuck it out. He came from a long way. Somebody that was never involved in any kind of sports at all until he was in high school. Then he made it for four years and he made all-conference. . . . [He got] along with everyone [and was] a real congenial person, [and] maybe no one bother[ed] him because he [was] on the football and wrestling team. All the kids knew him; [he was] almost like a celebrity.

The findings on children's outcomes are apparently unimpressive, based on the numbers. The suburban and city movers had very similar rates of behavior problems, similar grades, and similar class ranks. However, in this case, statistical insignificance may be substantively significant. Suburban movers entered schools with higher academic standards, higher behavior standards, and higher achievement standards. The fact that their relative standing was similar to that of the city movers is likely to reflect a higher level of performance.

NINE

Education and Employment Outcomes

THE EFFECTS OF DESEGREGATION ON BLACKS' SCHOOL ACHIEVEMENT

Research finds conflicting results on the effects of school desegregation. Different studies find that Blacks attending desegregated schools have better outcomes, worse outcomes, or the same outcomes as in segregated schools.[1] Some studies argue that the effects of school desegregation on Black and white students may be both positive and negative, depending upon other factors.[2] One of the factors may be how well accepted the Black students are.

Unlike most desegregation programs, which involve busing, Gautreaux created both residential and school integration, and it did so with little visibility, thus reducing backlash and stigma. Children arrived in the suburban schools as community residents, not as part of a busing program from a city every day. Moreover, residential integration provided the possibility for social integration of old and new residents. Seven years later, the basic question was whether transplanting ill-prepared poor children into suburban schools would put them at a competitive disadvantage. The *permanent disadvantage hypothesis* suggests that because suburbs have different standards than the city, low-income youth in the suburbs will suffer a permanent disadvantage and will have lower education and employment than city movers.

There are many reasons to expect that low-income youth may find it hard to meet suburban standards: their low-income background may

This chapter was adapted from Julie E. Kaufman and James E. Rosenbaum, "The Education and Employment of Low-Income Black Youth in White Suburbs," *Educational Evaluation and Policy Analysis* 14, no. 3 (1992).

make them less well prepared or less motivated than middle-income suburban youth; their low socioeconomic status may give them attitudes and behaviors deemed "undesirable" by the middle-income school staff or employers who make decisions affecting their education and employment; or racial discrimination may prevent them from being given full access to suburban resources. For any or all of these reasons, these suburban youth may have had less education and employment than city movers who did not face these barriers. A contradictory expectation is that rather than suffering from permanent disadvantage in the suburbs, suburban students will benefit from the higher educational and employment opportunities in the suburbs, and their suburban classmates will serve as role models for achievement.

School Academic Standards

The state of Illinois annually collects and publishes mean eleventh-grade reading scores, mean ACT scores, and mean graduation rates from all high schools in the state. This information provides a way to compare the schools the Gautreaux students attended. A reading test is administered to all eleventh-grade students in the state of Illinois, with scores ranging from 1 to 500. The state average for 1990 was 250. The suburban schools had significantly higher reading scores than the city schools in 1990 (259 in suburban schools versus 198 in city schools). The ACT is the college admissions test most often taken in Illinois, since it is required by the state colleges and universities. A perfect ACT score is 36. The national average in 1990 was 20.6, and the Illinois state average was 20.9. As with the reading test scores, mean ACT scores from city schools were significantly lower than those from suburban schools in 1990 (suburban schools, 21.5 versus city schools, 16.1). While these scores only represent the achievement of a fraction of students, they are an important group—those who aspire to college.

The state also computes high school graduation rates. The graduation rate was computed as the ratio of the number graduating in 1989 divided by the number entering high school four years earlier. The rates were much higher in the suburban schools than the city schools (86 percent for the suburbs versus 33 percent for the city). The numbers indicate not only a quantitative difference but also a major qualitative difference in the academic standards of city and suburban schools. Suburban schools' average reading and ACT scores are very close to the state averages, whereas the city schools' scores are significantly lower than the

Table 9.1 Youth Education and Job Outcomes: City-Suburban Comparison (percent)

Outcome	City	Suburb
Dropped out of school	20	5*
Grades	5.60	5.61
College track	24	40**
Attend college	21	54***
Attend four-year college	4	27**
Employed full-time (if not in college)	41	75***
Pay under $3.50/hour	43	9***
Pay over $6.50/hour	5	21***
Job benefits	23	55***
Skilled or semiskilled jobs (versus unskilled)	36	55
In school or working	74	90***

Note: Asterisks indicate significance level of difference between city and suburban samples, by chi-square or t test.
*$p < 0.10$; **$p < 0.05$; ***$p < 0.025$.

state averages. The information on graduation rates also suggests that city and suburban schools foster radically different expectations. Students attending suburban schools learn that it is normal to graduate with one's class, because this happens most of the time. On the other hand, students in city high schools learn that it is normal not to graduate with one's class.

The outcomes considered here follow a developmental progression in the school arena and in the employment arena. For the school arena, different outcomes were examined at different ages: for those seventeen or younger, whether the youth was still in high school, grades, and whether the youth was in a college or noncollege high school track. If the youth was eighteen or older, college attendance, type of college attended, and degree pursued in college were checked. In the employment arena two different outcomes are discussed: whether the youth was employed then and, if so, the status of the job in terms of pay, prestige, and job benefits (see table 9.1).

These outcomes not only showed the student's level of performance, but also served as indicators of future performance. Because children in the Gautreaux program were from a low-income, minority population, their mothers generally did not have college education or good jobs. Thus, Gautreaux students who were able to gain employment experience or attend college were likely to have more options as adults than is typical for low-income minority, urban populations.

High School Dropouts

The permanent disadvantage hypothesis predicts that a higher proportion of suburban youth than city youth will drop out of high school. Rather than suffer from the disadvantages of poor preparation and possibly race or class discrimination, suburban Gautreaux students would be more likely to drop out of this competitive situation than their city counterparts. However, for those seventeen years of age or younger, a higher percentage of city youth dropped out of high school than did suburban youth (20 percent in the city versus less than 5 percent in the suburbs). Gender had no influence on dropouts, and controlling for gender did not alter the suburban effect.

Instead of the anticipated disadvantage, youth of high school age in the suburbs had an educational advantage over those in the city—more of the suburban youth were in high school. Youth in the Gautreaux program seemed to benefit from the higher academic standards in the suburbs rather than suffering from a permanent disadvantage.

Grades

Grades are relative and at the same time represent a certain level of achievement. A C is the lowest acceptable grade. Because academic standards are much higher in suburban schools, a C in most city schools may represent less achievement than a C in most suburban schools. The permanent disadvantage hypothesis suggests that suburban Gautreaux children's grades would suffer from being in competition with suburban classmates who had always lived in the suburbs and in more affluent families, while urban Gautreaux students' grades would not suffer from this disadvantage, since they continued to attend city schools in low-income, Black neighborhoods. If a B city student moved to the suburbs, the higher academic standards would result in a lower grade for the same level of achievement. City movers would not experience this achievement decline. Contrary to the hypothesis, there was virtually no difference in grades (city, 5.60 versus suburbs, 5.61, n.s.; 5 = mostly C's, 6 = mostly B's and C's). Gender had no effect on grades, and controlling for gender had no influence on the suburban effect. These results show that grades did not suffer from the suburban move. In fact, if a C grade represents more achievement and learning in a suburban school than in a city school, the suburban movers' achievement might have been higher than that of the city movers. The benefits of being in schools with higher academic standards appear to outweigh the disadvantages.

College Preparation

Nearly all schools—including all schools in the sample—have different curricula for students who plan to attend college and those who don't. The phrase *college track* refers to the sequence of classes specifically designed to prepare students for college, as opposed to general track or vocational education track classes. Students in a college track have an educational advantage over students not in a college track.[3] The permanent disadvantage hypothesis proposes that suburban movers would be less likely to get into college track classes than city movers. The results contradict this prediction. A significantly higher percentage of suburban movers were in college tracks than were city movers (40 percent for the suburbs versus 24 percent for the city). Gender had no effect on track, and controlling for gender had no influence on the suburban effect. Suburban Gautreaux students were more likely to be in college tracks than city movers. Once again, the benefits of higher academic standards outweighed the barriers of competition.

College Attendance

The permanent disadvantage hypothesis predicts that suburban movers will be less likely to attend college than city movers. Fifty-five of the Gautreaux youth were age eighteen or older when they were interviewed. In this group, the rate of college enrollment was significantly higher for students in the suburban sample than for city students (54 percent versus 21 percent). Gender had no effect on college attendance, and controlling for gender had no influence on the suburban effect. It is important to note whether a student is attending a four-year institution that awards a bachelor's degree, a two-year junior or community college that awards an associate's degree, or a trade school that awards a certificate. Among those over seventeen, 27 percent of the suburban movers as opposed to 4 percent of the city movers attended four-year colleges. City movers had a very low rate of access to four-year colleges.

Of those not attending four-year institutions, two-thirds of the suburban movers were working toward an associate's degree, while just half of the city movers were. Taken together, suburban movers attended better types of colleges than city movers. Similarly, in response to the question, "What degree are you working toward?" almost half of the suburban college students said they were working towards their bachelor's degree, whereas only a fifth of the city college students were doing so. The outcomes for college attendance together with the college type and degree pursued show that the suburban students clearly benefit rather than suffer because of more challenging educational competition in the suburbs.

EMPLOYMENT

Regarding employment, the permanent disadvantage hypothesis suggests that suburban movers would be disadvantaged relative to city movers because they must compete with middle-income white youth whom suburban employers may prefer. On the other hand, the suburban schools may prepare students better for jobs, and suburbs may have more jobs than the city, so that suburban movers could have better employment outcomes than city movers. Better job availability could translate not only into more jobs, but also into jobs with better pay, higher prestige, and more benefits. Also, suburban youth may be influenced by new friends who may serve as role models and may encourage them to apply for jobs they might not otherwise consider.

For the employment outcome, youth answered the question, "Are you working now?" Contrary to the permanent disadvantage hypothesis, a significantly higher proportion of suburban youth than city youth were working (75 percent versus 41 percent). Males were slightly more likely to be working than females, but after controlling for gender, the suburban effect remained strong and significant.

Wages

Based on three categories of pay scale, suburban youth had a significant edge in wages. Forty-three percent of the city youth earned less than $3.50 per hour, whereas only about 10 percent of the suburban youth earned this little. On the high end of the scale, about 5 percent of the city youth workers earned at least $6.50 per hour, whereas over 21 percent of the suburban youth earned this amount. Gender had no effect on wages for these youth, and controlling for gender had no influence on the suburban effect, which remained strongly significant. The so-called permanent disadvantage did not keep suburban youth from getting jobs that paid at least as well as the jobs held by city youth.

Prestige

Prestige is one way of assessing the level of jobs. For these analyses, prestige is a three-category variable based on the level of skills needed for a job: 1 = unskilled; 2 = semiskilled; 3 = skilled. This is a gross distinction. The mean prestige for suburban jobs was higher than that for city jobs(1.78 versus 1.57). This difference is not statistically significant, but it is in the same direction as the other employment findings. Suburban youth were more likely to have skilled or semiskilled jobs than city youth (55 percent versus 36 percent), although this difference is not statistically significant. Skilled jobs were the only outcome significantly affected by gender (because of the secretarial and clerical jobs that females get); however, after controlling for gender, suburbs still had no effect. The suburban youth did not suffer in their employment experiences or opportunities and may have even profited by being in the suburbs.

Job Benefits
Suburban movers were significantly more likely to get job benefits than city movers. More than half of the suburban workers (55 percent) received at least one job benefit (such as vacation, sick leave, educational opportunities, or health coverage) and just over one-fifth of the city workers (23 percent) received at least one job benefit. Gender had no effect on benefits, and controlling for gender did not reduce the suburban effect.

YOUTH WHO WERE NEITHER IN SCHOOL NOR WORKING
Achievement outcomes not only help to assess children's current achievement but also serve as indicators for what types of education and employment opportunities they will have in the future. One of the greatest risks for youth is to be outside the school *and* employment systems—to be gaining neither education nor work experience. This is particularly a problem for low-income, Black youth.[4] The permanent disadvantage hypothesis predicts that the suburban movers would be less likely to be attending school or working than their city counterparts.

A significantly higher proportion of the suburban youth were either in school or working than were the urban youth (suburban, 90 percent; city, 74 percent). The suburban movers were less likely to be outside of the education and employment systems than the city movers. In contrast with the permanent disadvantage hypothesis, the suburban Gautreaux youth were more likely than their city counterparts to be working or in school.

PARTICIPANTS' VIEWS OF THE REASONS FOR THESE EFFECTS
Few Americans have lived in both the suburbs and the inner city, so the suburban movers had a distinctive vantage point that may offer new

insights on the differences between these environments. While long-term residents of suburbs or public housing lack a point of comparison, those who moved from housing projects to middle-class suburbs could see the differences clearly.

Participants identified several factors that may help explain this study's outcomes. When asked how youths' lives would have been different if they had not moved, both suburban and city respondents most frequently mentioned safety. Typical comments included the following: "He would be on drugs, dead or in a gang" and "The gangs were running my oldest son, and I moved out here, and he finished school without any problem." Getting out of the inner city dramatically improved the level of safety for suburban and city movers.

The two groups gave different responses for factors other than safety. The city movers mentioned improved housing quality and improved finances from rent supplements, but few noted motivational or educational changes. Indeed, most city movers went to schools that were similar to those they attended previously. Suburban movers noted that their new environment stimulated youths' motivation. For example, Claire Monroe noted that her daughter "wouldn't have the drive, the challenge, the desire to advance that's needed to get ahead in life . . . if we hadn't moved. She wouldn't be in college now." In contrast, consider a city mother's statement about the demoralization in public housing: "The housing project environment brings you down . . . makes you not care about the future . . . living in the type of environment where nobody wants nothing, nobody does nothing, nobody gets up and tries to have nothing." Another mother noted that "if it is cruddy around and run down, your drive is not there—you don't know any other way."

This increased motivation came about for several reasons. First, women noted that the suburban schools expected students to achieve at a higher level than city schools. Hallie Stickney stated, "A lot more is expected from you out here. A lot of emphasis on school. You have to succeed. If you don't go to school, you're not gonna be able to make anything of yourself." Darlene Williams observed, "The schools in the suburbs academically they are like a hop and a leap over the city. I'm glad I never had to raise my boys in the city. [Compared] academically to a Chicago student, I think they're still way ahead of them." Another mother compared urban and suburban experiences and expectations:

> They go to school with all nationalities—it's like the UN out here in DuPage [a suburban county]. They got to learn different lifestyles and

it makes them want a better lifestyle. They can go into the city now and look at the kids in the city. I hate to keep reflecting back into the city, but the teenage Black boys from Chicago versus the teenage Black boys who were raised out here—it's a whole world apart. It's a big difference.

This mother was careful to say she did not blame the people themselves, but she felt city children were offered very limited experiences.

The quality of suburban high schools was sometimes likened to college: "The high school program was really geared for college because they did give them work which I thought was college type of work. They really expected the best." Gloria Reno said, "[My son Anthony in high school] was ahead of me and could help me with my college work. The academics are ahead [of the city schools]."

An important aspect of school quality is *how* teachers teach. Suburban mothers noted teachers' expectations with comments such as, "Teachers want all the kids to do better" and "They know he can do better, so they expect him to do better." Suburban teachers suggested new behaviors, such as recommending that a student "check her answers if she finishes early." One suburban teacher offered encouragement to a young girl: "When [my daughter] doesn't do her work, the teacher says she's capable of doing it."

The kind of help teachers provide is also important. Many suburban students and their mothers report that teachers stayed after school to tutor them and to give them special lessons that would help them catch up. Even in high school, teachers were almost twice as likely to offer academic help in the suburbs than in the city (62 percent versus 35 percent). One mother noted that her son's "[suburban] teacher tries to help each individual as they need it. They didn't do that in the city." One city teacher actually told a mother that conditions in the city schools prevented her from helping capable students: "[My son's] teacher told me to try to get him away from the city—a city teacher told me that. . . . She told me . . . he's too smart to be in this school."

Teachers can make a huge difference in both encouraging their students to attend college and guiding them to resources that will help them get to college. Suburban high schools provided access to colleges. None of the city mothers mentioned this about city schools. A number of suburban mothers mentioned high school teachers and counselors who helped their children find out about college, prepare for college, and get in touch with colleges. One suburban mother said,

One of the teachers found out that [my son] wasn't taking advanced courses and he got him taking advanced courses, you know. Oh Lord, you know [my son] is very interested in school, and he puts it all there, so they be telling him about scholarships and things like that. Because they invited him to Purdue and the colleges are beginning [to] invite him . . . to look around.

Another said,

The counseling was very good. Now I did meet with the counselor several times. He would invite me in . . . so I would know what the plans, good plans, would be for her toward college. He worked real hard to try to make sure that she was placed in a school that he felt that she was capable of—that would be a challenge to her. The University of Illinois would definitely be a challenge. And, with her grades and her aptitude, she was able to handle that. She's doing real well in college [attending the University of Illinois].

Suburban mothers and youth also noted the influence of positive role models and peer pressure. One youth stated, "I saw that most of the kids in my classes wanted to go to college, and their older brothers and sisters were in college, so I thought I could do that too." Some suburban respondents compared their suburban and urban peers, noting that their peers in the city were negative models.

[What are the chances that you would have finished school in Chicago?] None. Like I said, peer pressure would bring you down. A lot of them are brung down. I seen this in my cousins. . . . The attitudes changed about life. That's all they think is to get high.

[How do you think your life would have been different if your family had not been in the Gautreaux program?] It would have been worse. I had so many friends in the city, and so many of my friends chose the opposite road than I did. I was a follower, so a lot of kids influenced me when I was younger. I think I would have took a different approach towards school. When I got out here, I met friends with more values—telling me that it was better to stay in school.

CONCLUSION

The permanent disadvantage hypothesis suggests that suburban movers will do worse than city movers in school and in jobs (1) because of higher academic standards in the suburban schools than in city schools and (2) because of discrimination by school staff or employers. Despite these expected barriers, suburban Gautreaux youths' academic and employment achievements were at least as good as their city counterparts, and often better. The higher academic standards may actually have had beneficial effects. Likewise, despite whatever fears suburban employers may have about hiring nonwhite youth who lack middle-class backgrounds, more of the suburban movers were working at higher wages and with better benefits than their city counterparts.

Compared with city movers, suburban movers were more likely to be (1) in high school, (2) in a college track, (3) in a four-year college, (4) in a job, (5) in a job with benefits, and (6) not outside of the education and employment systems. In addition, the grades of the city youth and suburban youth did not differ significantly. Given the higher educational standards of suburban schools, as evidenced by their higher ACT and eleventh-grade reading scores and much higher graduation rates than the city schools, the suburban children's grades may have been worth more in terms of achievement.

APPENDIX
Methods and Data

This chapter looks at the school and employment achievements of youth in the Gautreaux program, comparing suburban movers with city movers. When they could be located, the mother and a randomly preselected child from families interviewed in 1982 were reinterviewed in 1989. The interviews included both standard, closed-ended scales and open-ended questions.

The study interviewed children from families who entered the Gautreaux program between 1976 and 1981. As with the adult sample, the city and suburban samples of children's families were very similar (see table 9.2). In 1989, the children had similar ages (18.8 suburban,

Table 9.2   Characteristics of the 1989 Children's Sample: City-Suburban Comparison

	City	Suburb
Age (years)	18.2	18.8
Male (percent)	45.5	56.8*
Mother not married (percent)	88	86
Mother's education postmove (years)	12.03	12.09
Mother finished high school (percent)	43	47

Note: Asterisk indicates significance level of difference between city and suburban samples, by chi-square or t test.
*$p < 0.01$

18.2 city), with a range of 15–25 years in both groups. The families were predominantly female-headed in both the suburban (86 percent) and city (88 percent) groups. Virtually none of the mothers in either group had finished college, similar proportions had finished high school (47 percent suburban and 43 percent city), and their average years of education were virtually identical (12.09 versus 12.03). Thus, there were no differences between families who moved to the city and those who moved to the suburbs in such characteristics as education and previous work experience. The city movers are a good comparison group for the suburban movers.

Gender composition was the only difference between children in the suburban and city samples (males: 57 percent in suburbs, 46 percent in city). To remove the potential confounding influence, all the analyses examine the influence of suburb/city after controlling for gender.

TEN

Conclusion: The Road Ahead

The Gautreaux program has had a significant impact on the creation of other housing mobility initiatives and offers important lessons for housing policy as it affects low-income families and people of color. A number of factors combined in the late 1980s and early 1990s that resulted in the rapid growth of mobility initiatives. By the time the Gautreaux program reached its goal and stopped enrolling families in 1998, more than fifty mobility programs operated across the country. While these programs have different origins, their effectiveness has been influenced by factors similar to those that shaped the Gautreaux program. The experiences of the families in the Gautreaux program and others like it define the parameters of mobility efforts—their potential and their limitations, as well as the costs and benefits for participating families. These experiences, in conjunction with the competition for scarce federal housing subsidies to meet other important policy objectives, the shrinking supply of affordable rental units for low-income families in the private market, and the multiple factors underlying the persistence of segregated housing patterns, limit the possibilities for dramatically expanded mobility initiatives. Moreover, such programs cannot serve people who do not wish to move or who do not qualify. Thus, they must be part of comprehensive strategies that address the problems of deteriorating communities, improve the life chances of the people who live there, and give families realistic choices of where to live.

The first section of this chapter, "Gautreaux Progeny," discusses the confluence of demographic trends, changes in federal housing policies, and the specific events that led to the proliferation of mobility initiatives. It then looks at how the interaction of local situations with programmatic factors (e.g., administration, demand, supply, resources, and community response) affects the implementation and effectiveness of those initiatives. The next section, "Constraints," discusses issues that cut across the local variations in programs and will affect the expansion and role of mobility efforts into the twenty-first century. "Bottom Lines of the Gautreaux Program" provides an overall assessment of the Gautreaux program and the experience of the families who moved to the suburbs and stayed there for a substantial period of time. "Where Do We Go from Here?" applies the lessons of the Gautreaux program to recommendations for future mobility programs and housing policy generally, and identifies questions for further research. The conclusion summarizes the possibilities and the limitations for mobility programs and the families who participate in them.

GAUTREAUX PROGENY

In his 1997 study, *Poverty and Place: Ghettos, Barrios, and the American City,* Paul Jargowsky documented the increase in the concentration of poverty—particularly in the nation's central cities and inner-ring suburbs—that marked the latter part of the twentieth century. Between 1970 and 1990, the number of persons living in high-poverty neighborhoods (poverty rates of 40 percent or more) grew by 92 percent, while the number of poor people living in them nearly doubled. During the same time period, the number of high-poverty census tracts more than doubled, reflecting the geographic spread of poverty to more and more neighborhoods. By 1990, more than eight million people lived in high-poverty neighborhoods. Nearly half of them were Black, and nearly four out of five were members of minority groups.[1]

The growing concentration of poor people in central cities has been accompanied by the decentralization of metropolitan areas—a pattern of declining central city populations in relation to growing suburban populations. The continuing trend toward decentralization reflects an economic restructuring in which jobs are increasingly located in the suburbs. Middle-class whites and Blacks move out of inner-city neighborhoods in search of better opportunities, thus intensifying economic segregation and creating a locational mismatch between housing and jobs that severely affects access to employment for inner-city residents.[2] The need for greater access to jobs was reinforced by the 1996 welfare reform legislation, which established mandatory work requirements and time limits on benefits.[3]

Racial segregation, too, remains a feature of America's metropolitan landscape, attributable in part to the persistence of racial discrimination that continues to deny African-Americans full access to housing markets and the opportunities they offer for improving life chances. Mobility programs, by providing housing opportunities for low-income families outside areas of racial and poverty concentration, are one response to the problems of intensifying concentrations of poverty, the movement of jobs to the suburbs, and continuing racial discrimination.

Federal housing policy during the last two decades has opened the possibility of wider replication of mobility programs patterned after the Gautreaux program. Driven largely by concerns over the high cost of supply-side programs, the emphasis of national housing policy shifted during the last quarter of the century from subsidizing housing construction to providing assistance directly to tenants through vouchers and certificates—the core strategy of the Gautreaux program and other mobility efforts. Funding for additional public housing units was substantially reduced, and funding for Section 8 new construction and substantial rehabilitation subsidies was virtually eliminated. Since the mid-1980s, tenant-based assisted housing has accounted for virtually all of the additions to assisted housing. By the end of the 1990s, 1.4 million low-income households received vouchers and certificates, surpassing the number living in public housing.[4]

Moreover, under federal legislation enacted in 1996, large public housing developments determined to be no longer viable are slated for wholesale demolition or revitalization under plans that will substantially reduce the number of dwelling units.[5] In addition, HUD's efforts to close privately owned, severely troubled, subsidized developments and the conversion of viable, privately owned developments to market-rate housing as their federal contracts expire signal increasing reliance on tenant-based assistance into the next century.[6] Mobility programs utilizing certificates and vouchers became one of the relocation options for residents displaced by these activities. Another strategy to reduce concentrations of poverty is an increasing federal emphasis on mixed-income housing. By facilitating the movement of low-income people into middle-class buildings and neighborhoods, mobility programs are one means to that end.

Within the broader context of demographic trends and changing federal housing policies, a number of specific circumstances have fostered the proliferation of mobility initiatives. First was the Gautreaux program itself and the studies reporting its results. Several hundred low-income African-American families moved from Chicago's inner city each year for two decades, the majority of them to mostly white, middle-class suburbs, and the studies discussed in part 2 found that Gautreaux families who moved to the suburbs improved their lives. These studies became widely known. By the late 1980s and early 1990s, the Gautreaux program and the studies about it had garnered a substantial amount of local and national media attention, both in print and on television. Major daily newspapers in Chicago and the *Washington Post* and *New York Times* published significant stories and positive editorials about the program.[7] Network news, news magazines, and talk shows all featured the Gautreaux program and the studies about it.[8]

Meanwhile, conferences and informal networks of civil rights lawyers and fair housing experts spread the word to activists across the country. Lawyers representing plaintiffs in public housing desegregation litigation modeled on the *Gautreaux* case were an especially receptive audience since they too sought to develop beneficial remedial initiatives. In addition, a Gautreaux legal, administrative, and research team presented the Gautreaux program's experience to HUD and Congressional policy makers receptive to the idea of using the Gautreaux program as a model. The program's progress and the research results served as the basis for advocating expanded mobility programs. Also in the early 1990s, HUD Secretary Henry Cisneros embarked on a systematic campaign to settle the numerous desegregation lawsuits pending against the agency. Since the cases themselves were based on the Chicago litigation, the parties looked to the Gautreaux program as a basis for designing settlements. Most incorporated mobility remedies, usually with a special allocation of Section 8 certificates and HUD funding for counseling and housing search assistance.

Thus, mobility programs have had a variety of origins. More than a dozen have resolved desegregation litigation. Those initiatives generally emphasize racial desegregation in their selection of participants, residence of origin, and permissible destinations. They either require or strongly encourage members of the plaintiff class to move to predominantly white areas. Like the Gautreaux program, racial integration programs sometimes result in class mixing as well.

Impressed with the Gautreaux program's progress and early outcomes, the federal government initiated other mobility efforts. In 1992, Congress enacted Moving to Opportunity (MTO), which set up a controlled experiment to "assist very low-income families with children who reside in public housing or housing receiving project-based assistance under Section 8 of the Housing and Community Development Act of

1937 to move out of areas with high concentrations of persons living in poverty to areas with low concentrations of such persons."[9]

Thus, instead of the Gautreaux program's racial focus, MTO uses poverty to define eligibility and places of origin and destination. Also, instead of operating as an ongoing program, MTO was designed as a social experiment, with three distinct groups of low-income families to be studied: one moving to designated areas, a second moving any place they chose, and a control group not moving at all. HUD selected Baltimore, Boston, Chicago, Los Angeles, and New York to receive extra Section 8 and administrative funds to test and evaluate metropolitan initiatives. All the participating families moved within the first several years, but HUD funded a decade-long study to test the effectiveness of assistance and how the moves affected the families' educational and employment outcomes.[10]

Shortly after Congress created MTO, HUD incorporated the mobility approach into two of its own programmatic initiatives. Starting in 1996, it funded Regional Opportunity Counseling (ROC) at sixteen sites to facilitate regional mobility through the regular Section 8 program by incorporating family counseling and landlord outreach, and promoting collaboration among regional housing agencies. Moreover, beginning in 1995, HUD's Vacancy Consolidation Program gave seventeen local public housing programs modest funding for mobility counseling and housing search assistance ($1,000 per certificate) for public housing residents who received Section 8 certificates because their buildings were targeted for demolition. Like MTO, HUD's administrative initiatives aim to facilitate moves out of areas characterized by widespread poverty, but unlike MTO, they do not restrict where families can use their certificates. Race is not a consideration in selecting participants or in defining permissible destinations.

Several local public housing agencies, including those in Alameda County, California (Oakland and environs); Hartford, Connecticut; Baltimore; and Chicago, initiated mobility programs without litigation or special HUD funding. Cincinnati's mobility program had origins in both litigation and volunteerism. It was mandated by a consent decree from 1984 through 1990 and has operated voluntarily since then. The combination of litigation-based, federally developed, and locally initiated mobility programs expanded the field from a few fledgling efforts in the early 1990s to several dozen by the turn of the century. Their different origins help account for the proliferation of programs as well as their varied implementation experiences.

The factors that shaped the Gautreaux program's implementation have influenced its progeny as well. Contextual factors such as regional demographic and development patterns, law and policy defined by courts or HUD requirements, and local political and governmental structure provide diverse backdrops for these efforts. Programmatic factors, including administration, demand, supply, community response, and resources have substantially affected programs' progress. When the Gautreaux program "ended" in 1998, it was much larger than any of the other mobility programs, in part because of its substantial head start. In addition, the constraints that affected the Gautreaux program loom larger with many of its progeny. Most important, most programs have much more modest overall resources for rent subsidies—both absolutely and proportionately to their metropolitan populations—than did the Gautreaux program.

Administration

The two Chicago administrative experiences represent the spectrum of the commitment and capacity of administrative entities involved in mobility programs nationwide. Litigation-based programs sometimes make local public housing agencies unwilling participants in mobility programs, as happened with the Chicago Housing Authority (CHA). Under a 1987 consent decree, the Dallas Housing Authority is to build public housing in white neighborhoods. Its initial recalcitrance is reminiscent of the CHA's when ordered to carry out the scattered site program.

At the other end of the spectrum, nonprofit agencies in Cincinnati, Hartford, and elsewhere with fair housing missions like that of the Leadership Council are highly committed to carrying out their mobility programs. In the Moving to Opportunity program, organizations had to compete for the opportunity to take administrative responsibility by demonstrating their capacity as well as commitment.

The Leadership Council was fortunate to have bright and committed staff, but they did not start out knowing how to design and run such a program. Like the Council, other organizations have had to learn how to carry out such a program; but they have benefited from the Leadership Council's experience and advice.[11] Some of the Leadership Council's most experienced staff have shared their expertise with local program administrators.[12]

In addition to the quality of administration, implementation depends on the scope of services provided. The Leadership Council provided extensive counseling to help families locate housing, but much less assistance after their moves. With its limited staff, the Council primarily provided referrals to other agencies in the new communities, thus controlling program costs. Other programs provide different mixes of services, depending on political realities and the resources available.

Mobility programs also often require collaboration between nonprofit agencies and one or more public housing agencies. Continuing landlord participation often depends on efficient operation of these arrangements, including housing authorities' prompt apartment inspections and rent payments. Some programs have extended their partnerships to include community institutions, such as local businesses, local government agencies and officials, public and private social service agencies, schools, police, fair housing and legal services organizations, foundations and religious institutions.[13] Community partners provide additional program funding and post-move support services, encourage landlord participation, and help build community support when mobility efforts encounter opposition.

Demand

In the context of mobility programs, demand means the willingness of families to move to areas that programs designate, as well as their capacity to cope with the challenges encountered there.[14] Many Gautreaux families demonstrated those capacities by moving to mostly white middle-class communities, often far from their friends and extended families, where they coped with myriad forms of racial bias.

Like the Gautreaux program, other mobility programs were initially uncertain about whether low-income families would be willing and able to make the kinds of moves contemplated by other mobility programs—whether permissible destinations were defined by race or income. While the Gautreaux program's experience suggested there could be substantial demand elsewhere, earlier efforts to use housing vouchers to encourage racial or economic integration had been unsuccessful. The 1970s national Experimental Housing Allowance Program "had virtually no impact on the degree of economic and racial concentration experienced by participants."[15] Similarly, Project Self-Sufficiency in Cook County, Illinois, resulted in very few Black participants moving to mostly white suburbs.[16] In both programs, participants were reluctant to make these moves because of strong personal ties to their former neighbors, fear of discrimination, and unfamiliarity with distant suburbs.

However, the strong reasons for the high Gautreaux program demand carried over to other mobility programs. Many programs offer the same opportunity as the Gautreaux program to leapfrog long waiting lists and gain access to much-needed, increasingly scarce rent subsidies. In addition, by the 1980s and 1990s, inner-city deterioration was widespread. Even where program participants already receive rent subsidies, as in MTO, there are strong incentives to move to better neighborhoods. In the early days of MTO, fear of crime was the strongest motivation for participating, followed by access to better housing and schools. In Cincinnati, most movers want a better and safer environment and to a lesser extent, help with the rent, while finding a diverse area is of little concern.

In addition, program structure affects demand. There are trade-offs between integrationist goals and demand. The HUD-initiated programs encourage certain kinds of moves but do not have locational restrictions like Gautreaux or many other litigation-based programs. Some either encourage moves to low-poverty areas or leave the destination to relocatees. The emphasis on economic rather than racial integration mitigates potential participants' fears about encountering racial discrimination, while still permitting those interested in racial integration to choose accordingly. Having fewer and different locational restrictions increases both demand and placement rates, but at the cost of achieving less racial or economic integration.

Time limits on locating housing also affect demand. Under the Section 8 program, certificate holders are required to find housing within 120 days (with extensions). This is a problem where the destinations are restricted, or the housing market is tight, or when families need to resolve problems that might prevent them from using the certificate. Some programs, including the Gautreaux program, use a variety of mechanisms to extend the time to find housing.[17]

Programmatic incentives also generate demand for mobility programs. While services vary across programs, virtually all provide some counseling, which adds to their appeal. For example, administrators of Cincinnati's special mobility program attribute its high participation rate in large part to the extensive, up-to-date listing of available units they maintain.[18] The demographic and housing market characteristics in a particular region affect the kind of counseling needed for a successful program. Thus, special counseling is unnecessary to facilitate mobility to higher-income, predominantly white areas in Alameda County because of the relatively low racial and poverty concentration in the region. By contrast, special mobility counseling in highly segregated areas is essential because participants do not have extensive information about mostly white areas.[19] Some programs also provide van transportation to available sites, pay for moving expenses, or offer post-move services to ease the relocation adjustment.

Ongoing demand also depends on the experiences of previous movers. While some Gautreaux families returned to the city to live, about 70 percent of families moving before 1990 were still in the suburbs in 1998 and reported greater safety, better schools, and a degree of social acceptance. Similarly, other programs depend on the accounts of early movers to generate continuing interest.

Most mobility programs have found that demand far exceeds the limited opportunities available. They are in cities with substantial low-income and minority populations with limited housing and community options. In the HUD initiatives, the pool of potential participants is limited only by income, not by race and connection to the public housing program, as in the litigation-based programs. Moreover, most of the programs are small.

Only one mobility program has reported a lack of demand. During the six years of its operation, the Memphis special mobility program was unable to allocate all of the certificates awarded to it. The low demand was attributable to a combination of factors, including locational restrictions that applied not only to the initial moves but to moves after the first year, a requirement that families give up their place on the regular Section 8 waiting list, and a lack of cooperation by the Memphis Housing Authority with the program administrators.[20]

Supply

Since most mobility programs emphasize existing rental housing in the private market, the size, quality, cost, and type of units in the housing stock define the supply potentially available. In theory, large, long-term mobility programs could trigger construction to meet the demand they create. However, neither the Gautreaux program nor other programs have had the scale or duration to affect the available stock substantially.

Lack of units for large families is a common limitation in local housing stocks. A study of the Cincinnati program concluded that "one of the major limitations to housing choice in this program and other mobility efforts is the lack of affordable large bedroom units in most suburbs."[21] Dallas pays incentive bonuses to landlords for three- and four-bedroom apartments or houses, a strategy that program officials credit for their success in increasing the supply of badly needed larger units for the program.[22]

Rental housing costs and HUD's rent ceilings also play a crucial role in programs' access to existing housing. HUD's fair market rents, which limit the agency's subsidy for a unit, embody difficult trade-offs for mobility programs. Fair market rents often keep families from moving into middle-income areas by excluding more expensive housing; but increasing these ceilings reduces the numbers of families that can be assisted and also risks political backlash.

Until 1995, HUD set fair market rents at the forty-fifth percentile of area rents; but then they were lowered to be no higher than 40 percent of a metropolitan area's recently rented, decent-quality units. Lowering the percentage further impeded rentals in higher priced areas. However, the Gautreaux program found pockets of moderate rent units in many affluent suburbs and placed families in more than 120 suburbs throughout a large part of the six-county Chicago metropolitan area. The Orange County (California) Housing Authority established a rent gradient within its jurisdiction to encourage participants to search for housing in low-poverty neighborhoods. Allowable rents are capped well below the fair market rents (FMR) in some areas, while rents above the FMR are permitted in low-poverty areas where the market rents exceed the county average.[23]

Enlisting landlords remains one of the major challenges facing mobility programs. Over time, the Leadership Council established credibility with a number of landlords about the screening and counseling processes, but many landlords remained unwilling to participate. Despite landlords' presumed biases against low-income Blacks, Cincinnati's HOME program came to have a reputation among landlords as a "preferred provider of tenants" because of its screening process. Other programs have found greater resistance among landlords, and some administrators speculate that local realtor associations advise brokers not to get involved with the Section 8 program. At least one program established a Landlord Advisory Committee as a way to bring landlords closer to the program and into the marketing effort.[24]

The success of landlord outreach efforts depends partly on a program's locational restrictions. The more stringent the definitions of "low minority" or "low poverty" and the less choice movers have to opt out of those restrictions, the greater the assurance that the program will achieve its residential mix goals; however, the smaller the targeted housing market segment , the greater the likelihood of landlord resistance.

Programs originating in desegregation lawsuits emphasize the racial composition of destination communities, often precluding or limiting the number of moves to predominantly Black or largely integrated areas. The Gautreaux program had one of the most difficult challenges because the participants were low-income African-Americans, and the permissible destinations were largely middle-class, white, suburban communities. Not only was it difficult to find apartments within HUD's fair market rents, but many landlords were unwilling to participate in the program. Hard work by Leadership Council staff and individual homeseekers was required to enlist sufficient landlords for the Gautreaux program. Smaller litigation-based programs, such as those in Dallas, Memphis, and Cincinnati, have persuaded some white area landlords to rent to low-income Black inner-city families; but they also have encountered substantial resistance. In the Dallas area, major owners of rental properties accept Section 8 tenants in their Black neighborhood properties but not in the white area ones, and some landlords refuse to rent to African-American Section 8 families if there is a swimming pool in the development.[25]

HUD initiatives, such as Moving to Opportunity, Regional Opportunity Counseling, and public housing Vacancy Consolidation, instead emphasize moving to areas without concentrations of poor people. In MTO, where required destinations are low-poverty areas, it was sometimes easier to recruit landlords. Also, Regional Opportunity Counseling and Vacancy Consolidation programs use more permissive approaches, either "encouraging" moves to low-poverty areas or saying nothing about relocatees' destinations. Easier access to units results in higher placement rates in many of these programs.

Higher vacancy rates increase landlords' willingness to participate in mobility programs. Vacancy rates vary substantially across regions and over time. Moreover, the rates vary within metropolitan housing markets, so the definition of the target market determines which vacancy rates are relevant for programs' purposes.

Moreover, initial participation does not ensure that landlords will continue their involvement in a program. Their experience with having program families as tenants shapes their willingness to participate further. This presents a dilemma for mobility programs, because strict screening, which increases the chances of landlord satisfaction and continuation, excludes families that could benefit from the move. Since landlord acceptance is a limiting factor in placing families, many programs have followed the Gautreaux program's lead in specifying selection criteria meeting landlords' legitimate needs, such as past records in paying rent and maintaining property.

Community Response

Each year the Gautreaux program helped a few hundred families to move into widely dispersed, privately owned existing housing, increasingly to the suburban portions of the six-county region. The program's modest scale and pace and its demand-side emphasis gave it low visibility and led to minimal community response. Most similar programs are smaller than Gautreaux, of shorter duration, and rely heavily on the less visible rental of existing housing. Moving to Opportunity is at the other end of the scale and duration continuum from the Gautreaux program because it is more of an experiment than an ongoing program. Only about two to three hundred families moved in each of the five large metropolitan areas—all within a few years of the program's inception, and not all of them to places demographically different from their point of origin. There was a broad range between Gautreaux and MTO, but most programs have facilitated hundreds, rather than thousands, of moves.

Mobility programs have encountered community responses similar to the quiet reaction to the Gautreaux program. In the early years of the Gautreaux progeny, there was only one instance of intense and concerted community opposition. Even though it involved a small program with low-visibility, tenant-based assistance, the Baltimore MTO program's announcement in 1994 generated an extremely hostile response. Opponents organized mass meetings and garnered extensive media coverage. Hate groups joined the fray, and one white protester burned a cross on a lawn.[26]

Since the small size of the Gautreaux program helped to explain the lack of community resistance to it, the intensity of the Baltimore opposition may have been related to white suburban residents' concern that this would be a large program. The MTO announcement coincided with publicity about demolition of some of the city's high-rise public housing, thus planting the seed in some suburbanites' minds that MTO would help large numbers of public housing displacees to move to the suburbs.

Moreover, like the announcement of the CHA's original scattered site plans, the MTO announcement came during an election campaign. Candidates in local, state, and national campaigns exploited the issue for their political purposes, including tapping into the racial fears and economic insecurities of working-class, white, suburban residents, many of whom lived in neighborhoods that would not be affected.

Finally, the Baltimore program's information strategy added to the difficulties. Administrators were determined to announce the program publicly—unlike the Gautreaux program initiators—but the announcement was premature: the program structure was not fully developed, and answers to many questions from opponents in the community were not available.

Program administrators and proponents responded to the attacks on several levels. First, they expanded public education and outreach activities to allay community concerns. They met with public officials, journalists, and civic, union, and religious leaders. The Roman Catholic Archbishop initiated a letter of support signed by other prominent clergy. Proponents also tried to explain the program at mass meetings and in appearances on broadcast talk shows, as well as through letters and editorial opinion pieces in local newspapers.

In addition, administrators modified programmatic features to minimize community resistance. They intensified counseling and screening of families and made sure that poor families would be dispersed as they moved to the suburbs. After the election, the opposition died down as participants moved in without major incidents.

While program proponents calmed a serious challenge to the program, there were continuing adverse effects both locally and nationally. The stigma associated with mobility programs added to the difficulty of enlisting suburban Baltimore's landlords. More generally, Maryland Senator Barbara Mikulski, an original MTO proponent, succeeded in diverting funding intended for expanding the program nationwide.

Resources

Availability of resources has been the limiting factor in many mobility programs, especially those that did not originate as part of a court settlement. Resources for mobility programs generally take the form of special allocations of Section 8 rent certificates and administrative funding.

The level of Section 8 funds has varied substantially among programs, with litigation-based programs often receiving the most. At the other end of the scale, HUD's Regional Opportunity Counseling initiative was added to existing Section 8 certificates, adding no new ones. MTO and the public housing Vacancy Consolidation effort make small Section 8 allocations available for mobility purposes.

Similarly, administrative resources and activities differ significantly among mobility initiatives. While all programs provide counseling to home-seekers, the level of counseling ranges from general briefing sessions to in-depth training in doing housing searches or accompanying families on site visits. Moreover, most programs include landlord outreach. Some programs also help families with moving costs.

Administrative funding is built into litigation-based programs—about $500,000 annually in Dallas—with much more limited amounts for the smaller HUD initiatives.

Difficult trade-offs have emerged between the extent of services provided individual families and the numbers of families that programs can assist. Other programs could mesh with mobility initiatives to enhance families' experiences. Child care assistance is needed more in the suburbs, where relatives are not usually nearby to help. Additional education and training for adults can lead to better jobs. Also, assistance in obtaining a car can help with the job search and daily tasks, and facilitate children's involvement in after-school activities. But these additions can increase costs significantly, and perhaps trigger political opposition as well.

MTO instituted a third area of funding by incorporating an extensive research component building on the Gautreaux studies. Congress funded a ten-year research project to determine the program's effects in each of the five demonstration cities.

Mobility programs rely mostly on the federal government for both rent subsidies and administrative funds. Some programs, including those initiated locally, have obtained funds from state and local government sources, such as Community Development Block Grant funds, and private sources, such as foundation grants, to assist families with expenses such as security deposits and moving costs, or obtained in-kind contributions from local businesses, such as low-cost cars from rental companies. Still, federal financial support largely determines the scale and scope of mobility programs.

Constraints

Several factors evidenced at the turn of this century suggest limits on the expansion and role of mobility programs. The future of mobility programs depends on continued funding for tenant-based housing assistance, yet growth in the number of households receiving rental assistance has declined dramatically since the late 1970s. The average number of new households receiving assistance each year dropped from 224,000 between 1978 and 1982 to approximately 146,000 in the early 1990s.[27] From fiscal years 1996 through 1998, Congress provided no funding for new rental assistance to serve low-income families.[28] HUD's appropriation for fiscal 1999 included funding for 50,000 new vouchers to be used for a new welfare-to-work initiative.[29]

Funding limits make deciding how to allocate scarce resources even more difficult. Mobility initiatives must compete with other important policy objectives. For example, using certificates and vouchers to maintain income mix in areas undergoing revitalization or to support the choice of inner-city families who wish to remain in their current neighborhood limits their availability for mobility purposes.

At the same time, the supply of affordable rental housing in the private market for the nation's poorest families is shrinking. The gap between the numbers of low-income renters and affordable units in both central cities and suburbs is significant and growing.[30] In the six-county Chicago area, there were nearly two renters for every affordable unit in 1990.[31] A 1995 study of the potential supply of affordable units available for Section 8 recipients in low-poverty areas of the Chicago region estimated that there were nearly three families for every vacant unit, assuming that all of the units would meet HUD health and safety standards and that landlords would be willing to rent to Section 8 families.[32]

Public housing demolition and the conversion of privately developed subsidized housing to market-rate housing exert additional pressure on the supply of affordable housing, while potentially displacing large numbers of families. The number of public housing units is expected to decline with the 1995 suspension of the federal requirement of one-for-one replacement of public housing units lost through demolition or disposition.[33] In Chicago alone, the CHA plans to demolish some eleven thousand public housing units, only a fraction of which will be replaced.

Constraints on housing choice for low-income families continue to affect residential patterns, as suggested by locational outcomes under the regular Section 8 program. Studies in the early and mid-1990s revealed that while Section 8 recipients were less concentrated than public housing residents, many continued to live in racially segregated and economically distressed neighborhoods. This was especially true in central cities and for Blacks and Latinos.[34] While the preference of recipients to remain near family and existing social networks helps to explain these patterns, other factors were probably also at work—racial discrimination, discrimination based on Section 8 assistance, community opposition, lack of information about housing options, and excessive housing search costs.

THE BOTTOM LINES OF THE GAUTREAUX PROGRAM

The story of the Gautreaux program is too complex to capture in a single bottom line. At its peak, more than four hundred families annually moved to predominantly white, middle-class suburbs to which they had access only through the program's counseling and financial support; but it took more than two decades to reach the program's target number of placements.

The 1981 consent decree that formally established the program stipulated that 7,100 families were to be assisted through this initiative. Accordingly, when the agreed-upon goal was reached, HUD's obligation to fund the program ended. The final telephone registration process took place early in 1998. In the fall of that year, the last family who would relocate entered the program. Families already in the program continued to participate and receive the rent subsidies that had enabled them to relocate.

Well after ceasing operation, the Gautreaux program remained the country's largest mobility program and the standard by which other mobility initiatives were measured. Part of the reason for the program's continued preeminence was that it started well before most of the others. However, none of those that came along later have achieved a scale or pace comparable to those of the Gautreaux program.

The size, geographical scope, and duration of the Gautreaux program demonstrated both the promise and the limits of mobility efforts. It showed the possibilities for the scale of such initiatives, as well as the range of likely outcomes for program participants who relocated to the suburbs and stayed there for substantial periods of time.

The demand for the services of the Gautreaux program grew rapidly and remained very high throughout its life, despite the locational restrictions of the program—with its increasing emphasis on the suburbs—and families' continuing preferences to remain in the city. For many, the program offered desperately needed housing subsidies. Many were attracted by the prospect of a better living environment.

On the other hand, it appeared that the program was not for everyone. Some who were eligible did not apply. Others began the application process but withdrew before moving. Still others moved to the suburbs but returned to the city quite quickly. None of these responses was surprising in a region whose history was marked by racial and economic segregation, and by racial discrimination and even violence when Blacks moved into predominantly white city neighborhoods and suburban communities. Moreover, many families were committed to family and friends, and to improving the quality of life in their inner-city communities. Others feared the loss of their children's racial and cultural identities.

CONCLUSION: THE ROAD AHEAD   189

In addition, the program was not able to serve all of the eligible families interested in moving. The supply of private rental housing in predominantly white areas of the city and suburbs did not fully match the needs of eligible families, especially larger families who needed apartments with three or more bedrooms. Moreover, market forces and HUD regulations put much rental housing beyond the financial reach of the program. Also, many landlords and property managers accepted very few families through the program, or declined to participate at all.

The low-income Black families who moved to white middle-class suburbs assumed many risks in facing the unknown as pioneers. In doing so, they demonstrated courage and strength of will. The story of their capacities and motivations begins with their persistence in initially registering for the program, continues through the process of finding an apartment and convincing often skeptical landlords to accept them as tenants, and culminates with their coping with their new circumstances as strangers in a strange land to secure better life opportunities for themselves and their children. They persevered in spite of the things they missed in the city—family, friends and church—and the challenges they sometimes encountered—myriad forms of discrimination and social isolation. They also displayed openness to change and confidence in their ability to make a major adjustment and in their children's ability to meet the educational challenges of the more demanding suburban schools and the social challenges of a mostly white, middle-class environment.

Many of the families who moved to the suburbs were rewarded for those efforts. While the studies discussed in this book showed that families' experiences were very complex, they supported the basic premise of the concept of "geography of opportunity"—people who move to better areas can improve their opportunities and attainments. Contrary to pessimistic predictions of "culture of poverty" models that depicted low-income Black families as dysfunctional, families showed substantial ability to adapt to the middle-class environments where they relocated. The studies, which focused primarily on the opportunities afforded low-income Black children, indicate that many of the benefits are intergenerational. The early experiences of those children did not prevent them from benefiting from suburban moves in ways that may improve not only their own life chances but those of their children and future generations.

Compared with the children of city movers, the children who moved to the suburbs were more likely to be in school, in college-track classes, in four-year colleges, employed , and in jobs with benefits and better pay. However, these achievement gains were not immediate. Indeed, virtually all suburban movers experienced great difficulties in school initially, and many got lower grades in the first year or two. It took time to adjust to the higher suburban standards.

Suburban moves also led to social integration, friendships, and interaction with white as well as Black neighbors in the suburbs. Social integration was not total, and while racial harassment declined over time, some prejudice remained, and some children had little or no contact with white children outside of school. Women and their children developed coping strategies for dealing with racial bias, and at the same time many white neighbors and classmates accepted them.

In addition, suburban movers experienced greater safety and freedom from fear of crime than they did in the inner city. The racial harassment and threats they encountered did not pose the day-to-day physical danger they confronted in Chicago. Nor did they have to contend much with suburban gangs recruiting the children, a continuing threat in their city neighborhoods.

Moreover, the Gautreaux program as a whole encountered quite limited community opposition, in contrast to the experience with the scattered site program in the city. In particular, the program's modest pace, careful screening and counseling, reliance on the existing private rental housing, and dispersal policies limited its visibility, which in turn avoided local resistance.

WHERE DO WE GO FROM HERE?

The Gautreaux program has demonstrated both the potential and limitations of housing mobility strategies. It has also provided insights and information for future housing policy regarding who should be served and in what ways.

When the Gautreaux case began in the 1960s, many urban areas were still composed largely of Blacks and whites. Both the scattered site remedy and the Gautreaux program defined the urban landscape as if it contained only these two groups, with the goal of remedying the injury to African-Americans and furthering integration between them and whites. However, as in many metropolitan areas, Chicago's demographic landscape had changed significantly by the end of the century. Most dramatically, Latinos and Asian-Americans with roots in many Central and South American and Asian countries constituted substantial minorities in many large and middle-sized urban areas.

Housing programs generally, and mobility programs in particular, should be designed to take into account those demographic changes and provide assistance to a much more racially and ethnically diverse range of lower-income participants. An exception would be for mobility initiatives growing out of litigation, where the participating groups are defined by those whose rights are found to be violated in a particular case. The MTO program recognizes that housing needs cut across racial and ethnic lines and instead bases eligibility on income. Using such an approach also has the benefit of potentially attracting greater political support for the underlying expenditures, given the growing resistance to race-based programs and processes.

Counseling is fundamental to making mobility possible. One of the legacies and consequences of the history of racial and economic segregation in metropolitan areas is the lack of information about regionwide housing opportunities available to lower-income families and people of color. Because of the massive suburban migration of middle-class whites since World War II, middle-class white city residents have access to both formal and informal information sources—including family, friends, and religious and other institutions—about housing types, costs, and quality, as well as public services and facilities in a variety of suburban communities. Potential participants in demand-side housing programs require not only these traditional forms of information but also information about the climate of those communities for people crossing racial and class lines to move there. They need to know about the reception they are likely to receive in their new neighborhoods and the schools, based on the experience of other low-income families or people of color who have moved there. Counseling can provide much-needed assistance to enable families to make informed, reasoned decisions as they compare urban neighborhoods they have experienced with regionwide possibilities for relocating. Such counseling should be available generally to low-income families and people of color—those who generally have had the least mobility and for whom housing search costs may be a prohibitive barrier to moving to places that would improve their quality of life.

Comprehensiveness should also include post-move counseling to help families who may wish to move when their initial lease expires. Numerous participants in the Gautreaux program moved to other housing within the same community, to other suburban areas, or back to the city. Second-move counseling can help assure that families have information about the full range of housing options on which to base their decision.

Mobility programs should acknowledge and utilize the capacities of low-income families. For example, the Gautreaux program came to rely on the ability of families to find units and "sell" landlords on the program generally and on themselves as tenants. The ability of suburban movers to cope with the difficulties they encountered in the suburbs and to adjust to the white, middle-class, suburban culture suggests that current and past mobility program participants could play a role in the design and delivery of counseling and support services.

In all likelihood, only a fraction of low-income families will be served by mobility programs. Moreover, such programs cannot serve people who do not wish to move or who do not qualify, such as large, poor families or those with serious credit problems; nor can they quickly provide the kind of scale called for in the public housing demolition process. Most poor families will continue to live in urban neighborhoods or move away from those areas on their own if their incomes increase and they choose to relocate.

While the research discussed in this book begins the exploration of the impact of housing mobility initiatives, much more needs to be done. Some is already underway, including a long-term systematic evaluation of the Moving to Opportunity program. Moreover, James Rosenbaum has embarked on a major study of the impact of moves on Gautreaux families as the children reach adulthood. These studies will further test the "geography of opportunity" thesis.

Mobility programs have demonstrated that low-income families can make moves that facilitate racial or economic integration. First in Chicago and then elsewhere, vehicles have been invented and implemented that have assisted thousands of low-income families to move to better places with greater opportunities.

At the turn of this century, the Gautreaux program remains the best source of information regarding the possibilities for poor people to enhance their life chances by relocating to places where opportunities are greater. The Chicago experience tells a tale of possibilities and limitations—both for mobility programs overall and for the families who participate in them. This study has shown that when low-income Black families cross the class and color lines in society, they are capable of handling the difficulties that arise, and they experience many benefits from these moves. The question is, To what extent is American society willing to allow those families to have the chance?

NOTES

CHAPTER ONE

1. Sarah H. Bradford, *Harriet Tubman: The Moses of Her People* (1886; reprint, New York: Carol Publishing Group, 1994), 31.

2. "Black" is capitalized whenever it refers to Black people, in order to indicate that Blacks, or African-Americans (these terms are used interchangeably in the book), are a specific cultural group with its own history, traditions, experience, and identity—not just people of a particular color. Using the uppercase letter signifies recognition of the culture, as it does with Latinos, Asian-Americans, or Native Americans. See Kimberle Williams Crenshaw, "Race, Reform, and Retrenchment: Transformation in Anti-Discrimination Law," *Harvard Law Review* 101 (1988): 1331, n. 2.

3. *Gautreaux v. Chicago Hous. Auth.*, 296 F. Supp. 907 (N.D. Ill. 1969).

4. *Gautreaux v. Chicago Hous. Auth.*, 304 F. Supp. 736 (N.D. Ill. 1969), enforcing *Gautreaux v. Chicago Hous. Auth.*, 296 F. Supp. 907 (N.D. Ill. 1969).

5. *Hills v. Gautreaux*, 425 U.S. 284, 306 (1976).

6. John Calmore, "Spatial Equality and the *Kerner Commission Report:* A Back-to-the-Future Essay," *North Carolina Law Review* 71, no. 5 (1993): 1489.

7. *Title VIII of the 1968 Civil Rights Act, U.S. Code,* vol. 42, secs. 3601–19 (1994); In *Jones v. Alfred H. Mayer Co.*, 392 U.S. 409 (1968), the Supreme Court held that section 1982 of the 1866 Civil Rights Act applied to private discrimination.

8. *Southern Burlington County NAACP v. Mount Laurel Tp.*, 336 A. 2d 713 (N.J. 1975) (Mount Laurel I); *Southern Burlington County NAACP v. Mount Laurel Tp.*, 456 A. 2d 390 (N.J. 1983) (Mount Laurel II); *Urban League of Essex County v. Mahwah Tp.*, 504 A. 2d 66 (N.J. Super. L. 1984) (Mount Laurel III).

9. Anthony Downs has suggested that low-income Black families would seize opportunities to move to better neighborhoods, but might be reluctant to leave the city for the suburbs; see Anthony Downs, *Opening Up the Suburbs: An Urban Strategy for America* (New Haven: Yale University Press, 1973), 136–37.

10. Downs uses *cluster* to indicate organizing or placing individual households in geographic proximity to one another. His use of the term suggests that these groups of households would be scattered over some larger region; see Downs, *Opening Up the Suburbs*, 139. Douglas Massey and Nancy Denton use the term to denote "the tendency for black areas to adhere together within one large agglomeration, rather than being scattered about the metropolitan area"; see Massey and Denton, *American Apartheid: Segregation and the Making of the Underclass* (Cambridge, Mass.: Harvard University Press, 1993), 74–78.

CHAPTER TWO

1. Bessie Louise Pierce, *A History of Chicago* (New York: Alfred A. Knopf, 1937), 1: 12. Tradition holds that Du Sable had planned a colony of free Blacks along Lake Michigan near Chicago; see St. Clair Drake and Horace R. Cayton, *Black Metropolis: A Study of Negro Life in a Northern City*, rev. and enl. (New York: Harcourt, Brace and World, 1970), 1: 31.

2. According to one account, Du Sable owned a trading post and sold his property for about $1,200—a substantial sum at that time—when he left in about 1800; Rayford W. Logan and Michael R. Winston, eds., *Dictionary of American Negro Biography* (New York: W. W. Norton, 1982), 207, citing Milo M. Quaife, *Checagou: From Indian Wigwam to Modern City* (Chicago: University of Chicago Press, 1933).

3. William Cronon, *Nature's Metropolis: Chicago and the Great West* (New York: W. W. Norton, 1991), 27–28, 33; Bureau of the Census, *Population by Subdivisions of Counties, 1850* (Washington, D.C., 1853).

4. Chicago's Black population grew from 53 in 1840 to 955 in 1860; Bureau of the Census, *Population of Cities and Towns, 1860* (Washington, D.C., 1863).

5. The Illinois legislature banned racial discrimination in public accommodations in 1884, a prohibition that was enforced unevenly; see Donald L. Miller, *City of the Century: The Epic of Chicago and the Making of America* (New York: Simon and Schuster, 1996; New York: Touchstone, 1997), 501 (page citations are to the reprint edition).

6. Ann Durkin Keating, *Building Chicago: Suburban Developers and the Creation of a Divided Metropolis*, Urban Life and Urban Landscape Series (Columbus: Ohio State University Press, 1988), 123; Miller, *City of the Century*, 293.

7. Keating, *Building Chicago*, 3–4; Bureau of the Census, *Population by Subdivisions of Counties, 1850*; Bureau of the Census, *Population of Minor Civil Divisions, 1870* (Washington, D.C., 1873); Harold M. Mayer and Richard C. Wade, *Chicago: Growth of a Metropolis* (Chicago: University of Chicago Press, Phoenix Books, 1969), 132, 138, 140.

8. Keating, *Building Chicago*, 17.

9. The town of Pullman, which provided suburban living for the Pullman sleeping car company's workers, did not allow a single Black resident; see Thomas Lee Philpott, *The Slum and the Ghetto: Neighborhood Deterioration and Middle-Class Reform, Chicago 1880–1930*, The Urban Life in America Series, ed. Richard C. Wade (New York: Oxford University Press, 1978), 4–5, 52–53.

10. James R. Grossman, *Land of Hope: Chicago, Black Southerners, and the Great Migration* (Chicago: University of Chicago Press, 1991), 114, 116–17; Allan H. Spear, *Black Chicago: The Making of a Negro Ghetto, 1890–1920* (Chicago: University of Chicago Press, 1967), 11–12, 147. By 1900, most Blacks lived either in the Black Belt or in a ring of factories and laborer housing surrounding the city's central business district; see Drake and Cayton, *Black Metropolis*, 1: 16–17, 47; Miller, *City of the Century*, 275–76; Spear, *Black Chicago*, 17, 19, 146; Bureau of the Census, *Native and Foreign Born and White and Colored Population, Classified by Sex, of Places Having 2,500 Inhabitants or More, 1890* (Washington, D.C., 1893); Bureau of the Census, *Color or Race, Nativity, and Parentage, for Cities Having 100,000 Inhabitants or More, 1920*; (Washington, D.C., 1922).

11. Philpott, *Slum and the Ghetto*, x; Spear, *Black Chicago*, 142.

12. Philpott, *Slum and the Ghetto*, 149.

13. Spear, *Black Chicago*, 21. In 1917, the powerful Chicago Real Estate Board, the organization of real estate brokers, mandated that agents not sell homes to Blacks in areas that were more than 75 percent white. The Board viewed Black entry into white neighborhoods as a threat to their viability and to the city's well-being; Philpott, *Slum and the Ghetto*, 162–63. By 1930, white property-owner associations covered more than three-quarters of Chicago's residential property with restrictive covenants; Drake and Cayton, *Black Metropolis*, 1: 79, 182, 184.

14. William M. Tuttle, Jr., *Race Riot: Chicago in the Red Summer of 1919*, Studies in American Negro Life, ed. August Meier (New York: Atheneum, 1970), 64; Philpott, *Slum and the Ghetto*, 170, 173–74.

15. Devereux Bowly, Jr., *The Poorhouse: Subsidized Housing in Chicago, 1894–1976* (Carbondale and Edwardsville: Southern Illinois University Press, 1978), 18.

16. Ibid., 19–27, 30, 33.

17. Ibid., 27, 30; Martin Meyerson and Edward C. Banfield, *Politics, Planning, and the Public Interest: The Case of Public Housing in Chicago* (London: Collier-Macmillan, 1955; New York: The Free Press, 1964), 121–22 (page citations are to the reprint edition).

18. Drake and Cayton, *Black Metropolis*, 1: 8, 2: 434.

19. Some whites believed that speculators, Jews, Blacks, Communists, and city planners had formed a conspiracy to destroy what they had spent their lives building; see Arnold R. Hirsch, *Making the Second Ghetto: Race and Housing in Chicago, 1940–1960*, Interdisciplinary Perspectives on Modern History (Cambridge: Cambridge University Press, 1983), 194–96, 200–201, 210–11.

20. Hirsch, *Making the Second Ghetto*, 179–80; Nicholas Lemann, *The Promised Land: The Great Black Migration and How It Changed America* (New York: Alfred A. Knopf, 1991; New York: Vintage Books, 1992), 72 (page citations are to the reprint edition).

21. Hirsch, *Making the Second Ghetto*, 218–19, 230, 239. A 1940s complex that the CHA planned to have a 4-to-1 ratio of Blacks to whites could not attract whites at all; Meyerson and Banfield, *Politics, Planning, and Public Interest*, 123.

22. Hirsch, *Making the Second Ghetto,* 218, 230, 239.

23. Frederick Aaron Lazin, "Public Housing in Chicago, 1963–1971, Gautreaux v. Chicago Housing Authority: A Case Study of the Co-optation of a Federal Agency by its Local Constituency" (Ph.D. diss., University of Chicago, 1973), 74–75; Meyerson and Banfield, *Politics, Planning, and Public Interest,* 125.

24. Meyerson and Banfield, *Politics, Planning, and Public Interest,* 87, 128.

25. Taylor resigned the following year, and Wood was fired in 1954, in part due to disputes with CHA commissioners over racial policy; Meyerson and Banfield, *Politics, Planning, and Public Interest,* 242; Hirsch, *Making the Second Ghetto,* 234–38.

26. Bowly, *Poorhouse,* 111–24.

27. Ibid., 135.

28. Meyerson and Banfield, *Politics, Planning, and Public Interest,* 32.

29. Hirsch, *Making the Second Ghetto,* 28; Mayer and Wade, *Growth of a Metropolis,* 406.

30. In 1947, for example, 5,968 units were built in Chicago and 24,744 in the suburbs. In 1956, 13,625 were built in the city and 48,632 in the suburbs; Bowly, *Poorhouse,* 55.

31. Hirsch, *Making the Second Ghetto,* 27–28.

32. Elizabeth Warren, *Subsidized Housing in the Chicago Suburbs,* Urban Insights Series, no. 8 (Chicago: Loyola University of Chicago, 1981), 19.

33. Leonard S. Rubinowitz, *Low Income Housing: Suburban Strategies* (Cambridge: Ballinger, 1974).

34. Lazin, "Public Housing in Chicago," 63; Harold Baron, interview by Alan Mills, Chicago, January 1981.

35. Despite the uncertainties litigation involves, Dorothy Gautreaux risked the personal retribution that publicly resisting her landlord could entail. She believed that public housing residents should stand up for themselves rather than being mere victims of the city's political machine; see Business and Professional People for the Public Interest, "What Is Gautreaux?" (Business and Professional People for the Public Interest, Chicago, 1991, photocopy), 1.

36. Ibid., 4.

37. *Gautreaux v. Chicago Hous. Auth.,* 296 F. Supp. 907 (N.D. Ill. 1969).

38. The developments in white areas ranged from 93 to 99 percent white, as of 31 December 1967. Ibid. at 909.

39. The ruling, handed down three years after the case was filed, came too late for Dorothy Gautreaux, who died in 1968, in her early forties.

40. Abram Chayes discussed what he viewed as a new form of litigation, characterized in part by the need to construct relief. Abram Chayes, "The Role of the Judge in Public Law Litigation," *Harvard Law Review* 89, no. 7 (1976): 1281.

41. Alexander Polikoff, *Housing the Poor: The Case for Heroism* (Cambridge: Ballinger, 1978), 153.

42. *Gautreaux v. Chicago Hous. Auth.,* 304 F. Supp. 736 (N.D. Ill. 1969), enforcing *Gautreaux v. Chicago Hous. Auth.,* 296 F. Supp. 907 (N.D. Ill. 1969).

43. The buffer zone was held to be necessary to ensure that resegregation would not occur in areas where scattered site public housing was located; ibid.

44. *Gautreaux v. Chicago Hous. Auth.*, 304 F. Supp. 736 (N.D. Ill. 1969).

45. Plaintiffs' counsel opposed the use of quotas in those developments.

46. Both Black and white public housing tenants could have been reassigned, just as courts have required of public school students in hundreds of school districts. Indeed, a federal judge in Texas later ordered reassignment of public housing tenants in a case in which *Gautreaux v. Chicago Hous. Auth.* was the main precedent. See *Young v. Pierce*, 685 F. Supp. 986 (E.D. Texas 1988), in which the housing authority's site selection and tenant assignment policies and practices were held to have been racially discriminatory.

47. For a discussion of the necessity of protecting middle-class dominance as part of a strategy to expand low- and moderate-income families' suburban access, see Downs, *Opening Up the Suburbs.*

48. Mario Matthew Cuomo, *Forest Hills Diary: The Crisis of Low-Income Housing* (New York: Random House, 1974; New York: Vintage Books, 1975).

49. Leonard S. Rubinowitz, "Chicago, Illinois," in *Decentralizing Urban Policy: Case Studies in Community Development*, ed. Raul R. Dommel (Washington, D.C.: The Brookings Institution, 1982), 127.

50. Congressman Roman Pucinski, a Daley ally representing a largely ethnic district, said that the Gautreaux decision probably "dealt the death knell to public housing here" (Business and Professional People for the Public Interest, "What Is Gautreaux?," 6).

51. *Gautreaux v. Chicago Hous. Auth.*, No. 66 C 1459–60 (N.D. Ill. 1974).

52. At a meeting of twenty-five white homeowner associations, an attorney threatened: "If the construction really starts, we'll take action of some sort, and not letters or petitions. In the meantime, we'll put pressure on the aldermen to stop it. If they don't, we'll run them out of town on a rail"; see Roger Biles, *Richard J. Daley: Politics, Race, and the Governing of Chicago* (DeKalb, Ill.: Northern Illinois University Press, 1995), 173.

53. Ibid., 190.

54. Brian J. L. Berry, *The Open Housing Question: Race and Housing in Chicago, 1966–1976* (Cambridge: Ballinger, 1979), 393–97.

55. See *Housing That Works*, a videotape about the scattered site program produced by Video Services (1990) independently of the CHA, focusing on units on the city's north side, managed by the Housing Resource Center of Hull House, the first private manager with whom the CHA contracted. Staff suggested that careful screening was an essential ingredient in making the program work for the residents and the community.

56. Jay Miller, the ACLU executive director, acknowledged that the absence of a substantial constituency for the scattered site program hindered its implementation (Jay Miller, interview by Alan Mills, Chicago, 31 October 1980).

57. Lazin, "Public Housing in Chicago," 289–91.

58. HUD notified the CHA on 26 March 1974, that the moratorium had been lifted for Chicago. First Report of Special Master for the period 3 March

1975, to 3 September 1975, slip op. at 3, *Gautreaux v. Chicago Hous. Auth.*, No. 66 C 1459–60 (N.D. Ill. 1975).

59. This includes all units as of November 1997; see Rui Kaneya and Danielle Gordon, "Finding Sites for New Public Housing No Easy Task," *The Chicago Reporter*, March 1998.

60. John Schrag and Jorge Casuso, "A Delicate Balance: Open Suburbs Fight to Avoid Racial Tipping," *The Chicago Reporter*, December 1985.

61. George E. Peterson and Kale Williams, "Housing Mobility: What Has It Accomplished, and What Is Its Promise?" in *Housing Mobility: Promise or Illusion?* ed. Alexander Polikoff (Washington, D.C.: The Urban Institute, 1995), 85, table 19.

62. The 241 units of townhouse and low-rise developments slated for North Kenwood-Oakland were supposed to fulfill a commitment to the area's former housing residents who had been displaced from their development and whose buildings were ultimately designated for demolition.

CHAPTER THREE

1. *Gautreaux v. Romney*, 66-C-1460 (N.D. Ill. 1 September 1970).

2. *Gautreaux v. Romney*, 448 F. 2d 731, 739–40 (7th Cir. 1971); Leonard S. Rubinowitz, "Metropolitan Public Housing Desegregation Remedies: Chicago's Privatization Program," *Northern Illinois University Law Review* 12, no. 3 (1992): 598–99.

3. Memoranda in Support of Plaintiffs' Outline of Proposed Final Order Embodying Comprehensive Plan for Relief; Memorandum #2—The Additional Dwelling Units to Be Provided Should Be Located Throughout a Defined Metropolitan Area (3 July 1972).

4. *Gautreaux v. Romney*, 363 F. Supp. 690 (N.D. Ill. 1973).

5. *Milliken v. Bradley*, 418 U.S. 717 (1974). The lower courts had not adopted a specific remedy, but they had determined that the decree would encompass fifty-three suburban school districts in addition to the Detroit public schools; see *Bradley v. Milliken*, 338 F. Supp. 582 (E.D. Mich. 1971); *Bradley v. Milliken*, 484 F. 2d 215 (6th Cir. 1973).

6. *Hills v. Gautreaux*, 425 U.S. 284 (1976).

7. In *Milliken v. Bradley*, conversely, the majority of justices believed that the potential remedy would restructure dozens of innocent suburban school districts against their will; *Milliken v. Bradley*, 418 U.S. 717, 742–47 (1974).

8. *Hills v. Gautreaux*, 425 U.S. at 303; *Housing and Community Development Act of 1974*, U.S. Code, vol. 42, sec. 1437 (1994).

9. *Housing and Community Development Act of 1974*, sec. 1437(f)(c)(3) (Supp. IV, 1974) provides that the monthly assistance payment is the difference between the maximum monthly rental provided for in the contract and the rent the family must pay under the *Housing and Community Development Act of 1974*, sec. 1437(a)(2). The *Housing and Community Development Act of 1974*, sec. 1437(a)(a) (Supp. 1991) states that a family will pay the greater of: (1) 30 percent of the family's monthly adjusted income, (2) 10 percent of the family's monthly income, or (3) the portion of other welfare assistance designed to meet the family's housing costs. Moreover, the district court in 1975 had

brought the Section 8 program within the ambit of *Gautreaux v. Chicago Hous. Auth.* (unreported opinion of 5 May 1975).

10. *Housing and Community Development Act of 1974*, sec. 1437(f) (Supp. IV, 1974).

11. For a discussion of the ways in which HUD administered its programs on an areawide or metropolitan basis, see Leonard S. Rubinowitz and Roger J. Dennis, "School Desegregation versus Public Housing Desegregation: The Local School District and the Metropolitan Housing District," *Urban Law Annual 10* (1975): 145.

12. Alexander Polikoff, Plaintiffs' Counsel, interview by Leonard S. Rubinowitz, Chicago, 1995.

13. Alexander Polikoff, lead counsel for the plaintiff class, explained his views about the role of a lawyer in a class action suit during a congressional hearing chaired by Congresswoman Cardiss Collins, from Chicago's west side:

> *Mrs. Collins:* But you are not representative of all the people because you were neither appointed nor elected to do this.
>
> *Mr. Polikoff:* No representative of a class ever is, as Congressman Conyers will tell you, in a lawsuit. We have 40,000 families. There isn't any person in it or family which could be fairly represented other than in a legal sense in a class action. In that capacity we do represent the interests of that class.
>
> *Mrs. Collins:* Are you confident that you still speak for the plaintiff class?
>
> *Mr. Polikoff:* I was never confident I spoke for the plaintiff class on the day we filed the lawsuit. No lawyer worth his salt would respond affirmatively to that.
>
> *Mrs. Collins:* If it turned out you weren't, what could be done to see that you reflect their views?
>
> *Mr. Polikoff:* There is nobody, Congresswoman, no individual person, no organization who can speak for all of the 40,000 families, black and white, who . . .
>
> *Mrs. Collins:* I am talking about the majority of them.
>
> *Mr. Polikoff:* You don't take votes in class action cases.

U.S. Congress, House Hearings Chaired by Congresswoman Cardiss Collins, on the Impact of the Gautreaux Case, Chicago, Illinois, 1978 (statement of Alexander Polikoff, Plaintiffs' Counsel).

14. Quite different proposals might have surfaced in a more participatory process. In later congressional and court hearings, some Black, inner-city residents argued strongly for putting much-needed housing resources in their neighborhoods rather than facilitating families' moves to white city or suburban areas; ibid. See also *Gautreaux v. Landrieu*, 523 F. Supp. 665, 672–83 (N.D. Ill. 1981) (Fair Hearing Transcripts on the Gautreaux Consent Decree). Others would probably have argued for families having maximum autonomy to receive subsidies wherever they chose to live, regardless of the area's racial composition. In subsequent court testimony, some people objected to being told where to live, especially to moving to the suburbs; *Gautreaux v. Landrieu*,

523 F. Supp. 665, 672–83 (N.D. Ill. 1981). Some large, low-income families, the group that traditionally had the most difficulty in securing appropriate housing, might have pressed for renovating public housing, traditionally the most extensive source of affordable housing for large, low-income families.

15. *Gautreaux v. Landrieu,* 523 F. Supp. 665, 672–83 (N.D. Ill 1981), affirmed by *Gautreaux v. Pierce,* 690 F. 2d 616, 638 (7th Cir. 1982).

16. In one sense, the metropolitan provisions treated city-suburban boundaries as artificial and arbitrary. Since those lines did not significantly affect the families' movement in the private market, they would not limit the mobility of participant families. However, in another sense, the agreement treated the city-suburban boundary as critical, both for expanding opportunities for racial integration and for other benefits plaintiff class families could gain from moving to the suburbs.

17. The initial goals were 100 to 150 units for Cook County and approximately 25 to 40 units for each of the other five counties; "Full Text of Agreement between Plaintiffs and HUD Concerning Implementation of the Gautreaux Supreme Court Decision, 7 June 1976," *Bureau of National Affairs, Current Developments, Housing and Development Reporter* 4, no. 1 (1976), 40 ¶1(d).

18. Ibid., ¶1(a).

19. Some proponents developed "fair share" plans, based on the assumption that accommodation of lower-income households was a fiscal and social burden that should be shared equitably by a region's municipalities. Others stressed the political realities, that middle-class suburban residents would have to be assured of their continued dominance before they would permit the entry of housing for low-income families. The Gautreaux agreement's dispersal provision was consistent with these philosophical and practical approaches to achieving economic integration. For a discussion of regional housing allocation plans for low and moderate-income housing, including the first plan, adopted in 1970, by the Miami Valley Regional Planning Commission in the Dayton, Ohio area, see Rubinowitz, *Low-Income Housing,* 65–84. See also Downs, *Opening Up the Suburbs;* and David Listokin, *Fair Share Housing Allocation* (New Brunswick, N.J.: The Center for Urban Policy Research, Rutgers University, 1976).

20. "Agreement between Plaintiffs and HUD," ¶1(a).

21. Berry, *Open Housing Question,* Part 1. For the text of the Summit Agreement, which provided for the creation of the Leadership Council, see Alan B. Anderson and George W. Pickering, *Confronting the Color Line: The Broken Promise of the Civil Rights Movement in Chicago* (Athens, Georgia: University of Georgia Press, 1986), 441–46.

22. The Leadership Council started early in its history to assist Black families to move to largely white areas, but those early efforts bore little fruit. Few Black families moved through the "Equal Opportunity in Housing" program, which was among the least effective of the agency's undertakings. With that program having terminated, the Leadership Council did not have staff experienced at counseling families or securing access to housing for those families. See Berry, *Open Housing Question,* 19–68.

23. Several Chicago-area public housing agencies carried out a Section 8 certificate exchange program, but only a small number of families moved across jurisdictional boundaries through this initiative.

24. For discussions on why low-income Blacks might be unwilling to move to mostly white, middle-class suburbs, see Downs, *Opening Up the Suburbs*, 43–44, 81–83, 136–37.

25. "Agreement between Plaintiffs and HUD," ¶4.

26. Robert R. Elliott to Alexander Polikoff, Chicago, 1977 (Agreement between Plaintiffs and HUD, 1977 Extension).

27. Michael J. Rich, *Federal Policymaking and the Poor: National Goals, Local Choices, and Distributional Outcomes* (Princeton: Princeton University Press, 1993), 225–33. Most of those suburbs were predominantly white and middle-class. In 1979, Arlington Heights, Mount Prospect, Naperville, Schaumberg, and Skokie had poverty rates less than 3 percent, which placed them among the ten wealthiest "entitlement" communities nationally—municipalities with a population of fifty thousand or more were "entitled" to receive funds if their applications met specified requirements (ibid., 225).

The size of counties' grants depended in part on the population in communities that agreed to cooperate with the county. Although ninety-six Cook County suburbs agreed to participate in the county's block grant program in 1976, five others opted out. The primary reason for declining to participate was the fear that they would be required to accept housing for low- and moderate-income families. In an effort to secure municipalities' cooperation, county officials assured local leaders that they would not receive lower-income housing unless they wanted it.

28. In order to receive CDBG funds, communities had to prepare a plan to provide housing for low- and moderate-income families, including nonresidents who might be "expected to reside" in the community if affordable housing were available; Rich, *Federal Policymaking and the Poor*, 219–20. Arlington Heights, Berwyn, Cicero, Des Plaines, and Oak Lawn officials did not apply for the first-year CDBG grants set aside for their communities. Uncertainty about how the federal government would enforce this provision raised fears that the program would threaten communities' economic and racial homogeneity. Although the five places ranged from mostly working- and middle-class Cicero and Berwyn to quite affluent Arlington Heights, none had significant numbers of poor people. As of 1970, each was 99 percent or more white. Many of the residents were former Chicago residents who said they had fled racially changing neighborhoods and were unwilling to go through the experience again; ibid., 229, 233–34, quoting Jeff Adler and Michele Gaspar, "Why Five Suburbs Refused Federal Funds," *Chicago Tribune*, 14 June 1975, sec. 1, p. 12. Arlington Heights was entitled to $2.2 million over the first six years of the block grant program. The village board voted 6–3 not to apply for the first year, "out of fear that its acceptance would require the village to construct low- and moderate-income housing that could very well be occupied by nonresident minorities" (ibid., 229). Arlington Heights applied for block grant funds in subsequent years.

29. Rich, *Federal Policymaking and the Poor*, 237. At the time, about 30 of

the village's 65,000 residents were Black, and the community had no subsidized housing. A homeowners' association formed to oppose the development secured more than 3,000 signatures on a petition.

The district court ruled against the Metropolitan Housing Development Corporation (MHDC), but the U.S. Court of Appeals for the Seventh Circuit reversed. The Supreme Court upheld the village's zoning against an equal protection challenge, because the plaintiffs had not shown intentional racial discrimination by the village; *Arlington Heights v. Metropolitan Hous. Dev. Corp.*, 429 U.S. 252 (1977). The Court remanded the case for consideration of the applicability of the 1968 Fair Housing Act. The Court of Appeals ruled that if there were no land other than that held by MHDC suitable for assisted housing, then the village's refusal to rezone the property for multifamily housing violated the Fair Housing Act because of its racially discriminatory effect; *Metropolitan Hous. Dev. Corp. v. Arlington Heights*, 558 F. 2d 1283 (7th Cir. 1977). Ultimately, the parties settled the case by agreeing on an alternative site on unincorporated land that the village agreed to annex.

30. "Agreement between Plaintiffs and HUD," ¶1.

31. "Agreement between Plaintiffs and HUD."

CHAPTER FOUR

1. Pro-rating the goal over fifteen months would change the goal to 500. Actual moves reached only about one-third of that figure. Of the 168 families that moved, 146 went to general (white or integrated) areas of the suburbs and 22 moved within Chicago. Eleven went to the city's general area and 11 to the limited area. Sixteen of the 168 moved to one-bedroom units, 90 to two-bedroom units, 58 to three-bedroom units, and 4 to four-bedroom units.

2. *Gautreaux v. Landrieu*, 523 F. Supp. 665, 672–83 (N.D. Ill. 1981), *aff'd, Gautreaux v. Pierce*, 690 F. 2d 616, 638 (7th Cir. 1982). A 1979 HUD report on the program provided part of the basis for the consent decree; see Kathleen A. Peroff, Cloteal L. Davis, and Ronald Jones, *Gautreaux Housing Demonstration: An Evaluation of Its Impact on Participating Households* (Washington, D.C.: Office of Policy Development and Research, HUD, 1979).

3. The 7,100 does not include families assisted through the scattered site program. The decree also mandated that families not relocate into HUD-assisted developments in neighborhoods that were more than 30 percent Black—a requirement already in place for families using Section 8 certificates. Further, to avoid concentrating Gautreaux families in HUD-assisted developments, set-asides for them were limited to between 6 and 12 percent of the units; *Gautreaux v. Landrieu*, 523 F. Supp. at 677.

4. Leonard S. Rubinowitz and Katie Kenny, "Metropolitan Housing Opportunities for Lower-Income Chicago Families: Report on the Gautreaux Demonstration Program, Year 1" (Report for Leadership Council for Metropolitan Open Communities by the Investment Study Group, Center for Urban Affairs, Northwestern University, [1991]), 140–41, n. 25.

5. Kale Williams, interview by Leonard S. Rubinowitz, 10 March 1992; Real Estate Expert, interview by Leonard S. Rubinowitz, 9 March 1992.

6. One Leadership Council real estate counselor described this process as follows:

> After some initial research I began to visit the eligible complexes—those with vacancies in our FMRs. At that time I spoke with the resident manager or rental agent about the program, and left our Section 8 yellow folders . . . and my card. I filled out the apartment data sheet and toured the model, collecting whatever information the complex had available to hand out. Often as I drove, I stopped to "shop" apartments I had not previously called, leaving information.
>
> The next step was a phone call to the resident manager to find out if she was interested in hearing more about the program. She usually indicated that she wished to discuss the program with her property manager or owner to see if he was willing to explore the program further.
>
> We then set up a meeting with the resident manager or the property manager, whoever was empowered to make policy decisions. Most often it was the property manager who had an office away from the complex, sometimes downtown. At this meeting I explained Section 8 as well as the Gautreaux case and the Leadership Council's screening process. I used the enclosed file of materials as well as samples of tenant files. . . . If the property manager agreed to participate, I determined on what basis: how many units, what his qualifications were, who would sign the leases and review the files, etc. I then wrote him a letter outlining the arrangement as I understood it.
>
> Giving him time to inform his resident manager of his decision, I went back to the complex to brief the resident manager on the Section 8 forms and prepare her for the visit of housing counselor and client (memorandum from Mary Messer to Inez Tremain, 18 August 1976).

7. These agencies included the following: in Cook County, the Housing Authority of Cook County, Chicago Housing Authority, Oak Park Housing Authority, Lansing Housing Authority, Cicero Housing Authority, and the Maywood Housing Authority; the DuPage County Housing Authority; the McHenry County Housing Authority; in Lake County, the Lake County Housing Authority, North Chicago Housing Authority, and Waukegan Housing Authority; in Kane County, the Aurora Land Clearance Commission and Elgin Housing Authority, and in Will County, the Joliet Housing Authority. Rubinowitz and Kenny, "Metropolitan Housing Opportunities," 61–62.

8. Housing Authorities would receive their usual fee of 8–1/2 percent of the two-bedroom fair market rent for administration, but their start-up fee would be $100 per unit rather than the usual $275 per unit because of the assistance provided by the Leadership Council.

9. Housing officials in Oak Park, a racially mixed suburb bordering Chicago's west side, wanted assurances that the Gautreaux program would not disturb the community's carefully preserved racial balance. Blacks tended to cluster on the less-expensive east side of the village, adjacent to the city's mostly Black Austin neighborhood. Oak Park officials wanted to keep the number of

families moving in through the program small, and have them move to other parts of the community than the eastern portions.

10. The Waukegan Housing Authority, in an older industrial "satellite city" north of Chicago, may have already had its hands full because it administered one of the region's few sizeable public housing programs as well as a Section 8 program.

11. However, HUD rejected the DuPage County Housing Authority's request to control tenant selection as inconsistent with the Leadership Council's mandate; Rubinowitz and Kenny, "Metropolitan Housing Opportunities," 67–68.

12. A 1979 HUD study of the program found that only 12 percent of eligible families who did not participate in the program desired to live in the suburbs; see Peroff, Davis, and Jones, *Gautreaux Housing Demonstration*, 8, 35–36.

13. Mary Davis, Associate Director, Leadership Council for Metropolitan Open Communities, Presentation at Chicago Area Fair Housing Alliance Seminar, 24 June 1992.

14. The 1979 HUD study found that 43 percent of Gautreaux families said that their source of information about the program was a friend or relative; Peroff, Davis, and Jones, *Gautreaux Housing Demonstration*, 123.

15. Not all of the crowd were part of the demand for Gautreaux. Some were not sure what they were waiting for; some thought there were jobs at the end of the line. See "Multitude Drawn to HUD Offer," *Chicago Defender*, 24 January 1984. See also "Outline 'Dramatic' Need for Housing," *Chicago Defender*, 26 January 1984.

This situation was in stark contrast to the experience of Parma, Ohio, a suburb of Cleveland. A federal judge ruled in 1980 that Parma had deliberately excluded Blacks from settling there, and ordered the city to take steps, including advertising for minorities, to remedy the situation. By 1988 only three Black families had responded, with only 57 phone calls made even to inquire about housing for minorities; "Integration Proves Elusive in an Ohio Suburb," *New York Times*, 30 October 1988, sec. 1; "Suburb Runs Ads for Minorities, But Few Respond," *New York Times*, 26 September 1988, sec. 1. However, Parma was just one city, as opposed to the several counties involved in Gautreaux. Also, while the suburbs were part of the remedy in Gautreaux, they were not specifically cited as the problem, as was Parma; see Jeff Potts, "The Gautreaux Program: Factors Affecting Scale and Replicability" (unpublished paper on file with the author, n.d.).

16. Mary Davis, "The Gautreaux Assisted Housing Program," in *Housing Markets and Residential Mobility*, ed. G. Thomas Kingsley and Margery Austin Turner (Washington, D.C.: The Urban Institute Press, 1993).

17. In response, the Council invited reporters to observe the telephone lottery. The media presence and the participation of recognizable people such as Vincent Lane, then the head of CHA, and Alex Polikoff, the plaintiffs' lawyer, helped alleviate those suspicions.

18. Davis, "The Gautreaux Assisted Housing Program," 246.

19. However, the call-ins may have overestimated the numbers of families who were both eligible for the program and interested in moving through it. Some people did not fully recognize the implications of moving to the suburbs until well after they applied. An extreme example involved one of the first clients in the program, who changed her mind about moving while en route to her new apartment in virtually all-white DuPage County, about twenty-five miles from the city. Stuck in a rush hour traffic jam, she reconsidered her move because she was heavily involved in her church and had anticipated at least weekly trips to the city.

20. The permissible destinations varied at different times, depending on housing and certificate availability in the city and suburbs, respectively, and Leadership Council policy (Williams, interview).

21. A 1979 HUD study of the Gautreaux program found that 34 percent of participants judged good schools to be the most important factor in their decision to move; Peroff, Davis, and Jones, *Gautreaux Housing Demonstration*, 105.

22. William J. Wilson, *The Truly Disadvantaged: The Inner City, the Underclass, and Public Policy* (Chicago: The University of Chicago Press, 1987), 50; Gregory D. Squires et al., *Chicago: Race, Class, and the Response to Urban Decline* (Philadelphia: Temple University Press, 1987). See also Chicago Tribune Staff, *The American Millstone: An Examination of the Nation's Permanent Underclass* (Chicago: Contemporary Books, 1986); Alex Kotlowitz, *There Are No Children Here: The Story of Two Boys Growing Up In the Other America* (New York: Doubleday, 1991), 5; Mayer and Wade, *Growth of a Metropolis*; Sylvester Monroe and Peter Goldman, *Brothers: Black and Poor: A True Story of Courage and Survival* (New York: Ballantine Books, 1989).

23. Sections of some CHA high-rises were vacant and boarded up. In 1980, Chicago public housing complexes contained ten of the country's most concentrated areas of poverty. A four-block area of Robert Taylor Homes was the poorest community in the country; this segment's population of 5,681 had a per capita income of only $1,339; Squires et al., *Race, Class, and the Response to Urban Decline*, 94. Other accounts confirm the dramatic deterioration in the conditions of life in Chicago's public housing developments from the 1950s and 1960s to the 1970s and 1980s. See also Monroe and Goldman, *Brothers*, 295–96; "Dynamite or Condo: Fears Haunt Cabrini-Green," *Chicago Defender*, 5 July 1980; "Slayings Spark Citizen's Protest," *Chicago Defender*, 30 July 1985; "Complaints Rage At ABLA: 18 Vacant Apartments a Menace to Residents," *Chicago Defender*, 28 July 1986; "CHA Neglect Linked to Infant Mortality Rate," *Chicago Defender*, 11 August 1986. In the 1990s, CHA demolished many of the high-rises it had built in the 1950s and 1960s.

24. See, for example, Davis, "The Gautreaux Assisted Housing Program."

25. See "CHA Rent Subsidy Helping Families Find Decent Housing," *Chicago Daily News*, 25 May 1976; "130 Black Families Go Suburban in Test Plan," *Chicago Tribune*, 2 July 1977; "Project Dwellers Eye the Suburbs," *Chicago Sun-Times*, 24 August 1977; "Children from the Slums Get a Chance in the Suburbs," *Washington Post*, 11 June 1988, sec. A, 1; "U.S. Backed Chicago

Test Offers Suburban Life to Ghetto Blacks," *New York Times*, 22 May 1978, sec. A; "Some Chicagoans Are Moved Out of Projects Into a Future," *New York Times*, 3 February 1989, sec. A, 1.

The Chicago papers reported the results of research on families' experience in the program, done at Northwestern University's Center for Urban Affairs and Policy Research. See "Black Pupils Chalk Up Success in Suburbs," *Chicago Tribune*, 16 December 1981, 1; Editorial, *Chicago Tribune*, 22 December 1985, sec. 3; Editorial, *Chicago Tribune*, 9 May 1990; "Children from Projects Thrive in Suburbs—Study," *Chicago Sun-Times*, 9 October 1991, 1.

26. Peroff, Davis, and Jones, *Gautreaux Housing Demonstration*, 105.

27. Many families in the CHA's regular Section 8 program opted for "in-place" subsidies rather than moving. This suggests that subsidies, not relocation, were primarily important for many low-income families.

28. Mark Sheft, *A Place to Call Home: The Crisis in Housing for the Poor* (Washington, D.C.: Center on Budget and Policy Priorities, 1991).

29. Ibid., 18–19. In 1987, 26 percent of Chicago renters paid at least half of their income for housing. Among poor renters in the Chicago metropolitan area, the figure was 69 percent (ibid., 8). Poor Black households paid almost 80 percent of their income for housing in 1983; James W. Fossett and Gary Orfield, "Market Failure and Federal Policy: Low Income Housing in Chicago," in *Divided Neighborhoods: Changing Patterns of Racial Segregation*, ed. Gary A. Tobin (Newbury Park, Calif.: Sage Publications, 1987), 170–71.

30. Sheft, *A Place to Call Home*, 18–19.

31. Ibid., 35–37. The largest possible AFDC benefit, the primary source of public assistance for plaintiff class members, for a Chicago-area family of three with no other income, declined 54 percent between 1970 and 1991 (adjusting for inflation). By 1991, the fair market rent for a two-bedroom apartment in the Chicago metropolitan area was approximately 75 percent higher than the maximum AFDC grant for a family of three.

32. Fossett and Orfield, "Market Failure," 171–72. The loss of housing stock, primarily through demolition, exceeded additions through housing programs; Sheft, *A Place to Call Home*, 17–18. At the same time, middle-class migration to the suburbs declined, thus slowing the filtering process by which most low-income people secure their housing; Fossett and Orfield, "Market Failure," 165. Reducing the demand pressure, however, was a decrease in the number of low-income and Black people migrating from the South; Fossett and Orfield, "Market Failure," 162.

33. Sheft, *A Place to Call Home*, 21–22.

34. Sheft, *A Place to Call Home*, 23. In 1985, the CHA closed the Section 8 waiting list because it was receiving five thousand new applications per day. As of summer 1994, the closed list contained 46,812 names; Peterson and Williams, "Housing Mobility," 29.

35. One family persuaded an on-site manager to accept them as tenants after the Council had been unable to persuade the management firm to join the program.

36. Francis J. Cronin and David W. Rasmussen, "Mobility," in *Housing*

Vouchers for the Poor: Lessons from a National Experiment, ed. Raymond J. Struyk and Mark Bendick, Jr. (Washington, D.C.: Urban Institute Press, 1981), 107, 127–28; Glen Weisbrod and Avis Vidal, "Housing Search Barriers for Low-Income Renters," *Urban Affairs Quarterly* 16 (1981): 465.

37. John Yinger, "The Racial Dimension of Urban Housing Markets in the 1980s," in *Divided Neighborhoods: Changing Patterns of Racial Segregation,* ed. Gary A. Tobin (Newbury Park, Calif.: Sage Publications, 1987), 43, 46–47.

38. See Albert O. Hirschman, *Exit, Voice and Loyalty: Responses to Decline in Firms, Organizations, and States* (Cambridge, Mass.: Harvard University Press, 1990). Hirschman noted that moving into better neighborhoods was for Americans a "paradigm of problem-solving."

39. There were at least two particularly egregious incidents in 1984, unrelated to the Gautreaux Program; see Squires et al., *Race, Class, and the Response to Urban Decline,* 102. Stories about similar racial incidents also appeared in Chicago's Black newspaper, the *Chicago Defender.* See "Harass Family in Calumet Park," *Chicago Defender,* 10 September 1977; "Open Housing: A Nightmare," *Chicago Defender,* 10 May 1984; "Racists Hit 13 Homes in 85," *Chicago Defender,* 23 January 1986. See also "Racial Attack on Bus Driver Called Isolated Suburb Incident," *Chicago Tribune,* 24 May 1990, 9.

40. See Earnest D. Washington, "A Componential Theory of Culture and Its Implications for African-American Identity," *Equity and Excellence* 2 (1988): 24. Washington argues that too much difference between the culture of the community from which a student comes and that of the school which he or she attends may harm the child's development. See also Geneva Gay and Willie L. Baber, eds., *Expressively Black: The Cultural Bias of Ethnic Identity* (New York: Praeger Publishers, 1987).

41. Other literature that casts doubt on Blacks' willingness to move to mostly white areas includes T. F. Pettigrew, *Attitudes on Race and Housing: A Social-Psychological View* (National Academy of Sciences, 1973); Reynolds Farley, S. Bianchi, and D. Colasanto, "Chocolate City, Vanilla Suburbs: Will the Trend Toward Racially Separate Communities Continue?" *Social Science Research* 7 (1978): 319, 331. See also Reynolds Farley, S. Bianchi, and D. Colasanto, "Barriers to Racial Integration of Neighborhoods: The Detroit Case," *Annals of American Academy of Political and Social Science* (January 1979): 197–213; Joe T. Darden, "Choosing Neighbors and Neighborhoods: The Role of Race in Housing Preference," in *Divided Neighborhoods: Changing Patterns of Racial Segregation,* ed. Gary A. Tobin (Newbury Park, Calif.: Sage Publications, 1987), 15; G. Taylor, "Housing, Neighborhoods and Race Relations: Recent Survey Evidence," *Annals of American Academy of Political and Social Science* (January 1979): 26–40; Struyk and Bendick, *Housing Vouchers for the Poor,* 123; Paul B. Fischer, *Is Housing Mobility an Effective Anti-Poverty Strategy? An Examination of the Cincinnati Experience* (Cincinnati: Stephen H. Wilder Foundation, 1991), 5; Michael H. Schill, "Deconcentrating the Inner City Poor," *Chicago Kent Law Review* 67 (1991): 795.

Surveys of Blacks in Chicago and elsewhere have indicated an interest in living in communities that were about half-white and half-Black; see U.S. Department of Housing and Urban Development, *Survey on Quality of Community Life: A Data Book* (1978), 298–99. Very few such communities existed in Chicago, and they did not meet the Gautreaux program's integration goals.

42. Some participants said that their family and friends warned them about potential violence or discrimination. Suzanne Franklin was told that "immediately there would be cross burnings and lynchings," and Hazel Tucker was warned that "the water would be cut off, and I wouldn't have any water."

43. Williams, interview.

44. At a 1981 hearing regarding the consent decree between the plaintiffs and HUD, some residents of Black neighborhoods spoke out against the Gautreaux program's remedy, preferring instead that housing be developed in their neighborhoods. Others stated that they didn't want to move to the suburbs, where they knew no one and where access to needed services and transportation was extremely difficult (testimony of Jerome Butler, representing six plaintiff class members objecting to the consent decree, Fair Hearing transcripts, 19 January 1981, 10).

45. A HUD study estimated the supply of housing potentially available for the program—those meeting Section 8 requirements and Fair Market Rent criteria; see Peroff, Davis, and Jones, *Gautreaux Housing Demonstration*, 3, 43–49.

The analysis estimated the overall amount of rental housing in the region, vacancy rates, and units renting within HUD's Fair Market Rent ceilings—especially in mostly white and suburban areas. It estimated that about 73,500 rental units were vacant at any given time, a vacancy rate of 6.7 percent. Almost three-fourths of those vacancies (71 percent) were in the city of Chicago, and almost 40 percent of the total (12,000) were in parts of the city with 30 percent or more minority households—roughly the "limited area." An unknown number of vacancies were in "limited" areas in the suburbs. That still left as many as 19,000 vacancies, on average, that were suitable for Section 8 and located in predominantly white areas. Some of the vacancies were not likely to attract plaintiff class members because of their great distance from the city and lack of public transportation (ibid., 48–49).

However, the HUD study did not consider turnover, and therefore underestimated the amount of housing potentially available for the program. Appreciation goes to Professor Richard Sander for pointing this out.

46. Only those units that met Section 8 housing quality requirements and rented at or below 120 percent of HUD's Fair Market Rents (the program permitted up to 20 percent adjustment over the normal maximums) were potentially available to the Gautreaux program.

47. HUD required the Leadership Council to "avoid undue concentration of assisted families."

48. Chicago's public housing has generally accommodated a disproportionate share of large families by including a large percentage of apartments with three or more bedrooms. In 1976, 14,009 of the CHA's 30,518 family-type apartments had three or more bedrooms, about 45 percent. *CHA Facts 1977: Chicago Housing Authority Annual Report 1976* (Chicago Housing Author-

ity, 1978), 30. At that time, 28 percent of the applicant families required three-, four-, or five-bedroom apartments (ibid., 28).

49. The fair market rent concept was a Congressional compromise between providing low-income families access to decent housing in the private market and keeping the subsidy costs reasonable; Barry G. Jacobs et al., *Guide to Federal Housing Programs* (Washington, D.C.: The Bureau of National Affairs, 1982), 27–28; R. Allen Hays, *The Federal Government and Urban Housing: Ideology and Change in Public Policy*, 2d ed. (Albany: State University of New York Press, 1995), 140–41. Congress did not want poor people to have better accommodations than middle-class households because that would raise fairness questions and undermine support for the program (ibid., 159–60, 167–71).

50. Davis, "The Gautreaux Assisted Housing Program," 250–51; Real Estate Expert, interview by Leonard S. Rubinowitz, Chicago, Ill., 9 March 1992.

51. HUD can establish subregional fair market rents to reflect differing market rents within regions; see 42 U.S.C. 1437f(c)(1) (1988); 24 C.F.R. 888.113 (1991).

52. By the early 1990s, HUD permitted higher ceilings for northwest Cook County, thus facilitating expanded access there; but the DuPage County fair market rents precluded access to much of the rental housing. DuPage County's own Section 8 program absorbed most of the rental units within the fair market rents (Williams, interview; Davis, presentation).

53. Peterson and Williams, "Housing Mobility," 31.

54. *Gautreaux v. Landrieu*, 523 F. Supp. at 677. During the late 1970s and early 1980s, these set-asides were an important source of housing for the program. The federal government drastically cut the funding for construction programs during the 1980s. Nationwide, starts of subsidized new construction units peaked in 1971 at 441,000. Funding cuts beginning in 1981 caused a rapid decline of subsidized housing production, resulting in only 70,000 starts in 1985; George Sternlieb and David Listokin, "A Review of National Housing Policy," in *Housing America's Poor*, ed. Peter D. Salins (Chapel Hill, N.C.: The University of North Carolina Press, 1987), 29. Consequently, by the early 1990s, set-asides provided only a trickle of apartments for the Gautreaux program.

55. Jacobs et al., *Guide to Federal Housing Programs*, 45. See Michael A. Quinn, "Financial Tradeoffs and Landlord Participation in the Section 8 Rental Assistance Program," *American Planning Association Journal* (winter 1986): 33.

56. Davis, "The Gautreaux Assisted Housing Program."

57. In late 1976, a metropolitan daily newspaper ran a story on a Gautreaux family that had just moved to the suburbs and included the name of their development. As a result of the unwanted publicity, the management firm declined to make units available in its other developments.

58. In order to prevent concentration of these families, set-asides were limited to between 6 and 12 percent of the units in HUD-assisted developments. *Gautreaux v. Landrieu*, 523 F. Supp. at 677.

59. One study found that 58 percent of families with children experienced discrimination while searching for housing in Chicago, in spite of federal and state prohibitions; see Lawyers' Committee for Better Housing, Leadership Council for Metropolitan Open Communities and Metropolitan Tenants Organization, *No Children Allowed: A Report of the Obstacles Faced by Renters with Children in the Chicago Rental Housing Market* (1991), 18.

60. Real Estate Expert, interview.

61. *Fair Housing Act of 1968*, U.S. *Code*, vol. 42, secs. 3601–19.

62. Even those who are experienced at detecting racial discrimination cannot always discern subtle forms of bias. For example, two of the Leadership Council's professional "testers," one Black and one white, participated in a 1991 experiment in cooperation with the network television show *Prime Time*. The show used hidden cameras to videotape visits by each person over a period of two weeks to employment agencies, apartment buildings, car dealers, and stores in St. Louis. It found greater differences in treatment than either of them would have realized; "True Colors," *Prime Time* (ABC), 26 September 1991.

63. Some landlords participated initially on a very limited basis, accepting a family or two in a large development. This provided an opportunity to observe the impact of the tenants' presence. One of the largest Chicago-area management firms initially participated in the Gautreaux program as part of a settlement in a racial discrimination case, but it dropped out after a Black person was murdered near one of its white-area developments where a Gautreaux family lived. The family was not implicated in the murder, but the firm's concern about adverse publicity—because the family and the murder victim were both Black—led it to leave the Gautreaux program for a number of years.

64. Real Estate Expert #2, interview by Leonard S. Rubinowitz, Chicago, Ill., 9 April 1992.

65. One study revealed that landlords believe that maintaining Section 8 rental units is more expensive than typical market rental units, either because of the strict and continuous enforcement of quality standards or because Section 8 tenants more often damage the units. Fair market rents must compensate for these real or perceived increased costs for landlords to participate. Quinn, "Financial Tradeoffs," 33, 38–41.

66. 42 U.S.C. §1437f(t) (1988). Congress suspended this provision in 1996. U.S. *Statutes at Large* 110 (1996): 1327.

67. The owner may not evict a Section 8 tenant without filing a court action; see 24 C.F.R. 882.215 (1991). And the owner cannot terminate the tenancy except for serious violation of the terms of the lease, or for violation of the law, or for "other good cause"; 42 U.S.C. §1437f(d)(1)(B)(ii) (1988). Within 90 days of any termination, the landlord must submit a written notice to HUD and the tenant, so that HUD can determine the legality of the termination, or take steps to avoid it; 42 U.S.C. 1437f(c)(9) (1988).

68. Davis, presentation; Williams, interview. Conclusions on landlords' motivations must be tentative, because of the limited amount of direct evidence and reliance instead on impressions from program administrators and

participants, assessments by real estate experts and general data on Chicago area housing discrimination by race, income, and family size.

69. 42 U.S.C. §1437a(b)(1); 24 C.F.R. §882.109 (1991).

70. 42 U.S.C. §1439(a) (1977).

71. Letter from Jack Pahl, Chairman, Mayors' Steering Committee, Regional Housing Coalition, to All Mayors, Village Presidents, and County Board Presidents in the Chicago Region, August 1976.

72. While officials from Maywood, a largely Black, working-class western suburb, asked not to participate because it would upset the suburb's demographic balance, the village had already undergone substantial racial transition. Schaumberg, a largely white, rapidly developing, northwest community, also sought not to participate, because it already had subsidized housing. Officials from Joliet, an older, larger "satellite" city, Evanston, an older, racially and economically mixed, inner-ring northern suburb, and Crystal Lake and Woodstock, small, outer-ring mostly white communities, wanted to limit the size of the program and share the responsibility with other areas, but did not ask to be excluded.

73. Downs, *Opening Up the Suburbs*, 94–102. Downs refers to this as "middle-class dominance," the desire of an economic class to maintain dominance in its neighborhood.

74. The mayors were part of the Regional Housing Coalition, which officially ceased operation in 1975, citing the declining role of local elected officials in federal subsidy programs. Memorandum from Jack Pahl, Kale Williams, and Harry N. Gottlieb to the Board of Directors, 17 June 1975.

75. Resegregation of neighborhoods and communities occurred in many Chicago neighborhoods and some southern and western suburbs. See Berry, *Open Housing Question*, 255–57; Carol Goodwin, *The Oak Park Strategy: Community Control of Racial Change* (Chicago: University of Chicago Press, 1979); and Richard Sander, "Individual Rights and Demographic Realities: The Problem of Fair Housing," *Northwestern University Law Review* 82 (1988): 874. In a number of Chicago suburbs, local officials and community activists organized "integration maintenance" activities to keep their communities racially mixed and prevent resegregation. See Schrag and Casuso, "A Delicate Balance"; and Alexander Polikoff, "Sustainable Integration or Inevitable Resegregation: The Troubling Question," in *Housing Desegregation and Federal Policy*, ed., John M. Goering (Chapel Hill: University of North Carolina Press, 1986), 43.

76. Peterson and Williams, "Housing Mobility," 34, n. 6.

77. Barbara Garland Polikoff, "A Ticket Out of Misery," *Chicago Magazine* January 1987, 97–99; Barbara Garland, "Cabrini-Green to Willow Creek," *Chicago Magazine*, June 1977. There were critical op ed pieces as well, but the criticism was about the harm to Blacks and Black communities, not the threat to the suburbs. See also "Alice Doesn't Live Here," *60 Minutes* (CBS), 19 December 1993; "Gautreaux Program," *The Donohue Show* (NBC) 11 January 1994.

78. Chicago Tribune.

79. Local officials found block grants especially attractive because they

gave them a great deal of discretion in allocating the money. Rich, *Federal Policymaking and the Poor*, 219.

80. Peterson and Williams, "Housing Mobility," 30. HUD's designating certificates for particular geographical areas also constrained the Leadership Council's and families' flexibility in seeking housing, perhaps affecting moving rates as well.

81. See Alexander Polikoff, "Housing Policy and Urban Poverty," in Center for Housing Policy, *New Beginnings Project: A First Report* (Washington, D.C., 1994), 93.

82. Peterson and Williams, "Housing Mobility," 30.

83. A 1979 HUD study estimated that of the 43,374 families then eligible for the program, 22,655 were notified. Of those, 6,484 gave positive responses, 3,190 were invited to briefing sessions, 1,823 attended the briefings, 1,109 were visited at home, 971 visited housing sites, 487 applied for housing, and 455 were placed through March of 1979. *Gautreaux Housing Demonstration*, 36.

84. Peterson and Williams, "Housing Mobility," 30, based on Leadership Council estimates.

85. The Council was concerned that any certificates made available for the city would be used up quickly because so many families wanted to stay in Chicago. Others would then be frustrated and disappointed. Thus, the Council tried to equalize the situation as well as serve its goal of assisting families to move to predominately white suburbs. Davis, interview. As of mid-1994, however, about 2,600 Gautreaux families had moved within the city to integrated as well as predominantly Black neighborhoods. In the first several years, racial locational restrictions did not apply to project-based subsidies, so Gautreaux families moved into HUD-assisted developments in Black neighborhoods. The 1981 consent decree specified that project-based subsidies would be available only in predominantly white areas.

86. The most common destination was Northwest Cook County, a largely middle-income, predominantly white area experiencing great population and job growth.

87. Peterson and Williams, "Housing Mobility," 32, table 3.

88. The second round of interviews had far fewer accounts of negative racial experiences. There seem to be several possible explanations for that change: (1) much of this may suggest easing of racial tensions and problems over time, as people got to know each other as individuals; (2) reduced sample size may produce fewer accounts; (3) those who reported racial problems in the first round may have made up a disproportionate share of the attrition; (4) there may have been underreporting of negative racial experiences in the second round compared to the first round because people coped with the past by focusing on a better present and repressing or denying the earlier negative experiences.

89. Hank Zuba, Carol Hendrix, Almetta Rollins, Julie Fernandez, and Dolores Irvin.

CHAPTER FIVE

1. Most research on low-income Black families has focused on the inner city, including a great deal of writing about Chicago. See Wilson, *The Truly Disadvantaged*; Dempsey Travis, *An Autobiography of Black Chicago* (Chicago: Urban Research Institute, 1981), and *An Autobiography of Black Politics* (Chicago: Urban Research Press, 1987).

Alex Kotlowitz's *There Are No Children Here* looks at an all-Black Chicago public housing high-rise complex, focusing on a woman and two of her children who live there. Nicholas Lemann's *The Promised Land: The Great Black Migration and How It Changed America* (New York: Alfred A. Knopf, 1991), chronicles several generations of a family in Chicago's public housing. Lee Rainwater described life in public housing in St. Louis in the 1960s, in *Behind Ghetto Walls* (Chicago: Aldine Publishing, 1970). Carol Stack's *All Our Kin: Strategies for Survival in a Black Community* (New York: Harper & Row Publishers, 1974) is from the same era.

John Langston Gwaltney's *Drylongso: A Self-Portrait of Black America* (New York: New Press, 1993), brings together the narratives of "ordinary" Black people living together in a number of Eastern cities. The stories of inner-city children are told through their own words and pictures in Linda Waldman, comp., *My Neighborhood: The Words and Pictures of Inner-City Children* (Chicago: Hyde Park Bank Foundation, 1993). Sylvester Monroe's and Peter Goldman's *Brothers: Black and Poor—A True Story of Courage and Survival* (New York: Ballantine Books, 1989) and Mitchell Duneier's *Slim's Table: Race, Respectability, and Masculinity* (Chicago: University of Chicago Press, 1992) tell of the lives of Black men in Chicago, the former focusing on a group of men who grew up together in the Robert Taylor Homes public housing complex and the latter about a group of working men on the city's South Side.

Most accounts of middle-class suburbia emphasize the experiences of middle-class whites. See Herbert J. Gans, *The Levittowners: Ways of Life and Politics in a New Suburban Community* (New York: Vintage Books, 1967); William H. Whyte, *The Organization Man* (Garden City, N.Y.: Doubleday, 1956), about Park Forest, south of Chicago.

2. John Gehm's *Bringing It Home* (Chicago: Chicago Review Press, 1984) discusses an effort which bears some resemblance to the Gautreaux program and which also assisted families to move out of Chicago's public housing. However, the scale was very different, with only six families moving out of one development—Cabrini-Green. The families moved to Valparaiso, Indiana, a virtually all-white community which is well beyond the Chicago metropolitan area. Also, the Valparaiso families purchased homes rather than renting, which required special financing and made the effort highly visible.

3. Section 8 subsidies have enabled low-income families to move from predominantly poor neighborhoods to working-class or even middle-class communities, but rarely have they resulted in moves to predominantly white middle-class suburbs. See Michael Vernarelli, "Where Should HUD Locate Assisted Housing? The Evolution of Fair Housing Policy," in *Housing Desegregation and Federal Policy*, ed. John Goering (Chapel Hill: University of North

Carolina Press, 1986), 214–34; Robert Gray and Steven Tursky, "Location and Racial/Ethnic Occupancy Patterns for HUD-Subsidized Family Housing in Ten Metropolitan Areas," in *Housing Desegregation and Federal Policy*, 235–52. Earlier programs, including public housing itself, as well as the Rent Supplement program and Section 236 rent subsidies, facilitated a degree of economic integration, but the Gautreaux program's racial and economic integration exceeded that of earlier programs.

4. Mari Matsuda, "When the First Quail Calls: Multiple Consciousness as Jurisprudential Method," *Women's Rights Law Reporter* 14 (1992): 297.

5. Julie Kaufmann, "Low-Income Youth in White Suburbs: Education and Employment Outcomes" (Ph.D. diss., Northwestern University, 1991), 21.

6. Twenty-five percent of the suburban group had not completed high school, 28 percent had high school diplomas, 9 percent had post–high school training such as nursing or technical school, and 38 percent had attended some college. Twenty percent of the city group had no high school diploma, while 37 percent had graduated from high school, 4 percent had post–high school training and 37 percent had some college. Less than 2 percent of the women from either group had graduated from college.

7. Peroff, Davis, and Jones, *Gautreaux Housing Demonstration;* cf. Marilynn J. Kulieke, "The Effects of Residential Integration on Children's School and Neighborhood Environments, Social Interaction, and School Outcomes" (Ph.D. diss., Northwestern University, 1985), 51.

8. James E. Rosenbaum and Susan J. Popkin, "Employment and Earnings of Low-Income Blacks Who Move to Middle-Class Suburbs," in *The Urban Underclass*, ed. Christopher Jencks and Paul E. Peterson (Washington, D.C.: Brookings Institute, 1991).

9. James E. Rosenbaum, Stefanie DeLuca, and Shafra Miller, *The Long-Term Effects of Residential Mobility on AFDC Receipt* (Institute for Policy Research, Northwestern University, 1999).

10. Interviewers recorded respondents' answers to the open-ended items verbatim, and each interview was taped as a back-up. The open-ended items were entered on FactFinder, a database management system for the Macintosh which allows the data to be sorted by themes and keywords. To get a representative sampling of participants, the sampling design was stratified by the year the respondent first entered the Gautreaux program and by location—suburb versus Chicago. Respondents who moved in three years—1980, 1983, and 1986—were randomly selected. The refusal rate on interviews was less than 7 percent. There are no systematic differences between the interview and survey respondents, but the interview sample is used only for qualitative analysis. Responses to self-administered questionnaires were consistent with those from the in-person interviews, suggesting that the respondents were able to read and understand the questions and that they gave accurate and truthful answers.

11. Peroff, Davis, and Jones, *Gautreaux Housing Demonstration;* Kulieke, "The Effects of Residential Integration," 51.

12. Peroff, Davis, and Jones, *Gautreaux Housing Demonstration.*

13. U.S. Dept. of Health and Human Services, *Characteristics and Finan-*

cial Circumstances of AFDC Recipients 1986 (Washington, D.C.: U.S. Dept. Of Health and Human Services, 1987).

14. To address this issue further, Gautreaux participants were compared with a random sample of AFDC recipients in Chicago; Susan J. Popkin, "Welfare: A View from the Bottom" (Ph.D. diss., Northwestern University, 1988). Gautreaux participants are similar to the Chicago AFDC sample in their time on public assistance (above seven years) and their marital status (about 45 percent never married, 10 percent currently married). However, Gautreaux participants are less likely to be high school dropouts (39 versus 50 percent), tend to be older (median age of 34 versus 31), and have fewer children (mean of 2.5 versus 3). They are also more likely to be second generation AFDC recipients (44 versus 32 percent). In sum, while Gautreaux participants may be slightly higher status than the average public assistance recipient, most differences are not large.

15. Other research on the Gautreaux program examined women's employment experience before and after their moves within the city or to the suburbs. See James E. Rosenbaum et al., "Can the Kerner Commission's Housing Strategy Improve Employment, Education, and Social Integration for Low-Income Blacks?" *North Carolina Law Review* 71 (June 1993); Rosenbaum and Popkin, "Employment and Earnings of Low-Income Blacks," 342–56.

16. The complexity of these stories suggests the need to avoid oversimplified "good" or "bad" assessments. Sarah Lawrence Lightfoot, *I've Known Rivers: Lives of Loss and Liberation* (Reading, Mass.: Addison-Wesley Publishing, 1994).

17. In the 1982 study, five women who were contacted declined to be interviewed. One interview ended prematurely, at the woman's request.

18. Wilson, *The Truly Disadvantaged.*

CHAPTER SIX

1. From 1979 to 1988, Chicago averaged more than twenty-five murders per hundred thousand residents, ranking eighth among the largest cities in the country, above New York and Philadelphia. U.S. Dept. of Justice, *Uniform Crime Reports for the United States, 1980–89* (Washington, D.C.: Government Printing Office). The crime statistics reported throughout this chapter—from the late 1970s to the early 1980s—encompass the time period in which families moved to the suburbs and both sets of interviews were conducted. While communities differed, the crime data and trends reflect the overall picture of safety in Chicago and in the suburbs, and the changes in the metropolitan Chicago area over time.

2. In 1983, for example, more than half of the city's murders and assaults took place in seven of twenty-four police districts, areas with high percentages of low-income Black and Latino residents; Wilson, *The Truly Disadvantaged,* 25.

In 1988, residents of Chicago public housing reported a 50 percent higher rate of violent crime victimization than residents of the city as a whole. James Garbarino, Kathleen Kostelny, and Nancy Dubrow, *No Place to Be a Child: Growing Up in a War Zone* (Lexington, Mass.: Lexington Books, 1991), 135.

See also James Garbarino et al., *Children in Danger: Coping with the Consequences of Community Violence* (San Francisco: Jossey Bass, 1992), 46.

3. Specifically, 11 percent of the city's murders, 10 percent of its aggravated assaults, and 9 percent of its rapes took place in the Robert Taylor Homes. Garbarino, Kostelny, and Dubrow, *No Place to Be a Child*, 133; Wilson, *The Truly Disadvantaged*, 25.

Other CHA complexes experienced similar levels of violent crime. In 1981, following a series of murders in the Cabrini-Green development, former Mayor Jane Byrne moved into an apartment there for three weeks to try to bring the violence under control. "Byrne Moves into Cabrini; Gang Raided," *Chicago Tribune*, 1 April 1981, sec. 1.

4. According to a *Chicago Tribune* analysis of 1990 Chicago crime statistics, the Wentworth police district, which includes the Robert Taylor Homes and Stateway Gardens, has the highest rate of homicides, sexual assaults, robberies, and serious assaults and the second highest rate of burglaries among the city's twenty-five police districts. The statistics include 99 homicides, 318 sexual assaults, 3,686 robberies (2,186 were armed robberies), 3,707 serious assaults (including 1,200 shootings), and 1,886 burglaries. "City's Top Crime Rates Still Haunt Poor Areas," *Chicago Tribune*, 15 April 1991, sec. 1, p. 1, North Sports Final edition.

5. Alex Kotlowitz chronicles the struggles of LaJoe Rivers and her children, including eleven-year-old Lafayette and nine-year-old Pharoah, amidst the violence and gang influences in the Henry Horner Homes public housing development in Chicago in the late 1980s; Kotlowitz, *There Are No Children Here*.

6. Police departments may wrongly "unfound" a reported crime (determine a crime to be "false or baseless") and fail to press charges for a variety of administrative and political reasons. Studies show some police departments may unfound the crime of rape, for example, by 50 percent. See Margaret T. Gordon and Stephanie Riger, *The Female Fear* (New York: Free Press, 1989), 34; Wesley G. Skogan and Michael G. Maxfield, *Coping with Crime: Individual and Neighborhood Reactions* (Beverly Hills: Sage Publications, 1981), 28–29.

7. Perhaps the most significant limitation of crime statistics is that they reflect only crimes reported to police. Victimization surveys, which focus on victims and their experience with crime, may include crimes that are both reported and unreported to police. See U.S. Dept. of Justice, Bureau of Justice Statistics, *Report to the Nation on Crime and Justice*, 2d ed. (March 1988), 11.

Robert F. Kidd and Ellen F. Chayet, "Why Do Victims Fail to Report? The Psychology of Criminal Victimization," *Journal of Social Issues* 40, no. 1 (1984): 42–48. Victims feel powerless and believe they have no control over events. Contacting the police becomes costly and time-consuming. Many victims report lost time from school or work and long waiting times. Reporting a crime further requires the victim to re-experience feelings of pain and vulnerability. With the belief that little will be accomplished, victims seek to avoid further victimization by the authorities and the criminal justice system.

8. Residents of public housing are acutely aware of the consequences of

reporting crime to police, even fearing that they or their families will be killed. See Garbarino, Kostelny, and Dubrow, *No Place to Be a Child*, 146.

Kidd and Chayet, "Why Do Victims Fail to Report?" 46. Previous studies found that minorities are generally more distrustful of police and public agencies.

9. Wesley G. Skogan, "Fear of Crime and Neighborhood Change," in *Communities and Crime*, vol. 8, ed. Albert J. Reiss Jr., and Michael Tonry (Chicago: University of Chicago Press, 1986), 210. Studies confirm the relationship between people's fear and official crime and victimization rates. One Chicago study found that people who felt unsafe outside at night lived in communities with high crime rates. Another Chicago study found that people who rated specific crimes as "big problems" in their communities lived in areas with higher rates of these specific crimes.

10. Other aspects of inner-city life exacerbated women's fears. Inner-city residents may be especially fearful if they know victims of serious crimes. Skogan and Maxfield, *Coping with Crime*, 166; Skogan, "Fear of Crime," 211. Skogan and Maxfield conclude that victimization plays only a limited role in people's fear of crime; *Coping with Crime*, 60.

11. Skogan and Maxfield, *Coping with Crime*, 69–74.

12. Inner-city residents view observable signs of physical deterioration and social disorganization within a community as warnings of potential dangers which indicate criminal activity. These "signs of disorder" include abandoned and vandalized buildings and automobiles, garbage on streets, vacant lots, gang graffiti, teenagers congregating on street corners, and open drug use. Dennis P. Rosenbaum, "Community Crime Prevention: A Review and Synthesis of the Literature," *Justice Quarterly* 5, no. 3 (Academy of Criminal Justice Sciences, September 1988): 358–59; Skogan and Maxfield, *Coping with Crime*, 91–94; Wesley G. Skogan, *Disorder and Decline: Crime and the Spiral of Decay in American Neighborhoods* (New York: Free Press, 1990), 47–49.

Inadequate maintenance and security contributed to the physical deterioration of CHA buildings, creating more opportunity for crime—and fear—to flourish. A 1984 study of CHA family buildings found that at any one time almost two-thirds of the elevators were broken. See Robert A. Slayton, *Chicago's Public Housing Crisis: Causes and Solutions* (Chicago: Chicago Urban League, Dept. of Research and Planning, 1988), 2.

13. The Chicago Police Department estimated that as of 1992 there were approximately fifty thousand gang members in Chicago and at least twenty thousand additional "wannabes and hangers-on"; see "Inside Look at Violent World of Street Gangs," *Chicago Tribune*, 17 December 1992, sec. 1, p. 6.

High vacancy rates allowed public housing complexes to become centers of gang activity. While vacancy rates vary by complex and year, buildings in the Robert Taylor Homes averaged about one-fifth vacancy, and Cabrini-Green reached one-third vacancy in 1987. See Slayton, *Chicago's Public Housing Crisis*, 9–13; Nicholas Lemann, "Four Generations in the Projects," *New York Times Magazine*, 13 January 1991. Gang members are attracted to low-occupancy buildings and use empty apartments, particularly on the upper floors of high-rises, to store drugs and guns and shoot at rival gangs. "Compromise Cabrini Plan: Mayor, CHA Boss Detail 'War' Effort," *Chicago Tribune*, 20 October 1992, sec. 1, p. 1. Police report that 80 percent of crime in Chicago public housing is caused by up to 70,000 illegal residents, many of whom are gang members who move into empty apartments or live with girlfriends. "Chicago's Uphill Battle," *Time*, 17 June 1992, 30.

14. In an effort to remove gang members and drug dealers from public housing, the CHA began to conduct surprise sweeps in 1988 for weapons, drugs, and unlawful tenants under a twenty-year-old rule prohibiting guns on CHA premises. In 1990, police confiscated 817 weapons from public housing complexes in Operation Clean Sweep; "Chicago's Uphill Battle."

In 1991, gang violence caused 115 of the 924 reported homicides in Chicago; "Bystanders Paying Price in Gang Wars," *Chicago Tribune*, 27 January 1992, sec. 2, p. 1, North Sports Final edition. In October 1992, following the death of seven-year-old Dantrell Davis from sniper fire as he walked to school—the third fatal shooting of an area child due to gang violence in eight months—Chicago Mayor Richard Daley outlined an eleven-point plan to tighten security at Cabrini-Green and Chicago public housing complexes. "Compromise Cabrini Plan." The plan included vacating and sealing up four low-occupancy, high-rise buildings, conducting sweeps at CHA buildings for weapons, improving lighting, reorganizing police and security, and expanding tenant patrol programs.

15. Rival gangs often controlled neighboring buildings, turning complexes into "war zones," and wielded their power by imposing curfews and terrorizing residents. Garbarino, Kostelny, and Dubrow, *No Place to Be a Child*, 131.

In *The Youth Gang Problem: A Community Approach* (New York: Oxford University Press, 1995), Irving Spergel disputes media and police reports that associate drugs with increasing gang violence. Still, Spergel documents the increase in gang-related violence (p. 33).

16. The striking analogy between gang-controlled urban neighborhoods and war zones has been well-documented. Garbarino, Kostelny, and Dubrow, *No Place to Be a Child*, 131.

17. Elijah Anderson chronicles the interactions of residents in two adjacent urban neighborhoods in an eastern city, including the racially and ethnically diverse and changing community of Village-Northton. He describes the "female old head," who was well respected in the community. Elijah Anderson, *Street Wise: Race, Class, and Change in an Urban Community* (Chicago: University of Chicago Press, 1990), 69–74.

18. LaJoe Rivers warned local gang members that she would call police if they continued to pressure her son Lafayette into joining a gang. "I'll die first before I let them take one of my sons," she said; Kotlowitz, *There Are No Children Here*, 31.

19. Irving A. Spergel et al., *Youth Gangs: Problems and Response, Executive Summary, State 1: Assessment, National Youth Gang Suppression and Intervention Research and Development Program* (School of Social Service Administration, University of Chicago, in cooperation with Office of Juvenile Justice and De-

linquency Prevention, U.S. Justice Department, May 1990), 7. See "Inside Look at Violent World of Street Gangs," *Chicago Sun-Times*, 17 December 1992, 6.

20. Spergel, *Youth Gang Problem*, 97. Spergel argues that the "need for recognition, reputation, or status is the common denominator" among those who join gangs (98).

21. See Lemann, *The Promised Land*, 296, for a discussion of gang recruitment. Spergel generally disputes the assumption that forcible gang recruitment is pervasive. Still, he acknowledges that a child who refuses to join a gang can be attacked and severely injured. Spergel, *Youth Gang Problem*, 91.

22. Garbarino et al., *Children in Danger*, 46; Garbarino, Kostelny, and Dubrow, *No Place to Be a Child*, 135. Throughout the 1980s, the risk of victimization continually increased for public housing residents. Slayton, *Chicago's Public Housing Crisis*, 3. The relationship between the physical design characteristics of public housing and criminal opportunities and activities is well documented in other major cities, as well. See Oscar Newman, *Defensible Space: Crime Prevention Through Urban Design* (New York: Macmillan, 1972).

23. Anderson notes that while some residents leave a changing community, residents who remain develop a "peculiar etiquette for surviving in public places," which he defines as "street wisdom." They develop "a repertoire of ruses and schemes for traveling the streets safely." Anderson, *Street Wise*, 6. See also Wesley G. Skogan, "Disorder, Crime, and Community Decline," in *Communities and Crime Reduction*, ed. Tim Hope and Margaret Shaw (London: HMSO, 1988), 53; Dennis P. Rosenbaum, "Community Crime Prevention," 330–31. Avoidance behaviors are generally more common among people who live in high crime areas or who have been victimized. Dennis P. Rosenbaum, "Community Crime Prevention," 333. While risk-avoidance behaviors are effective in reducing victimization, especially for women and senior citizens, they do not necessarily lower fear. Studies have found that people who restrict their behaviors are significantly more fearful of crime and feel unable to control their environment (333–35).

24. Public housing residents are often unable to avoid the very areas of their buildings and complexes which they most fear. Three-fourths of CHA residents surveyed felt that the high rise buildings were unsafe. Most residents believed that the public spaces in their buildings—hallways and elevators—were dangerous, even during the day. Metropolitan Planning Council Task Force on CHA Rehabilitation and Reinvestment, *Untapped Potentials: The Capacities, Needs and Views of Chicago's Highrise Public Housing Residents* (Chicago: Metropolitan Planning Council, 1986), 33–34.

25. Victimization produces fear and anxiety, particularly about one's safety and security. The experience is often sudden and uncontrollable, and sometimes physically injurious. Such an unpredictable event makes a person feel violated or vulnerable. Kidd and Chayet, "Why Do Victims Fail to Report?" 41–42.

26. Ibid., 42.

27. Arthur J. Lurigio and Patricia A. Resick, "Healing the Psychological Wounds of Criminal Victimization: Predicting Postcrime Distress and Recov-

ery," in *Victims of Crime: Problems, Policies, and Programs*, ed. Arthur J. Lurigio, Wesley G. Skogan, and Robert C. Davis (Newbury Park, Calif.: Sage Publications, 1990), 53–55.

28. Skogan, "Fear of Crime," 216. In *There Are No Children Here*, 12–13, Alex Kotlowitz described residents' isolation in the Henry Horner Homes.

29. Skogan, "Fear of Crime," 215–16.

30. See Dennis P. Rosenbaum, "Community Crime Prevention," 358–59; Skogan, *Disorder and Decline*, 13, 15; Skogan, "Fear of Crime," 215–16.

31. Garbarino, Kostelny, and Dubrow emphasize the difficulties inner-city and public housing residents faced in identifying "the enemy"; *No Place to be a Child*, 145–46.

32. Skogan, "Disorder, Crime, and Community Decline," 53. See also Skogan, "Fear of Crime," 215–16.

33. Skogan, "Disorder, Crime, and Community Decline," 53. Inner-city residents also fail to call police because they fear retaliation by gang members or know the offenders. See Kotlowitz, *There Are No Children Here*, 34–35; Garbarino, Kostelny, and Dubrow, *No Place to Be a Child*, 146.

34. Skogan, *Disorder and Decline*, 13.

35. Skogan and Maxfield, *Coping with Crime*, 245. Although Blacks were more likely to express their desire to move, they reported that they probably would not actually move. Follow-up studies found that many who wanted to move could not.

36. Many inner-city residents, particularly residents of public housing developments, lived in the same communities and often the same apartments, for years. For example, residents surveyed in three CHA complexes lived in CHA housing for an average of twelve years and in their current apartments for eight years. Thirty percent of residents lived in their current apartments from eleven to twenty years; Metropolitan Planning Council Task Force, *Untapped Potentials*, 61.

37. Larry V. Dykstra, *Violent Crimes in Illinois* (Criminal Justice Information Systems and Illinois Law Enforcement Commission, March 1981), 2. In 1972, for example, 94 murders (a rate of 2.7 per 100,000 population) were committed in the combined counties of Cook (minus Chicago), Kane, Lake, DuPage, and Will, as compared to 711 murders (a rate of 21 per 100,000) in Chicago. See Illinois Department of Law Enforcement, *Crime in Illinois*, (compilation of statistics for years 1975–91, prepared by the Bureau of Identification).

38. Reported violent crime declined in Chicago in 1975; nonetheless, murder was six times more likely in the city than the suburbs, rape almost four times more likely, robbery almost seven times more likely, and aggravated assault more than twice as likely in the city than in the suburbs. Although Chicagoans were four times more likely to be victims of violent crime, they were only slightly more likely (1.39 times) to be victims of serious property crimes, such as burglary or theft. "Property Crimes Up, Violence Ebbs in 6-County Area," *Chicago Tribune*, 26 August 1976, sec. 7, Metro/South edition.

39. "Drugs, Gangs Tied to 10 Percent Suburb Crime Hike," *Chicago Tribune*, 30 July 1989, 1. In both 1990 and 1991, violent crime rose approximately

4 percent in suburban Chicago, but increased 10 percent in suburban Cook County in 1991. Cook, Kane, McHenry, and DuPage Counties reported increases in 1990. DuPage County, one of the nation's wealthiest, experienced a 25 percent increase in violent crime. "Violent Crime Rises By 4.5 percent in Suburbs," *Chicago Tribune*, 10 November 1991, sec. 1, p. 1; "Violent Crime Soars 10% in Cook Suburbs," *Chicago Tribune*, 8 November 1992, sec. 1, p. 1.
40. "Violent Crime Soars."
41. A strong relationship between sexual street harassment and women's fear of rape has been asserted in the legal literature. See Cynthia Grant Bowman, "Street Harassment and the Informal Ghettoization of Women," *Harvard Law Review* 106 (January 1993): 517. Dierdre Davis, in "The Harm That Has No Name: Street Harassment, Embodiment, and African American Women," *UCLA Women's Law Journal* 4 (1994): 133, emphasizes the different realities of street harassment for Black women (156–61). Bowman argues that historically Black women faced even greater degradation and abuse by white men, who treated Black women as sexual property during slavery and still may perceive them as sex objects or prostitutes. Black women may suffer more intensely from street harassment, as they associate it with a history of sexual abuse by white men. Bowman, "Street Harassment," 532–34.

CHAPTER SEVEN
1. Wilson, *The Truly Disadvantaged.*
2. Douglas S. Massey and Nancy A. Denton, "Trends in the Residential Segregation of Blacks, Hispanics, and Asians: 1970–1980," *American Sociological Review* 52 (1987): 802–25.
3. Carolyn R. Zeul and Craig R. Humphrey, "The Integration of Black Residents in Suburban Neighborhoods: A Re-examination of the Contact Hypotheses," *Social Problems*, 18, no. 4 (1971): 462–74.
4. W. Scott Ford, "Interracial Public Housing in a Border City: Another Look at the Contact Hypothesis," *American Journal of Sociology*, 78, no. 6 (1972): 1426–47.
5. Robin M. Williams, *Strangers Next Door: Ethnic Relations in American Communities* (Englewood Cliffs, N.J.: Prentice Hall, 1964).
6. James E. Rosenbaum, Leonard S. Rubinowitz, and Marilynn J. Kulieke, *Low-Income Black Children in White Suburban Schools* (Evanston, Ill.: Center for Urban Affairs and Policy Research, Northwestern University, 1986), 61–64.
7. Paul S. Schnorr, "Denied a Sense of Community: Problems of Class, Race, and Community Form in a Voluntary Resettlement Effort" (Ph.D. diss., Northwestern University, 1993).
8. Berry, *The Open Housing Question.*
9. Internal sense of control was measured by respondents' answers to four items on a four-point scale from strongly agree to strongly disagree: (1) Good luck is more important than hard work for success; (2) Every time I try to get ahead, something stops me; (3) When I make plans, I can usually carry them out; (4) Planning only makes a person unhappy because plans hardly ever

work out anyway. These four items were combined to make an index of fate control.

CHAPTER EIGHT

1. Design for Change, *Caught in the Web: Misplaced Children in Chicago's Classes for the Mentally Retarded* (Chicago: Designs for Change, 1982).

2. Cf. Kulieke, "The Effects of Residential Integration," 89.

3. Ibid., 93.

4. Rosenbaum, Rubinowitz, and Kulieke, *Low-Income Black Children in White Suburban Schools*, 106.

5. Ibid, 108. This question was not asked to the city movers group.

6. The Gautreaux children were enrolled in dozens of different school districts, which administered many different standardized tests, as well as different forms of the same test, given at different times of the school year and in different grades. Moreover, because many schools did not provide transcripts even with consent forms, grades from only forty-two transcripts were available.

As a result, analysis of the children's academic accomplishments relied on the mothers' accounts of children's grades. While mothers could exaggerate their children's performance, comparing mothers' reports with the transcripts that were available found a very high correlation. While mothers did tend to report their children's grades as somewhat higher than the transcripts indicated, the exaggeration was fairly uniform across mothers. Mothers' reports tended to be about one-half grade higher than indicated in the transcripts. Even though grades are not objective measures of achievement, they indicate how teachers regard children's achievements.

CHAPTER NINE

1. See Robert L. Crain and Carol S. Weisman, *Discrimination, Personality and Achievement: A Survey of Northern Blacks* (New York: Seminar Press, 1972); Jon W. Hoelter, "Segregation and Rationality in Black Status Aspiration Processes," *Sociology of Education* 55 (1982): 31–39; Alyce Holland and Thomas Andre, "Participation in Extracurricular Activities in Secondary School: What Is Known, What Needs to Be Known?" *Review of Educational Research* 57 (1987): 437–66; Linda Grant, "Black Females' 'Place' in Desegregated Classrooms," *Sociology of Education* 57 (1984): 98–111; Harold B. Gerard and Norman Miller, *School Desegregation: A Long-Term Study* (New York: Plenum Press, 1975).

2. Nancy St. John, *School Desegregation Outcomes for Children* (New York: John Wiley & Sons, 1975).

3. Joyce L. Epstein, "After the Bus Arrives: Resegregation in Desegregated Schools," *Journal of Social Issues* 41 (1985), 23–43; James E. Rosenbaum, *Making Inequality: The Hidden Curriculum of High School Tracking* (New York: Wiley, 1976).

4. One variable combines employment and education outcomes, that is, whether the youth were in school or working, grouping youth who were then in high school or college or working.

CHAPTER TEN

1. Paul Jargowsky, *Poverty and Place: Ghettos, Barrios, and the American City* (New York: Russell Sage Foundation, 1996), 35, 39, 61–62, 185.

2. Ibid.; see also Wilson, *The Truly Disadvantaged.*

3. *Personal Responsibility and Work Opportunity Reconciliation Act of 1996, U.S. Statutes at Large* 110 (1996): 2105 (codified at 42 U.S.C. §601 (1998)).

4. U.S. Department of Housing and Urban Development Office of Policy Development and Research, *Rental Housing Assistance—The Crisis Continues: The 1997 Report to Congress on Worst-Case Housing Needs* (Washington, D.C.: HUD, April 1998), 5.

5. *Omnibus Rescissions and Appropriations Act of 1996, U.S. Statutes at Large* 110 (1996): 1321.

6. Lauren Allen, *Changing the Paradigm: A Call for New Approaches to Public Housing in the Chicago Metropolitan Region*, Metropolitan Planning Council, October 1996, 8; Rutgers University Center for Urban Policy Research, *Case Studies of Vouchered-Out Assisted Properties*, prepared for U.S. Department of Housing and Urban Development Office of Policy Development and Research, May 1998, xxvii–xxviii.

7. See, for example, Marc Fisher, "Giving Ghetto Children a Chance in the Suburbs," *Washington Post*, 11 June 1988, 1; Editorial, "Chicago's Housing Pioneers," *New York Times*, 1 November 1988, 30; William Schmidt, "Some Chicagoans are Moved out of Projects into a Future," *New York Times*, 3 February 1989, 1; Albert Shanker, "Doing Well in School," *New York Times*, 16 July 1989, E7; Sharman Stein, "Moving from Fear, Joblessness to Hope," *Chicago Tribune*, 29 April 1990, 3; Dirk Johnson, "Move to Suburbs Spurs the Poor to Seek Work," *New York Times*, 1 May 1990, A9; "Children from Projects Thrive in Suburbs," *Chicago Sun-Times*, 9 October 1991, 1; "Location Is Key in Seeking Better Life," *Chicago Sun-Times*, 9 October 1991, 1; "Study: Poor Blacks Who Move to Suburbs More Likely to Go to College," *Chicago Defender*, 10 October 1991; "Inner-city Children Tackle Suburban Life," *Chicago Tribune*, 19 July 1992, 1; Jason DeParle, "An Underground Railroad from Projects to Suburbs," *New York Times*, 1 December 1993, 1.

8. See, for example, Louis Richman, "Housing Policy Needs a Rehab," *Fortune*, 27 March 1989, 92; "Housing Opportunities in Chicago," *Today Show*, NBC, 23 November 1989; Cathy Slobogin, "The Nation's Agenda: A House Divided," Cable News Network, 20 September 1992; "American Agenda: The Power of New Surroundings," ABC *World News Tonight*, 4 February 1993; Kenneth Labich, "New Hopes for the Inner City," *Fortune*, 6 September 1993, 83–90; Lou Waters, "Low-Income Families Move to Suburbs," Cable News Network, 6 December 1993; "Low-Income Families Move to Suburbs," *60 Minutes*, 19 December 1993.

9. *Housing and Community Development Act of 1992, U.S. Code*, vol. 42, sec. 1437f (1994).

10. U.S. Department of Housing and Urban Development Office of Policy Development and Research, *Expanding Housing Choices for HUD-Assisted Families: Moving to Opportunity for Fair Housing Demonstration, First Biennial Report to Congress* (Washington, D.C.: HUD, April 1996).

11. Judith D. Feins, Mary Joel Holin, and Anthony A. Phipps, *MTO: Moving to Opportunity for Fair Housing Demonstration, Program Operations Manual*, prepared for U.S. Department of Housing and Urban Development Office of Policy Development and Research (Cambridge, Mass.: Abt Associates, July 1994).

12. Mary Davis, Senior Vice President of the Leadership Council and the only staff person involved throughout the life of the program, and Kale Williams, the agency's executive director for much of that period, provided extensive technical assistance to HUD and local agencies starting mobility programs.

13. Margery Austin Turner and Kale Williams, *Housing Mobility: Realizing the Promise*, Report from the Second National Conference on Assisted Housing Mobility, September 1997 (Washington, D.C.: The Urban Institute, January 1998), 128–29.

14. Programs could also be so selective that they chose people who would have succeeded even without the program, so that personal successes are not really program effects.

15. Cronin and Rasmussen, "Mobility," 123.

16. James E. Rosenbaum, "An Evaluation of Project Self-Sufficiency in Cook County" (Center for Urban Affairs and Policy Research, Northwestern University, 1988).

17. Feins, Holin, and Phipps, *MTO*, 9–6; Turner and Williams, *Housing Mobility*, 108.

18. Peterson and Williams, "Housing Mobility," 37.

19. Ibid., 18.

20. Ibid., 14, 54; John Goering, Helene Stebbins, and Michael Siewert, *Promoting Housing Choice in HUD's Rental Assistance Programs: Report to Congress* (U.S. Department of Housing and Urban Development Office of Policy Development and Research, April 1995), 56.

21. Fischer, *Is Housing Mobility an Effective Anti-Poverty Strategy?* 6.

22. Peterson and Williams, "Housing Mobility," 42.

23. Meryl Finkel et al., *Learning from Each Other: New Ideas for Managing the Section 8 Certificate and Voucher Programs*, prepared for the U.S. Department of Housing and Urban Development Office of Policy Development and Research and Office of Public and Indian Housing (Rockville, Md.: Abt Associates, September 1996), 30–31.

24. Judith D. Feins et al., *State and Metropolitan Administration of Section 8: Current Models and Potential Resources: Final Report*, prepared for U.S. Department of Housing and Urban Development Office of Policy Development and Research (Cambridge, Mass.: Abt Associates, April 1997), 4–12, 4–13.

25. Michael M. Daniel, "*United States v. Walker*: The Problem of Implementing Remedies to End Segregation in Subsidized Housing Against Federal, State, or Local Government Officials" (paper presented at the John Marshall Law School Conference on housing desegregation and affordable housing, Chicago, Illinois, 3 April 1998); Turner and Williams, *Housing Mobility*.

26. Steve Inskeep, "Moving to Opportunity Housing Program," *Morning Edition*, NPR, 25 March 1998, 8:21 A.M..

27. HUD, *Rental Housing Assistance*, 13.

28. Section 8 Program Reservations for Fiscal Years 1996, 1997, and 1998 (U.S. Department of Housing and Urban Development).

29. HUD Press Release No. 98–509, 21 October 1998.

30. HUD, *Rental Housing Assistance*, 11–12, 18–19.

31. Allen, *Changing the Paradigm*, 9.

32. Paul B. Fischer, "Housing Affordability in the Chicago Metropolitan Area: A Study of the Potential Supply of Fair Market Rent Units in Low Poverty Areas," 2 August 1995 (paper on file with the author), 13.

33. Allen, *Changing the Paradigm*, 12; W. David Koeninger, "A Room of One's Own and Five Hundred Pounds Becomes a Piece of Paper and 'Get A Job': Evaluating Changes in Public Housing Policy from a Feminist Perspective," *Saint Louis University Public Law Review* 16, no. 2 (1997): 451, 463.

34. Goering, Stebbins, and Siewert, *Promoting Housing Choice*, ii, 5–29 (Blacks); Margery Austin Turner, "Moving Out of Poverty: Expanding Mobility and Choice through Tenant-Based Housing Assistance," *Housing Policy Debate* 9, no. 2 (Washington, D.C.: Fannie Mae Foundation, 1998): 377–82 (Blacks and Latinos).

SELECTED BIBLIOGRAPHY

A number of articles that are not part of this book have come out of this research project. Readers who are interested in exploring different aspects of the research may also refer to: James E. Rosenbaum and Julie E. Kaufman, "Educational and Occupational Achievements of Low-Income African-American Youth in White Suburbs" (unpublished paper on file with the authors, 1991); Susan J. Popkin, James E. Rosenbaum, and Patricia M. Meaden, "Labor Market Experiences of Low-Income Black Women in Middle-Class Suburbs: Evidence from a Survey of Gautreaux Program Participants," *Journal of Policy Analysis and Management* 12, no. 3 (1993); James E. Rosenbaum, "Black Pioneers—Do Their Moves to the Suburbs Increase Economic Opportunity for Mothers and Children?" *Housing Policy Debate* 2, no. 4 (1994); James E. Rosenbaum, "Changing the Geography of Opportunity by Expanding Residential Choice," *Housing Policy Debate* 6, no. 1 (1995); James E. Rosenbaum, "Closing the Gap: Does Residential Integration Improve the Employment and Education of Low-Income Blacks?" in *Affordable Housing and Public Policy,* ed. Lawrence B. Joseph (Chicago: Center for Urban Research and Policy Studies, University of Chicago, 1993); James E. Rosenbaum, Nancy Fishman, Alison Brett, and Patricia Meaden, "Can the Kerner Commission's Housing Strategy Improve Employment, Education, and Social Integration for Low-Income Blacks?" *North Carolina Law Review* 71 (June 1993); James E. Rosenbaum and Julie E. Kaufman, "Low-Income Black Youth in White Suburban Schools: Long-Term Educational Outcomes" (paper presented at American Educational Research Association annual meeting, Chicago, Ill., April 3–7, 1991); James E. Rosenbaum, Marilyn J. Kulieke, and Leonard S. Rubinowitz, "Low-Income Black Children in White Suburban Schools: A Study of School and Student Responses," *Journal of Negro Education* 56, no. 1 (1987); James E. Rosenbaum, Marilyn J. Kulieke, and Leonard S. Rubinowitz, "White Suburban Schools' Responses to Low-Income Black Children: Sources of Success and Problems," *The Urban Review* 20, no. 1 (1988); James E. Rosenbaum and Patricia Meaden, *Harassment and Acceptance of Low-Income Black Youth in White Sub-*

urban Schools (Evanston, Ill.: Center for Urban Affairs and Policy Research, Northwestern University, 1992); James E. Rosenbaum and Susan J. Popkin, "Employment and Earnings of Low-Income Blacks Who Move to Middle-Class Suburbs," in *The Urban Underclass,* ed. Christopher Jencks and Paul E. Peterson (Washington, D.C.: Brookings Institution, 1991); James E. Rosenbaum, Susan J. Popkin, and Karen McCurdy, *Social Integration of Low-Income Black Adults in White Middle Class Suburbs* (Evanston, Ill.: Center for Urban Affairs and Policy Research, Northwestern University, 1990); James E. Rosenbaum, Susan J. Popkin, Julie E. Kaufman, and Jennifer Rusin, "Social Integration of Low-Income Black Adults in Middle-Class White Suburbs," *Social Problems* 38, no. 4 (1991); James E. Rosenbaum, Leonard S. Rubinowitz, and Marilyn J. Kulieke, *Low-Income Black Children in White Suburban Schools* (Evanston, Ill.: Center for Urban Affairs and Policy Research, Northwestern University, 1986); James E. Rosenbaum and Susan J. Popkin, *Economic and Social Impacts of Housing Integration: A Report to the Charles Stewart Mott Foundation* (Evanston, Ill.: Center for Urban Affairs and Policy Research, Northwestern University, 1990); and Leonard S. Rubinowitz, "Metropolitan Public Housing Desegregation Remedies: Chicago's Privatization Program," *Northern Illinois University Law Review* 12 (1992).

INDEX